APPROACH WITH(OUT) CAUTION

JAMES HASKELL

WITH RICHARD WATERS

APPROACH WITH(OUT) CAUTION

The 5-Step Plan to Take Control of Your Life

HarperCollins*Publishers*

HarperCollins*Publishers*
1 London Bridge Street
London SE1 9GF

www.harpercollins.co.uk

HarperCollins*Publishers*
Macken House, 39/40 Mayor Street Upper
Dublin 1, D01 C9W8, Ireland

First published by HarperCollins*Publishers* 2023

1 3 5 7 9 10 8 6 4 2

A catalogue record of this book is
available from the British Library

HB ISBN 978-0-00-849584-8
PB ISBN 978-0-00-849585-5

Printed and bound in the UK using 100%
renewable electricity at CPI Group (UK) Ltd

For my daughter Bodhi, who has given me a
whole new understanding of love

To hell with that old spinster called Prudence
I want a lap dance with Providence.

CONTENTS

INTRODUCTION

A LIFE BEYOND EAT, SLEEP, SHAG, REPEAT

'Why another book?' I hear you cry. Will it be another roller-coaster of humour and behind the scenes stories of debauchery and carnage that littered my playing career, sandwiched between the highs and lows of professional sport? Well, sadly no, it's time for me to put my sensible hat on. Just for a short while at least. So before you put this book back where you found it, I promise you there will be some real value within these pages, some nuggets of information or perhaps just a different perspective that will possibly help you navigate this wonderous journey we call life.

I get extremely frustrated by what I see happening in the world today and decided to write this book to suggest a different approach to cut through the red tape, the social hypocrisy, the bullshit and fear. I think we have lost our way in the world, and rather than sticking our heads in the sand and waiting for society to become sane again – it never will, it never was – it's time to tackle some of the *unmentionables* many of us are quietly grappling with. There is no straight talk any more, and it's increasingly hard to find the truth. Everyone is shit-scared about saying what they really think and feel in case they offend anyone, and we're spending our days walking on eggshells. Someone needs to draw a line in the sand. Enough is enough. I am going to attempt, dear reader, to draw that line, but in the process I may myself get cancelled. However, I am currently on my fifth cancelling and I still got to publish this book, so maybe like a cat I have four more lives before I am forced to retire to a small seaside village, with limited internet and forgiving local inhabitants who don't mind a Z-list pariah living in their midst.

By the way, when did being offended or offending someone become a problem? When did the rhyme 'sticks and stones may break my bones but names will never hurt me' become redundant? People and jokes are being labelled as offensive. No, they are not offensive, *you* find them offensive. Being offended is a feeling you feel, it's not a physical thing. 'What that person said I don't like, I find him offensive.' Great, that's called experiencing human emotions. The answer is: move on and find things you do like. It's not to try and eradicate the feeling of being offended, or to stop everyone being offended. I know people who get offended at the very sight of me, let alone when I open my mouth. Do I care about these people? No, I don't give them a second thought. It's like when you are channel hopping on the TV, you come across something you don't like and you skip to the next channel. Even if I came across something offensive on TV, I have never thought to post about it on social media or contact the stars of the show and give them a piece of my mind. When people don't like me, I don't get offended that they are offended. I don't call the police or Ofcom and say, 'I find these people offensive so I'd like to complain.' I just roll my eyes and move on. That's how the system works.

Not in 2022, it's not.

There are some undeniable facts of life … death, taxes, vegans telling you they are vegans. Each and every one of us has doubts, fears and – contrary to what social media makes you think – good days and bad days. We are not happy *all* the time! If we were, we'd look like a crowd of North Korean civilians pressganged to attend a nuclear military parade, smiling so hard their cheeks are cracking. Life is shit, life is hard, but it's sometimes also unique and beyond joyous. We are guests for a limited time on this beautiful blue and green ball suspended in a dark eternity. We're here for one primary reason – to play rugby. Joking. It's to be born, live, procreate and die. End of story.

Or is it for a much simpler reason? One that a wise old head told me on my first day as a professional rugby player, suggesting it as the panacea for everything we do, from the moment we wake up until we go to bed: 'Life is all about Stash, Gash, Cash and Lash?' Now while a lot of those things are great to have, collect and aim for, there is a much deeper-rooted reason. It sounds wanky – and I can assure you, you are still reading a book by James Haskell – but I believe what most of us are striving for whether we know it or not is to be happy; to do things each and every day that make us proud, challenge, scare and develop us as a person or at the very least make us feel satisfied we are not stagnating. To make something out of nothing. To utilise this incredible body and mind we have been given. To make the journey from birth to death as fulfilling, fun, successful and happy as possible.

Keeping that last sentence in mind let me tell you a little story. Ever heard the creation story of Prometheus? In ancient Greek mythology he was one of the titans, the giants that lost the war with Zeus and the gods. While the rest of his brethren were sent to hell for life, Prometheus was excused for not taking part in the war. Instead, he was charged with the task of creating creatures to populate the earth. Every one he made from clay and each animal had an attribute that made it special: lions were brave, birds could fly, whales could hold their breath a long time, chameleons could change colour, donkeys could carry loads of stuff and had huge cocks, and so on.

The last animal he made he wanted to do something special with, and that was man. The problem was he couldn't endow us with flight, might, or even the ability to jump really high (which the flea had just bagged) because all those attributes had already been given out. You'd think we'd have formed a group and complained – if we'd been French or named Karen we probably would have done, or at the very least blockaded something in an aggressive fashion – but we were thick as porridge cavemen being eaten all the time by these animals with their sharp jaws, expert claws and massive paws.

So Prometheus – whose name ironically translates as 'he with foresight' – took a rather extreme risk. He snuck up Mount Olympus, the home of the gods, and nabbed a branding iron from the fiery forge of Hephaestus, taking it back down to the thicko humans – think front-row forwards – and gave it to them to light their minds and pull their finger out.

'Improve yourself, my children,' he said, thinking to himself, *You lot couldn't be any more useless than you are currently.* For his theft from the gods, Zeus had Prometheus chained to a rock, and each day a vulture would fly over to him and slowly peck out and eat his liver only for it to regrow overnight and be eaten every day, for all eternity. And you thought the current social media pile-ons and cancellings were bad. I think the only thing to rival having your liver eaten out of your body every day would be being forced to watch reality TV on a loop.

Anyway, back to the cavemen. Despite burning each other a few times they soon got the hang of fire and were cooking up mammoth zinger burgers in no time. Pretty quickly they made leaps and bounds in language, weaponry and early forms of pornography on the walls of their caves. With fire in their hands to protect them and keep them warm, their special attribute was the freewill to be whatever they wanted.

We are not so different today. Our freewill gives us the freedom not to exist on a hamster wheel of shagging, sleeping, eating and hunting – though I have to say that sounds rather nice, and ironically people spend their whole lives trying to work to get enough money to live in the rarefied atmosphere where they can sit around all day eating, shagging and sleeping. The hunting not so much. Yet the bizarre structure of our capitalist society that we have shackled ourselves to means that when you do normally attain the ability to act in the aforementioned way, you are too old to do it and then you die.

However, what freedom will provide is the ability to do more than service our primal drivers; it gives us a choice to make something of ourselves out of our bare clay, to envision the life we want and slowly fashion it into being. On the other hand, we can just be like we were in the cave before fire was given to us. Who needs purpose and identity with that kind of simplicity? A nice kip, wake up and get your leg over, a spot of shooting before dinner and roast beef and Yorkshire pud every night – sounds like Heaven. Only we're human, so we would soon get bored of that (or at least if you had a modicum of intelligence you would). I am making the assumption that if you have bought this book you may think there is a life beyond eat, sleep, shag, repeat. Or something with more purpose to add to that list at the very least.

Substitute fire for the internet. The web can illuminate us at the tap of a button; we can discover all the treasures of the Ancient World – from the stories of Alexander the Great and the Seven Wonders of the World to the secrets of the Pyramids of Giza – and we can also use it for finding out what someone had for lunch and whether their bum looks big in a bikini. Genius.

Freewill is as much a curse as it is a blessing, because when we don't challenge ourselves and keep active and curious about the world around us, we become miserable and defeated and end up wasting our days. I am going to make a statement backed up by nothing more than my own assumptions and experiences of life: I would suggest that those who give in to every pleasure – food being one example – and who don't exercise or challenge themselves physically and mentally, more often than not become unhappy and suffer from health and mental health issues. We are not meant to waste our days sitting at screens, eating poorly, being caught up in the rat race of home, work, then back to home.

This book is not about arson. It's about making the most of your clay.

At any given moment you can decide to shape yourself into something you always wanted to be and make significant changes to your life. Remember earlier when I said we are here on earth to be happy, or at the very least strive for our own personal view of what happiness is? Context is critical here. What makes me happy won't make you happy. In order to find this contentment within ourselves, it takes a little work. To find our joy we have to be brave enough to chase what we love doing, to work at it, seek advice from others to improve, and possess the grit to stick at it. And if we haven't found what makes us tick yet, we need to keep trying new things until we do. En route to our goal, we can progress and become better versions of who we are every day. It's about keeping things simple. *Simple* is key: work out what you want, who you want to be with and where you would like to go, and you're well on your way to a happy life.

What you'll quickly learn is it's far more about the journey and how we apply ourselves on it, than it is to do with reaching the end goal. For example, do we ever make all the money we want, or achieve the body we dreamt of? I would argue very hard that we don't. But having something tangible to give us in this journey of success, failure, heartache, love and everything else in between is key. It's never about the *what*, it's often about the *why* and more importantly the *how*.

I am a firm believer that we need to be vocal about our issues and our concerns, but only by matching these with action will it make a difference. Focusing on mental health, for example, and encouraging men to talk is great, but if you don't match the talk with action you get nowhere. This book is not meant to be just an observation on life and to pick holes in how we do things – though there will be plenty of that – but rather to give you practical tools to take away and use in your own life the way you see fit. I have mentioned that context is key. We are all experiencing this thing we call life, differently. That's why we should never be quick to pass judgement or criticise how someone else chooses to live their own life.

However you want to get from birth to death is your choice, but we all share mostly the same problems, and I would argue there are better and worse ways to deal with them. That's why I have created the system of the '5 Pillars' that can be utilised to handle any problems or pitfalls you come across. The idea is not to never have a bad day again, or not to feel heartache, loss, stress or whatever normal human emotion you experience, but it's about getting you back on track again quickly and in the right way. It's about helping you formulate a plan of attack to achieve the things you want in life. It's a set of principles and actions that I use every day, that I believe can change how you approach life and will lead to your happiness and success in the areas you want.

Every one of these 5 Pillars – Recognise, Reflect, Resist, Change and Progress – has been formed over time from working with the best psychologists, psychiatrists, life coaches and CEOs, and they come from my own personal experience of failure, loss, success, injury, media scandal and heartbreak. You will read a lot more about these as you progress through the book.

Another powerful reason for me to write this book, beyond my selfless desire to help people – I say that with a mild hint of sarcasm, as you all know I love the sound of my own voice, and love having an opinion, so this is as much for me as it is for you – was because of the overwhelmingly (and surprisingly) positive feedback I received from my autobiographies, *What a Flanker* and *Ruck Me*. I've been inundated with messages regarding my upbeat attitude to failure and negativity, how I've dealt with adversity and ultimately kept a positive outlook on life. I would get a dozen messages a day from people for months telling me they loved the way I approached life, the things I said regarding mental health and the lessons they took from it that they could use in their own life. Some went as far as to say that my approach to life is what got them through lockdown. I am sure it was hyperbole, but I had clearly struck a chord, albeit an unintentional one.

I have had much the same feedback through my podcast *The Good, The Bad & The Rugby*; that people, especially men, have found real value and benefit in the straight-talking and no-nonsense approach that I and my co-hosts Alex Payne and Mike Tindall take when it comes to important issues, from mental health, social media and everything else in between.

Let's be clear. I'm neither a life coach nor a guru. I have no qualifications to speak of. I am a trained barista and can drive a 360 JCB excavator on any UK building site, but I guess that's not particularly useful to anyone reading this book, unless you'd like me to make you a coffee or dig you some foundations. My main goal is that I'd like to share my experiences and some hard-earned lessons that can be applied to your own life, and perhaps save you from making some of the mistakes I made. Eighteen years as a pro sportsman working in the best (and worst) teams around the world has taught me a thing or two. I have a mouth as wide as the Ganges, and it's often flowing with an equal amount of shit. More than once have I put my foot in it. I have fucked up a lot and had my fair share of scandal, so from that perspective I have a lot to say about what works and what doesn't in the pursuit of being a better person.

I hope this book will help you reshape the way you view past failures and to jettison any unnecessary baggage you may still be carrying, to make you lighter on your feet to reach success. I will give you some user-friendly, idiot-proof tools that really work; well, they worked for me. I'll challenge you to examine your current mindset, in a straight-talking way, and no, you won't to have to ask the Universe for anything or transfer your life savings over to J Haskell Industries. Most of these techniques for self-mastery I've learnt from some of the best coaches, therapists, gurus and players in the sporting world. I have seen first-hand from the likes of Eddie Jones, the

England rugby head coach, what it takes to get the best out of people. How a new person can come in and create an environment of accountability, aspiration, self-reliance, success and fun. I have seen that if you don't invest in the players and their individual needs, you can on the surface have success but under the mildest of pressures see it fall apart as quickly as it took to form in the first place. I have sat in changing rooms with people with more talent than I could have ever mustered but who failed to deliver because they never took responsibility for their mental health or who lacked the direction and grit to achieve their own personal goals. Equally, I have seen players who have achieved more than I could have ever hoped to, and when you look into why they have done this, it's not some magic formula or God-given talent (for the record, I don't believe God exists, but each to their own). What you find when you look under the bonnet of their success is a simple set of principles that they fall back on time and time again.

Success is not something you write down in your journal and revisit once. It's something you have to come back to every single day, until it's second nature; and even when it seems the norm you have to double down again to make it consistent. Nothing ever came easy unless you have a trust fund or are named Donald Trump. You have to make the most of the tools you are born with and learn along the way.

Life, I have found, is not fair; there is not an equal distribution of talent, ability, wealth and intelligence, and you certainly can't choose who your parents are. Anyone who believes we can balance this all out and help the slowest man catch up with the fastest is deluded. Yes, you can and should aim to help those who are less fortunate than yourself, but there is a limit. For some, all they will ever achieve is mediocrity or worse, and for them that's okay but for others it's not. What you can do is not use any of these as an excuse for your own personal limitations and reasons for failure. You either decide to make a difference and change what you can, or you give up and allow yourself to be defined by your past and current life circumstances.

What I want to do is show you how, through a daily regimen of self-improvement and a process to support it, I can take you to where you want to go. I am not here to fix your mental health – I'm probably more qualified to perform open-heart surgery – but I hope this book will help you see things differently, shift your mindset, and encourage you to empower yourself and understand more about what you can and cannot control.

Time to remould your clay. I can't make any promises on the donkey cock thing (I'm good, but not that good; if I was, I would have sorted myself out in that department) but I can promise you one hell of a journey getting to your final destination.

1

THE PROBLEM WITH THE WORLD IS ...

THE ANGST OF CHOICE

When I was a lad, three years old to be more specific, Burger King had only just arrived in the UK and the first cappuccino had been sold only a year earlier. It was either a lacklustre Wimpy or if you could find one, a McDonald's. As for an oat milk skinny latte, forget about it. But wind the clock forward to the present and there are too many fast-food joints to mention, and more kinds of ways to have your coffee and coffee house brands than you could list in a 12-point font on the generously sized arse of one of the Kardashians. Don't play coy with me, you know exactly what I am talking about. I can picture exactly what you're thinking. So stop it! As an aside, when I go in to order my favourite coffee, a flat white, and they ask with normal milk and I say yes, they look at me like I am the mental one for saying yes and for not having some obscure milk drained from something nonsensical. Since when did having normal milk become so odd?

It's not just food and coffee that we're swamped with too many options for. The world is now at a tipping point where humanity has never had so much choice, and never had it so easy, and yet we're no happier because of it; if anything we've never been so miserable, anxiety levels have never been higher and depression is as common as white vans in Croydon. We waste more time looking at the joy in other people's lives on our phones (then worrying about the *lack* in our own), wondering who we are, what we stand for, who we need to please and how we should present ourselves to the world (i.e. the world of social media), than ever before. Everything is available to kids at the touch of a button, and while some access dollops of dopamine-releasing praise from their followers, they can just as easily be cancelled, bullied, ignored or derided.

Meanwhile, the likes of Alexa, Echo and Siri are lurking in the background of most houses, quietly listening to your conversations – next time you're on Instagram, try saying out loud, 'I need a new pair of jeans' and see what shortly appears as a pop-up ad in the photo feed. Self-drive trucks are hitting the road imminently, drones are now commonplace and we're unknowingly having our first customer service-related conversations with a bot pretending to be human. Technology has already outpaced mankind in terms of evolution and is moving at a pace we won't ever be able to catch up with. Entre-nous, I've been keeping tabs on the sex droids and they're coming along very nicely. Before you judge me, just think all of the sex and none of the hassle. Want some alone time? Switch it off or pop it in the cupboard. It's as easy as that. Just let that sink in for a minute while you read on. Chloe, my wife, is trying to make out that only perverts would buy and sleep with a sex doll. I just think deep down she knows her days are numbered if those crazy Japanese get their act together and release that Shagbot 3000. I will have it on pre-order before you can say pump and dump.

When I want to watch something, a film, documentary or mini-series, I must now choose between Amazon Prime, Hulu, Apple TV, Netflix and so many more. You then end up scrolling for hours on end, much the same way as you fall down a rabbit hole looking at porn. Then, utterly defeated, having wasted so much energy, you can't be arsed to actually watch anything. They need to invent a TV series that you can watch while scrolling on your phone – it would be a smash hit, as that is all anyone is doing now. Back in the day, I had to choose between *Quantum Leap*, *Lovejoy*, *Grange Hill*, *The Really Wild Show* and *Poirot*, and that was much easier: no stress, very few choices. Too much choice is not always a good thing. Essayist and boxing pundit Norman Mailer once said, 'I think the internet is the greatest waste of time since masturbation was discovered.' Clearly, he hadn't played *Fortnite*, but I tend to agree with the old grumps.

I believe no-one is eternally happy – well, next to no-one – though you may find a monk halfway up a mountain who has found inner peace. But if he knows it, he isn't sharing it as he's probably taken a vow of silence or doesn't mix in the real world, which is probably why he is so happy (or he's narrowed his viewing options down to one streaming service).

CLIMATE CHANGE AND BELLENDS

Life moves in cycles. Some days are good and bursting with possibility, others you feel like someone has hexed you by chalking a giant sign on your back that reads 'Kick Me'. Have you taken a look at the 'real world' lately? We are in the era of fake news, disinformation, extremism and depravity on a whole new scale. I am not a religious man but the world does resemble those biblical cities of Sodom and Gomorrah. People are having sex in public and doing crazy things filming themselves all in the name of making 'content', and then just sending them on or uploading them. If you don't believe me, then give 'Influencers in the Wild' a follow on social media. You won't have appreciated how bad things have got until you see some of the stuff that's getting posted. If you still don't believe me, just accept an invite to a WhatsApp group (full of men) and before you know it's severed heads, death and group sex that are landing in your inbox before you can say, 'Please, no!'

Now every muppet has a voice thanks to social media. For all those God-fearers waiting for Judgement Day, Ragnarok, or Sodom and Gomorrah to return I have bad news. It's already here. We are in the last bastion of civilisation, speeding toward a Mad Max-type future where instead of petrol currently being the commodity everyone seeks (which, ironically, when I first put pen to paper for this book was not an issue, but then we ended up in a fuel crisis caused by fake news and now, some 12 months later, we are paying the best part of £2 per litre), it will be water and shelter from the intolerable sun. That, and intelligent company. Is it me or are we getting more stupid? Whatever happened to common sense? I can see it now: it's just going to be me and my dog roaming the lost highways looking for someone to chat with and annoy.

Now you may think, 'Oh, James, you are playing fast and loose with your examples, things are not really that bad.' Well, I say this to you, dear reader, if anything I am playing things down, I am putting a spin on it … I am going all Monty Python and looking on the bright side of life. At the time of writing this particular chapter we are in day 6 of a fuel crisis that appears to have no end. The panic buyers are out in force blocking forecourts, fighting each other and anyone in their way, following fuel tankers around just to intercept them when they stop. They are queuing for mile upon mile to fill up cars, petrol containers and, I shit you not, plastic bags with fuel. What kind of pond scum thinks that filling up a 'bag for life' with petrol is a good idea? I will tell you who, the average man in the street. This is not caveman stuff, this is prime-time 2022 at its best.

They are like armies of the dead intent not for blood to satiate their lust, but fuel. Fuel they don't need but must have because some fuckwit in our shambles of a government suggested there is a shortage due to a lack of HGV drivers. This was then played on repeat across all our vile media outlets. On the one hand they are all telling us, 'This shortage will last for months,' and then on the other hand saying, 'Look at these idiots panicking.' It's so odd that we let this happen. Go onto the *Daily Mail* online app, for example, in fact any of the tabloid news outlets will do, and in a 5-inch screen space there are usually four or five contradictory stories. You have a writer slamming the government and asking all the tough questions like 'How did we run out of drivers?', 'Why did we let this happen?', 'Why haven't we got the Army in?' Then you have this washed-up hack of a social commentator writing another article further down saying, 'There is nothing wrong, it's scare-mongering, these people are subhuman and should be locked up.' Then you have another article blaming immigration for the lack of jobs for our brave young Tommies and no-one can get an HGV licence as all the exam slots are being taken up by those of a non-British ethnicity. Then finally you have an article that suggests because of Brexit and the idleness of the British worker, we have no foreign workers to fill the drivers' seats. Who do we believe? Who is to blame? Well, I'd like to say that this was a one-off, and that there are lots of smart people out there, and perhaps it was just a bad day for humanity.

But that would be bullshit. Cast your minds back to the first COVID-19 lockdown, when people were panic-buying – wait for it – bog roll, with aisle upon aisle empty in every shop in the country. Come to think of it, people were panic-buying everything for some reason. There was no shortage of food, no-one had mentioned a forthcoming shortage of anything, but lo and behold society's human flotsam, the dense and the mindless, were out stacking trollies to levels never reached before even in the heyday of Dale Winton and the popular TV show *Supermarket Sweep*. They were dashing from shop to shop grabbing whatever they could. However, their real penchant was for toilet roll.

When I first heard of this, I had to check that I hadn't misread the symptoms of COVID-19 and that once contracted you didn't suddenly erupt into something that could only be described as a 'poocano', your bowels erupting every half-hour. Upon checking the list of things that happened when you caught COVID-19, nowhere did it say you were at risk of shitting yourself to death. Then I thought perhaps you got a cold that was so bunged up with mucous you needed reams of toilet roll to just mop it up. No again, symptoms were a cough and respiratory problems.

So why are these fuckwits hoarding toilet roll? The answer is no-one knows, as nobody will admit to it, so you can't ask them. But they are out there. Some reader of this book by the mere odds alone must have hoarded the stuff. I can only think it's down to mob mentality. It has to be. The fuel crisis proves that. Just tell someone they don't have something and then you see your mate getting that very thing. You think, 'Well, I must do it too,' and that's how quickly the world unwinds. All this fear propelled on the wings of social media is just fanning the flames of the madness.

In short, the world is fucked, people are stupider than ever, and the ability to link to like-minded cretins is easier than ever before. Nobody checks the facts; we all believe what we read and do nothing to dispel any of it. Well, nothing until you read *Approach With(out) Caution* and we start changing this nonsense, by isolating the hoarders and generally kicking ass (rather than wiping it). At least, at its most basic, that is the idea of the book. To raise some awareness and become shepherds of our own lives as opposed to sheep.

Putting people's stupidity to one side for a moment, there are other issues at stake that must be noted. The planet is heating up at a pace never witnessed before in human history, with vast sheets of Antarctic ice the size of Donald Trump's ego detaching themselves from the South Pole. Fortunately, at a time when the fate of the earth hangs in the balance, we can rely on corporate billionaires to conquer space in their penis extensions. There was widespread heartbreak recently as the CEO of the world's most profitable 'pee in a bottle or you're fired' company returned safely after a successful 11-minute orbit in his high-powered phallus. Honestly, look me in the face and tell me that his rocket's *cock*pit is not modelled on a bellend. We all know he's Dr Evil despite his best attempts to disguise it with a 10-gallon hat. At any moment, you can imagine him addressing the UN and demanding he has control over the world or his moon 'laser' will destroy a continent of his choice at the touch of a button.

With a massive migratory footfall expected over the coming decades from the Middle East and African nations, as more and more flee drought, famine and exposure to humanly intolerable heat, it's comforting to know that those with silly amounts of dosh will be spending it not on helping reverse climate change but by fleecing celebs and – groan – social influencers to play out their spaceman fantasies in our celestial back garden. These are weird times.

I don't want to sound alarmist but almost everything that could go wrong *is* going wrong. We have lost our way so badly that the next eight years leading up to 2030 are said to be the most critical yet for our earth's survival. Little wonder we've not had any contact with aliens. I imagine they would just fly up to Earth, drop the window on the UFO, have a look at this mess we have got ourselves into and think, 'Fuck it, I'm not going down there!' and then fly off. The juice is not worth the squeeze when it comes to interacting with the human race in its current state. Of the 4.5 billion years the earth has existed, mankind has been around for only about a couple of hundred thousand years. If you condense Earth's history to 24 hours, humans have been around for a mere three seconds – and look what they have done to it.

I heard a story of an experiment in which two high-powered computers were given access to the history of the Earth and tasked with planning the survival of the planet. Left to talk to each other, it took them only two days to conclude that the most crucial action that could be taken was to annihilate the human race before they wiped everything out, including themselves. Now you may take that with a pinch of salt, but you know there is an element of truth to it when Elon Musk has gone around warning the governments of the world about artificial intelligence and the fact that we cannot under any circumstances set it free. They are now fitting sniper rifles and rocket launchers to Chinese robotic dogs and teaching them to shoot with pinpoint accuracy. Did we learn nothing from every movie where machines are made self-aware? Skynet – the fictional AI system that threatened to take over the world in the *Terminator* movies – is a real possibility, and when it works out we are the biggest threat to it and Earth, we are going to need something pretty special to stop the inevitable. Not even Arnie can save us if that happens.

POUNDLAND POLITICS

If the average IQ in the UK is 100 (source: worldpopulation-review.com) then we have a large proportion of people below the average still voicing their opinion, even getting to dictate life and policy through the pressure of social media; which I believe is entirely wrong. The old adage 'opinions are like arseholes, everyone's got one' holds true. We can no longer afford to countenance everyone's concerns. I don't try and perform brain surgery, so why are we letting people who can't tie their own shoelaces and think a can of Coke and a Mars bar is a healthy lunch call for someone's head, or for us to leave the European Union? It's barmy.

It's way easier to constantly be shouting at everyone else as you don't have to focus on your own situation. Instead of addressing the problems and looking at our own side of the street, we get involved in pseudo crusades and current affairs sideshows that mean we become distracted from our own reality and do anything and everything to avoid making the changes and putting in the hard work required to make a positive difference. Changing and having real success is hard, tiring and littered with failure. But it's that challenge that improves us as individuals.

The Olympics have been and gone while I have been writing this book. The fanfare to mark the start of the world's greatest event was muted to say the least; apart from the athletes no-one bar a few local Japanese was in the stands cheering. Multiple sackings within the Japanese Olympic Committee took place, including the director of the opening ceremony three days before it took place for making a Holocaust joke back in 1998, and the head of the Japanese Olympic Committee for making sexist remarks. At the Rio Olympics, officials distributed 450,000 condoms, but apparently at these games there were only 150,000 given out, and solely to athletes as they left for home. Given the ruling that Olympians should shield themselves and never leave the Olympic village apart from attending their event, it added up to a lot of spare time in their rooms. Shouldn't they have given them the condoms at the outset of the games, or did they assume that giving them that many condoms was a green light rather than a deterrent to start shagging other members of the numerous Olympic participant countries? I mean they will anyway, hence the large amounts they normally give, but there's nothing like human nature to think, well, if we just only give them a smidge, they will get the message. I want to know what happened to the other 300,000? Maybe they went into the production of a giant rubber bubble – like the one in *The Prisoner* that chases Patrick McGoohan across the beach – to police errant Olympians keen on sightseeing in a country where before the Olympics just 7 per cent of the population had been vaccinated against COVID-19.

You've got to hand it to the Japanese Olympic Committee for being more consistently inconsistent than Boris Johnson's 2020 'Stay Alert' to COVID speech. First, it was 'Yeah!' to Asahi beer sponsoring the event in a desperate bid to assuage the crippling $15.4 billion it was costing Japan to stage the Olympics. Then perhaps having witnessed the fine bottle-throwing techniques of a minority of England football fans at the European Championship final – at what should have been an occasion to savour in British sporting history but instead turned into a display of idiocy and thuggery – they performed a rapid about-turn.

NEWSFLASH: TINTIN GETS SHAFTED IN THE CONGO!

I'm not going to gripe for the whole of this book, just most of it. You see, there's a lot wrong with the world at present. Do I sound like a broken record yet? Bear with me as I am just setting the scene and making sure you understand that I have not succumbed to media hysteria, but I am in fact basing my fears on actual fact, which should encourage you to take some action and become self-reliant and in charge of, at the very least, your own destiny. At a time when we need clear thinking and action, the average person is confused and beset by fear and feels tongue-tied with anxiety when it comes to expressing their views. Then again, what constitutes an average person these days?

I hear you say, 'How dare you pigeon-hole anybody as *average* when we are all made of stardust!' When Dr Seuss gets cancelled for his whimsical illustrations of Chinese men and black people being deemed 'over exotic', we know we're in dangerously unchartered waters. Apparently in the USA, one in four toddlers' first reading adventure is with a Dr Seuss picture book. Given the population is 328 million, that's 82 million people now scratching their heads and soul searching whether they've been racist bigots since birth. Let's just blame all racism on poor old Dr Seuss, that's convenient. Woke staff at Dr Seuss Enterprises have withdrawn six of his books in a proactive move that has sent his other books' sales into hyperspace (as opposed to the bell-ended rocket that travelled a mere 66.5 miles). Maybe I should try and withdraw one of my books. Watch this space, reader.

Admittedly, the world is less racist than it was when *Tintin in the Congo* was published in 1931. But sadly, while colonialism is a thing of the past, the superior attitudes displayed towards people of colour back then still run through today's society in a more diluted way. Undoubtedly, there is unconscious bias – where a white person behaves differently towards a black person without realising it. Some black people would compare living with unconscious racism as like starting a game of chess in which you are already several moves behind. There aren't the same job opportunities as there are for white people, and there is brazen inequality. These are facts, not just the rhetoric of the liberal left. There is clearly still a problem.

Just as Miami was built on the proceeds of Colombian cocaine, we all know the British Empire was founded on theft and pillaging, slavery and racism. The East India Company were essentially a bunch of pirates in uniform with our monarchs' blessing to do as they wished to make the Empire rich. But let's be practical, we can't remove the sins of our forefathers by toppling any statuary evidence of their existence. Instead, isn't it better to address what is unacceptable and offensive to black people by listening to them and educating the white masses on institutional racism? The simple fact that must be remembered in any argument, whatever your thoughts are on racism, whether we are, or we aren't, whether we have improved or we haven't: no-one is born racist. It's learnt through our parents, and whoever exerts influence on our children. These are picked-up habits that we either dismiss or absorb. Just let that sink in for a moment. A child does not understand racism; he or she is taught to be that way. So, with that logic we can unteach or set better examples moving forward to stop this in its tracks.

While the KKK still marches through parts of America, we have work to do. Let's not worry about trying to right past wrongs; going back and holding the past to account is pointless, it's the past for a reason, we are meant to learn from it and then change what we do now. You cannot go back and cleanse yourself and society of what happened. You don't have to champion them as heroes, but you must understand that context is everything. Without context nothing makes sense. The media and social media give you no context, they give you bite-sized edited chunks that play to a narrative, that are there to cause conflict and unrest. You never get the whole story, and most people don't bother to understand, they just react. Once you understand this, you then see how dangerous jumping on the bandwagon can be. What used to happen, doesn't happen now, because we have learnt that it wasn't right. Put your energy into changing now, not cancelling the past. I think pulling down statues and all the posturing is a substitute for taking action now. People are frustrated but they don't know where to channel it, and it's too easy an option to mob together and smash stuff up and call people out than actually worry about what they do and how they live, and fixing the world by being the best version of themselves. If they were healthier, more hard working, looked after their own metaphorical garden and focused on sorting the things they can control, that would make a real difference. It's how people act now that matters, not how they used to act. Without wanting it to sound like the lyrics from a song, children are our future. We need to protect them from our fears and prejudices. I will leave this with you one more time: NO-ONE IS BORN RACIST.

PROTECTING YOUR BOTTOM LINE WITH SOME GOOD OLD TOKENISM

In an act of rapid penitence, or more likely transparent panic for their profit margin, big corporate brands have lately been showing off their 'wokeness' by insisting on BAME-people placement in almost every advert on TV. Who cares if it's pure tokenism to BAME people and the brands don't mean a word of it? So long as consumers continue to buy their product, that's all that matters.

It's not just the corporate fat cats and their PR gurus scrabbling to react appropriately to wokeness and milk its indignant tit for all it's worth; the average (there you go again Haskell with that odious label) well-meaning person is in such a state of anxiety over what everyone thinks and will say about them if they get it wrong, they prefer to keep quiet altogether. A typical conversation with a woke grandson and his grandmother living in Herefordshire might be:

'There's a nice coloured couple from London moved in next door.'

'You can't say coloured anymore, Nan, you have to say black.'

'But we called them *black* before, and we were told that was the wrong thing to say, so we had to say *coloured* instead.'

'Just so you know, Nan, black people are proud to be black.'

'Well, dear, I am sure they are but I am now very confused as to what the right thing to say is.'

No-one can see anything other than through the optics of their nature and nurture. However well-meaning you are, you can't do anything these days without upsetting *someone*. Which is not a problem, by the way. Who cares if you upset a few people? That's actually a normal thing. It's just now everyone is pretending to be whiter than white that it's seen as really bad. It's almost a badge of honour to find something upsetting. I can't remember the last time anything really rattled me. I am too busy doing all the things I need to be doing to stop and look, or even acknowledge, what other people are up to, let alone complain, be outraged, pass comment, or worse, dedicate my life to their destruction. I would suggest you worry about yourself and your own life, before you think you are in the rarefied position to even comment and complain about others. Trust me, you have things you could be doing that are much more worthwhile and will actually help you to be healthier and happier.

How shit would life be if everyone agreed with what you had to say? I can only imagine how middle of the road you would have to be to keep everyone happy. The world is closer than ever and has only shown just how different we are. I post stuff on social, and I actively hope it causes a difference of opinion; it at least shows I am saying something that courts a reaction positive or negative. I am not sensationalist for the sake of it, I am not Piers Morgan. I just might post something that I find funny that 80 per cent of people will also, but others won't. I posted the other day about having a spa and using it in the sun but I captioned it like this:

'Whatever the weather looking after yourself inside and out is important. Do whatever you can to achieve this. Lucky @layzspauk has temperature controls and you can take things down a notch and still relax 🕶️🤟🤐🐟'

It was clearly an ad for a product. This is a genuine response I got, and goes to show just how stupid people are and how your life context and your point of view versus mine is everything:

'Read this initially and was inspired, genuinely thought you were posting about mental health and looking after yourselves, thought great to have someone in your position promoting mental health in response to Ryan Jones' news today and window lickers like me with PTSD who struggle each day. I know banter and jokes play a part in dealing with things, and that's how I try to deal with things, but to come to the end of your post with pretty much a sales job for hot tubs was disappointing to say the least. You enjoy that tub, lucky you can relax, lucky you can have a luxury like that at home. Just a very disappointing post, you could do so much more supporting those with mental health and still plug your sponsors in a less brash way.'

I'd like to say this was unusual, but it's not. This is the state of play most days. So when I say I don't care about people not agreeing or having a problem with me, I really don't. I *want* people to disagree, as I see the world very differently to this bloke and plenty of others.

Having a difference of opinion should not be such a problem. After all, isn't that what makes democracies great – we debate, argue, vote and then we get on with it? There is a huge degree of arrogance being shown by anyone who thinks that their opinion should never be countered. Just as there will be those who read this book and don't agree with a word of what I am saying, which is okay (so long as you bought the book).

What's not okay is where people once used to disagree and move on, or just avoid going near things they didn't like, they now seem to always be on the offensive, actively seeking out conflict; and dear reader, they don't just disagree, now they want to burn your house down with you in it. Healthy debate has turned into all-out war.

TALK TO TRACY

Are we trying too hard to be all things to all men (*and* women, I quickly add, before your 'woke' little brother hits you on the head with the *Guardian*)? All this over-pandering has got the BBC in a spin; as a public service broadcaster funded by TV licence payers, they are terrified of someone complaining about their lack of diversity and so are cramming each news segment with people of every creed, colour and social demographic, which is pointless, long-winded and frankly detracts from the main story.

Who gives a shit what Tracy at No 5 thinks of the Brexit policy? She can't even spell it! When she voted for us to leave, she assumed the powers that be were going to round up all 'immigrants' – basically anyone not described by the police as IC1 (a white person) – into a big boat and ship them off to where they came from. So that's next door but one. Imagine when she discovered that was not the case, she would have been so livid she probably went to Iceland for another bucket of ice cream. No, not Reykjavik sadly ... Before you think what I'm saying is nonsense, look back at the old media coverage of the people who voted for Brexit, and in the ensuing days they honestly felt lied too. They thought that the NHS would get all this money, and that they would never see a person who 'spoke funny' again. I think some genuinely believed that they would round up anyone with different coloured skin or different ethnicity from that of a pale, badly tattooed, overweight, poorly teethed individual and load them on big boats and send them back from whence they came. Sadly for these morons, this was not what Brexit meant, and I would suggest that now we have been in a post-Brexit world for some time, we have learnt a few things. Namely, nothing has actually been sorted and this Brexit deal is pretty shabby and threatens the Good Friday Agreement; the hospitality and service industries are completely screwed as we have no work-force (it turns out the unemployed British don't want to do these menial jobs, and that it wasn't foreigners taking 'our' jobs, it was automation); and we're now experiencing a general malaise from a situation these thickos thought Brexit would fix. This is what happens when you give the masses a vote and feed their desires with lies and rhetoric. No-one bothers to question anything – 'Oh, if it's come from the media and politicians, it must be true.' I imagine the Russians under Putin and the North Koreans under Kim Jong-un feel the same way until they are shown to have been fed a pack of lies. We are not in a dictatorship, but we get played the same way.

What everyone's forgotten is what you get when you ask five hundred people in a room a question. Namely, a shitload of different answers – some will agree, some will disagree, some will answer a question you didn't ask, others will come up with something so leftfield and bizarre it will make you shudder, and some will have fallen asleep. Others may start fighting in disagreement, but at the very least you should get a consensus or an element of common sense that dictates what the answer should be. If you still have any lingering doubts, get an expert – preferably one with letters after their name – who has spent ten years studying that subject, not Karen off Facebook who thinks that the Milky Way is something you have for a nutritious snack after your Greggs' bacon sarnie. And just as an aside, why is it all these so-called experts look as if they're the lovechild of a mangled Barbie doll and a fairground ride operator?

Do you remember that during the height of COVID-19, the sister of Terry's mate Janice knew someone in the Army who said they were going to take to the streets? It never happened but thank you Facebook for the hype. Or during the two-day heatwave when the media were live reporting tarmac temperatures and they shut schools and nobody went to work? Yes, sadly there were some fires but it again turned out to be just a really hot couple of days. Did we need the hype, the bullshit and hysteria? No, we didn't. We needed to hydrate, wear a hat and get the fuck on with it.

PANDERING TO HYPOCRISY

Sadly, in current times common sense has gone out the window and been replaced with an obsessive focus on inclusion and equal opportunity. We can't afford to risk having an opinion for fear that others may get offended, so instead we tiptoe around getting nowhere, perpetually apologising for things we didn't do in the past. Yes, there has been, and still is, an enormous imbalance in so many areas of life that needs addressing; you only have to look at the fact there was *apparently* only one Japanese 'gay' in the Tokyo Olympic Village, or reflect on the white-hot racist fury poured on the three young black men who missed their penalties in the Euro 2020 Final – that twisted minority may as well have sung '*It's coming home, it's coming, lynching's coming home ...*' Race should never have come into it. They were three young men trying their best, and do you know what, it's a game, sport is a fucking game. Win or lose, nothing changes, the sun sets and rises regardless. Things only change for those involved; even if you feel your life would be better if they had won, it would only have papered over the cracks in your reality until the endorphins ran out and you were back to your reality. At times like that, even a man with a steely disposition and a positive outlook on life starts to get really down about humanity. I actually turned to my wife after the final penalty miss and said those lads are going to get it and it's going to be horrible and racist. I was already dreading the morons' responses. She said no, people are better than that. Sadly, they're not.

Yes, we have had it backwards for so long now regarding gay rights, race and sexism. And yes, we must put in place some tough changes to make things better, but rather than spur of the moment stupidity, we need to give these subjects the time they deserve, not blind reacting but considered proacting. It's not about being seen to be doing the right thing, which I think most brands are guilty of. Just look on social media during big moments in time, like Black History Month, Gay Pride or International Women's Day. All these brand companies are so eager to post their PR-managed posts that tick all the boxes and demographics. But frankly they are bullshit and so transparent. If you were to ask them if they have extended paid maternity/paternity leave or put in a structure of equal pay for women, most would look the other way or pretend you hadn't asked the question. They do fuck all in real terms; it's all about being seen to be doing the right thing for that magic social media moment in time.

I attended Pride a while ago and all these people were proudly marching while holding signs from the big companies. I said to one person, 'It's great that your company lets you have time to do this.' 'Oh, no,' she said, 'we had to take unpaid leave.' 'Well, why the fuck are you promoting that company?' The answer came back, 'Because they asked us to!'

It's virtue signalling of the highest order by these brands. I personally hate it and have experienced it first-hand. I have been hung out to dry by more brands than I've had hot dinners, not because they feel I did anything wrong, but because they need to be, and I quote, 'seen to be doing the right thing'. No-one makes a decision or stands for anything anymore, it's just groups of people sitting in boardrooms all trying to be holier than thou and nobody can risk getting it wrong, because everyone is so vocal on social and we live in such a litigious world. So they all just panic and go with the path of less resistance. Because these brands who have money stand for nothing, it means that the incoherent ramblings of a muppet on social media now actually have traction. Critics used to just criticise, maybe in the media, maybe at work and probably in the pub; now if they shout loud enough they can actually make things happen. Online, three voices sound like 300, 300 like 3,000, 3,000 like 30,000 and so on. The vocal minority have been given a voice and power by weak companies and brands tripping over themselves to be all things to all (wo)men, not realising they have made a rod for their own backs and set unrealistic expectations that will ultimately be their undoing. One mishap from an employee, one loose corporate outing and they have to burn themselves in a super-stringent way to match the precedent they have set.

When the news came out that most top-paid broadcasters at the BBC were men who were all paid considerably more than their female counterparts, many men were instantly replaced in a kneejerk reaction to save political and public face. I have always believed that you should employ the best person for the job, rather than selecting them on what sex, social demographic or race they are. I will say this though to counter my own belief. We've perpetuated such a skewed system for so long, that while some recent female promotions may not have been the best candidates, at least young women at school and university will see women they admire in positions of success and power. Perhaps in five to ten years we'll have a crop of real quality to fill many of those big-cheese jobs, because suddenly women feel like they can get to the top.

Random question: how many of those knobheads tossing glass bottles at Wembley were women? A second part to that question: how different would the world be if we had women in all the top positions of power? I am going to say very different and in a good way.

What all this pandering hypocrisy has created is a game of who can be seen to be whiter than white, for want of another expression. There are so many people out there who now live to be outraged; being offended is the default position for not only *Daily Mail* readers but those that make a full-time job of ganging together to get behind a cause. They have no direction or focus and are completely rudderless. They have no idea how to fix their problems so join crusade after crusade to detach themselves further from actually having to go through some turmoil to change what they dislike about themselves.

Just like a shark dies if it stops swimming, if these people stopped being outraged and asked themselves 'What's my life like?' or 'What's my side of the street like?', I think they would hate what they see. If they made an effort to fix that and everyone took social responsibility to firstly do better each day themselves, the world would be better. Trust me on that. It's easy to be galvanised when you feel part of a struggle. That's why I'm wary of people who have never played sport or been part of a proper team, or at the very least strived for a goal that required them to make a personal sacrifice, go through some emotional and physical turmoil or do something that required them to put others before themselves. (I do not include supporting Arsenal in that bracket, even if it is a rollercoaster of all of the above.) These people don't know what it's like to fight for a cause, or truly work hard and be made to feel accountable. It's one thing letting yourself down, it's another thing knowing that your actions will affect others. That's why I feel strong teams play such an important role in personal development; they teach you many lessons you'd never have if you've never been part of one. Even on a really base level, the stats of those people who find success and change their bodies when they train with a partner versus those who don't, show that having a partner means you are much more likely to fulfil your goal and actually do it, as opposed to lying in bed and just hitting snooze.

Obviously, being part of a professional sports team is not a reality for most people, but the principles of accountability to yourself and others can be carried forward. I will talk later on about some of the methods you could put in place to replicate the benefits you would get from a team, and to identify what these benefits are and to police yourself instead of having others do it.

QANON MEETS THE SATANIC CANNIBALS

There are some disadvantages, however, to partnering up when it's fuelled by hate. Being outraged and joining others to create an even bigger ball of outrage makes people feel like they are part of a cause, no matter how inflammatory or misguided it may be. As individuals we possess an opinion, but put us together, united in a cause, and we can become a very ugly herd and do terrible shit. It's as if our eyes glaze over like they are on herd autopilot. There are people out there ready to kill or maim, and the worst thing about it is that they are thriving like bacteria, spurred on by conspiracy theories, hatred, envy and mistrust. Or maybe they've lost the collective brain cell they share. I mean, come on, you have to be a demented sheep to follow the twisted narrative of QAnon – who believe a cannibalistic, satanic cabal of paedophiles, led by Biden, Obama and Gates, is ruling the world out of a pizza shop.

When you delve a little deeper into their world, you see how tenuous their hold on reality is. The problem with this organisation, run by 'Q', an alleged shadowy government insider keen to reveal all on sites like 4chan for the good of mankind, is that they were too specific with the dates for the events they predicted – like when a bomb was going to be dropped on North Korea, and never happened, or when 'the storm' would break where Hillary Clinton and her merry band of devil-worshipping paedos would all be arrested (that didn't happen either); and when in true biblical fashion, JFK Jr (who apparently never died in a plane off Martha's Vineyard) would come out of hiding and reign with big Orange Donny. Guess what? That also never fucking happened. Even the Charles Manson lookalike with the bison-horned helmet who led the charge on Capitol Hill must have felt like a knobhead if he didn't already. Helmet indeed.

Another by-product of this outrage is that it has now given us a whole load of false idols to follow. The more extreme the views, the more extreme the figurehead we need to fall and prostrate ourselves beneath. Just look at Trump, the embodiment of the extreme, the lead actor in his own reality TV show, the king influencer of the social media world. Fake news, blatant lies and inciting the masses to act. Shock horror, there were people waiting in the wings for the blue touch paper to be lit, and Trump was out there with a flamethrower. Half of the people who stormed Capitol Hill did it for no other reason than to say, 'I was there' and 'To film it for ...' you guessed it, 'social media'. It was a fun day out for the trailer trash loonies from the boonies. They wanted to live out all of their constitutional fantasies and to finally justify the right to bear arms. This was their moment, the reason they have AR-15s in every colour of the rainbow and vehicle-mounted grenade launchers. Americans even have in their constitution the much-quoted Second Amendment:

'A well-regulated Militia, being necessary to the security of a free State, the right of the people to keep and bear Arms, shall not be infringed.'

If it says it in the Second Amendment to the US Constitution, then it must be right and cannot be argued with. We'll conveniently overlook the fact that it was written for a different time when the arms they could bear were muskets, which let's be honest give you a lot of time for reflection during the loading process. (I imagine halfway through stoking the muzzle, loading the ball, and adding the wadding and black powder, you would get over whatever fucked you off in the first place and led you to pull your giant cumbersome rifle out in anger. Or if you did shoot someone, I'm not sure you would have the energy to go again.)

These lunatics have weapons that most armed forces in the world would be proud of. There's nothing like giving your average US citizen military-grade weaponry, after the most stringent of over-the-counter security checks as follows:

'What's your name?'
'Are you going to kill anyone with this?'
'No? Okay then, I'm happy. Might I recommend this anti-aircraft gun, sir?'

The mob felt their freedoms were in jeopardy. Suitably armed, they were ready to protect themselves from a terrible enemy: an army of satanic nonces, hell bent on world domination and sacrificing kids. So they stormed a building and achieved nothing.

There is some great footage of Trump's rabid supporters climbing the walls of Capitol Hill. It was powerful, symbolic, and it made for great TV, especially as every now and then some fuckwit with the athletic capability of a house brick would get halfway up and just fall down. Funny as this was, what made it even worse was there was no need to climb; the idiots could have put their *Call of Duty* fantasies on hold and used the stairs. Yes, that's right, there were stairs. These muppets were climbing walls for no reason.

WE NEED MORE SPACEMEN

Remember as a kid when a relative asked you, 'What are you going to be when you grow up?' and you fired back an answer without thinking. Maybe it was an astronaut, a fireman, but whatever it was, and however ambitious it sounded, you didn't censor yourself, did you? On the cusp of answering, 'I want to be president of the USA' you didn't suddenly stop yourself as that voice in your head, the doubting Thomas, told you it was ridiculous and too over-reaching. Actually bin that, it's a shit example, as these days, even orange people made of plasticene can reside in the White House. My point is the older we get the more we limit the reach of our dreams and goals based on the evidence of what we have done so far. Your dream might be to become a successful fiction writer, but because thus far your novels have been rejected or you haven't written a word, you doubt yourself.

I read somewhere of a study conducted on kids' self-belief and how quickly reality bit as they got older. When pupils at primary school around four or five years of age were asked what they wanted to be when they grew up, they shouted things like 'spaceman' or 'fighter pilot', 'ballet dancer', 'pop star' and 'soldier' (these days they'd probably just yell, 'famous!'). Nothing to these young children seemed too far-reaching. They had full licence to shoot for the stars. And when they were asked who was the quickest in the class, or the strongest, kindest, or funniest, most of them would put their hands up, unabashed. Fast forward a few years to around the age of seven and when now asked who was the quickest, strongest etc. the kids had already decided who that was in the class; they no longer put their hands up but just pointed the individuals out. In terms of what they wanted to become when they were older, there were markedly fewer spacemen.

Socialisation had already taught them it wasn't clever to boast, just as experience had taught them they were not the best runner or cut out for ballet dancing. Is this a good or bad thing? A little reality isn't a bad thing as it preps you for the disappointments of later life, but it's sad how quickly the imagination and freedom to believe we can be anything start being policed by our environment at such a tender age. If only we could return to that time when the self-belief begins to slip and interject by saying, 'You might not be brilliant at it now, but if you put your mind to it and really believe in yourself you will get there.

'The first thing you need to do if you want to be a space-man, sorry spacewoman, spacethingy – Ah fuck it, astronaut! – is you need to work hard on your maths and physics and read a lot of books on space and then try and meet an astro-naut, or write to Tim Peake ...' Possibly the shittiest advice in the world ever given to a child, but the point is if you can teach something someone is interested in, in a way that they will receive and absorb it, breaking things down to gradual chunks, then the sky or the stars *are* the limit. Equally, we need to stop pretending all things are possible to all people. Yes, if you want to be an astronaut then you will need the above-mentioned, but if you don't have the prerequisite skills then it's never going to happen and no amount of positivity or self-belief is going to change that. There is no point me sitting here at 37 with a wrecked body going, 'I'd like to win the Tour de France.' It's never going to happen, not even if I took Lance Armstrong-sized amounts of performance-enhancing drugs. Yes, I might be able to do a stage without dying and in a time that you might be able to beat by walking fast, but that's about it. So, while we need to keep the faith and under-stand that the world is our oyster when we are younger, we also need to stop selling false dreams. That's why no-one is happy doing the simple things in life anymore. Everyone wants to be an influencer, YouTuber, model or a performance car reviewer. Adidas says impossible is nothing, which I don't agree with, but it's great marketing. In my mind if it looks impossible and sounds impossible then it probably is. Have faith and you can achieve things in areas you never imagined, and you can always keep repeating successes until you die. You just can't be a spaceman or fighter pilot if you can't see and are as thick as Boris Johnson's skin.

THE YOUBANK

Did Mr Amazon ever dream he was going to take over the world and hold us to ransom from his willy-shaped space rocket for, wait for it … *one million pounds*!? Probably. I mean, out of his garage he created one of the biggest businesses the world has ever seen. Growing up, boxers Tyson Fury and Muhammad Ali made a point of boring anyone who would listen that they were one day going to be the heavyweight champion of the world. The difference between the 'Louisville Lip' and the 'Morecambe Mouth' to the average Joe is that they believed it themselves and had the mindset and physical skills to achieve it. It takes a strong character to keep the flame of a dream alive long enough for it to become an ambition; and then keep it alight until it is realised as a truth. The fuel that keeps it burning is self-belief and most of us run out of wood too soon to even get to the starting line. By pure accident, I hereby gracefully circle back to Benjamin Button.

The story of a person born as a withered old baby-sized man who grows younger on the outside as his mind grows older, and falls in love in the middle of his life when his looks are in balance with his mind, before ending his life cared for by his lover as a baby with dementia who has forgotten everything, has nothing to do with my point – which I can't remember anyway. But Benjamin had this to say: 'For what it's worth, it's never too late, or in my case too early, to be whoever you want to be. There's no time limit ... start whenever you want ... you can change or stay the same. We can make the best or worst of it.'

As I have said, I don't entirely agree with starting whenever you want; ideally it would have been better to become a mixed martial artist before playing 18 years of international rugby, when I wasn't reduced to a hobble. But the essence of it is true: all change starts with an intention, and through the repetition of will, amazing things are achievable.

The day you stop thinking you can do better is the day you might as well pack it all in. I guarantee any idol worth his salt will always be on this path of self-development. Look at Cristiano Ronaldo: he has everything, and has done everything, but try telling him that; he is hungrier than ever. He wants more and is prepared to do what it takes to be 3 per cent better today than he was yesterday. Look at Adam Peaty, two times Olympic champion and the most dominant athlete in a single event that Britain has ever produced. His mantra 'always be better than yesterday' is what he lives by, forever pushing himself on.

The German philosopher Friedrich Nietzsche believed we must craft our identity from the clay of our own intention. Happiness for him was found through facing a problem and countering its resistance so you felt in control. We'll meet this firebrand philosopher a lot over the coming pages. His empowering phrase *amor fati*, meaning 'love your fate', teaches us that every good and bad thing that happens to us is absolutely necessary, part of our individual journey and something that we can learn and self-develop from if we choose to.

2

IDENTITY AND MEANING

WHO THE HELL AM I?

Knowing who you are, what you stand for, the tribe you belong to and what you are made of, are all key elements that form your identity. In short, your identity is who you think is looking back at you when you see yourself in the mirror. Take away any one of these elements and you can easily feel lost, vulnerable and isolated, like a knight who has mislaid his armour. When we lack a clear identity we spend our precious time running around as if we are trying to find our shadow; we're restless and unsated, unfocused and frustrated at not knowing what we want or what our inner purpose is. We look outside for the answers rather than finding them within ourselves. We lead a shallow, repetitive existence, knowing we could be more than we currently are. We become people pleasers.

Lack of identity causes us to make non-specific, poor choices, choose any old job, run with any pack of idiots and constantly underestimate ourselves. Our lack of self-esteem ensures we pick partners that are not best suited to us, and because we're unclear what our values are we're easily led and end up doing things that don't feel right; like falling in with the wrong crowd and standing by as they bully someone else, or ending up with the wrong partner. Identical is what we are when we play it safe, when we lose our identity, when we are herd creatures.

When I retired from rugby, one day I was someone, an England player and athlete, the next I wasn't. As a professional sportsman, I knew when I had to wake up and what I needed to do to get the best out of myself. I knew when it was work time and when it was time to chill. Suddenly, when I retired, I had to go on a journey once again to find out who I was. Most people develop their identity over time and it takes years. I had found mine and then at 35 I had to find it again. If you follow me on social media, you will know that I tried many things – MMA, DJing, music production, podcasting, stand-up, public speaking and social media influencing to name a few. Some I found fitted well with me, others I chose out of a misguided attempt to fill a void that I now had in my life. I didn't get the balance right. I went away from what made me happy: training, routine and work. I partied a lot, I travelled a lot, I got into things I didn't like. I must battle this lack of identity every day, but because I used the tools I learnt on my first experience of life, most of them in this book including discipline and a desire to be successful, I finally feel that I once again have an identity and I am not defined by what I used to do. There is nothing worse than meeting a former sportsperson and all they talk about is what they used to do. I always want to ask the question, 'Yeah, that's great, but that was 25 years ago. What the fuck have you been doing with the rest of your time?'

If you've ever been kicked in the head, fallen and hit your head, been punched on the head – or whatever it was you did to your bloody head – you might have experienced temporary amnesia. It can be really scary when all of a sudden you don't know what your name is, who the people around you are and where you are from. I only got properly knocked out once in my career and that was on my comeback game for Wasps after eight months out with a toe injury. I ran up to smash Freddie Burns but at the last minute he rotated, and I hit his hip bone with my temple. That was all she wrote and I was out like a light. My great comeback ended after 28 seconds. I will never forget waking up and having no idea where I was and what had happened. I was convinced that I had let the team down, that I had let the opposition score a try. I must have asked our poor physio Ali James the same questions over and over again. 'What happened?' 'Did we win?' 'Did I let them score?'

Memory allows us to frame the present and make sense of it by looking back on thousands of experiences that act as reference points for how to act. Having experienced amnesia, I remember what a lovely gift it was as the mist of forgetfulness gradually started to clear and those slightly hysterical questions of 'Who am I?' 'What am I doing here?' 'Who the fuck are you?' 'What's my Xbox Live sign-in?' slowly found answers as the puzzle of my psyche reformed and I knew exactly who I was again. I had an identity!

PULLING YOUR PARENTS OFF THEIR PEDESTAL

A weak identity equals a lack of self-control. That's because your identity helps keep you on track; it's a code of honour you've developed over the years from watching your parents and sponging off how they do things. If your mum and dad break up or one of them falls from grace, you can suddenly experience an identity crisis as you realise that the two people who brought you up and taught you most of everything you know are as flawed as the rest of humanity. It feels like the ground has been pulled from beneath you and you suddenly question the truth of everything they've ever said and that you believed was absolute. When we pull our parents down from their pedestal, we then advance into the next realm of identity, that of choosing a new tribe other than that of our family. We find this in our friendship groups. It's here that we start to redefine our view of the world and our place in it. I can remember the exact moment when I realised that my parents were flawed. That sensation of, 'Oh, hang on, perhaps the world isn't quite as you have said it is and your way of doing things might not be the best way', or 'I don't agree with your perspective or approach to life.' I think every child goes through it. For me, I was lucky it took a while as my parents were great and I wanted for nothing. Some children learn this very quickly as their parents let them down from day dot. I am about to be a father and I hope that I don't fall into the same trap of trying to teach my children that the Haskell way is the only way, when in fact I get more things wrong than right.

WARPED IDENTITIES

Identities are the lens through which we see ourselves. And sometimes this lens needs a damned good clean. What we perceive ourselves to be is not always the same as what everyone else is seeing. An extreme example of this is David Brent from *The Office*. He believes he's gifted, creative, charismatic and irresistible to the opposite sex, but he's actually a one hundred per cent nightmare of a creature, and yet because he's the boss nobody tells him. A real example would be Orange

Donny: he won't entertain the fact he was the worst president in the history of the United States and is planning on running again. It's a big problem when your identity is so skewed in your favour that you become flawless in your own eyes.

Trump doesn't realise or care about the destruction he's caused to the state of his nation in the space of four years: the evisceration of Obamacare with no healthcare plan to replace it; withdrawing from the Paris Agreement on climate change in favour of returning to coal and open-pit mining (the equivalent of dumping Netflix and going back to Blockbuster); and promoting his own business interests. Like the time the Saudis booked five hundred nights of rooms at Trump's Washington hotel, and shortly after Trump failed to condemn the assassination of *Washington Post* journalist and American citizen, Jamal Khashoggi, despite the evidence irrefutably proving his murder at the Saudi embassy in Turkey as being directly sanctioned by Crown Prince Mohammed bin Salman. Then there was Trump's racism, with inhumane immigration policies like child separation, where kids were removed from their parents and put in cages as a deterrent to others trying to cross the border from Mexico. I could go on, but I won't.

Yes I will! Trump has an ego thicker than rhino skin. He hears only what he wants to hear; in the world of Orange Donny everyone else is fake but him. The brazen way he would go on TV and deny he'd said something, even if it was recorded and played back to him, was extraordinary. Even when there was proof against him, he would simply swipe it away and call it *fake news*. Any strong feedback that came from staff around him resulted in immediate dismissal and then a further shredding of their reputation on Twitter. The fact he was lying most days in front of billions of people across the world, be it about swallowing bleach to cure

COVID-19 or the supposed odious crimes of Hillary Clinton, it didn't trouble him, there was no glimmer of any conscience in his eyes. Nothing got through to the man.

Why didn't Donald Trump listen to any feedback? Now it might be because he was a complete narcissist, or if that wasn't the case then perhaps he was so used to being Mr Big throughout his entire career (even if it was built on delusion) that nobody had ever dared to give him straight feedback. When he found himself in the White House in a position where top military brass shot from the hip, he couldn't handle it and everybody was given short shrift and was fired from their jobs.

And then there's that other mentally distorted, equally deluded ego currently waging genocide on the Ukraine. Vladimir Putin brazenly removes any resistance to his regime, be it from journalists or political opponents, by having them spiked with poison. There is a dedicated team of chemical killers – all of them keen to visit provincial churches like the one in Salisbury – working round the clock. Putin's apparatus of control works through fear, and having perverted the course of democracy by making himself lifetime president, he's free to ride bare-chested in his homo-erotic fantasy of world domination, showing off his latest Botox treatment while innocent women in Ukraine are raped and butchered in front of their kids by Russian soldiers. The thing that Hitler, Trump, Putin and Crown Prince Mohammed bin Salman all have in common is their warped sense of self-identity.

MONSTER EGOS

A person's personality, according to Sigmund Freud, is composed of three things: the ego, id and super-ego. The id is the wild part of us given to primal behaviour. It is driven by the pleasure principle and impulsively demands immediate gratification for sex, food and needs. As kids we are ruled by our impulses to sleep, eat and drink. If we don't get what we want, we cry until we get it. As adults if we took what we wanted when we wanted it, the world would be reduced to a Mad Max dystopia. Fortunately, as we grow up we develop the super-ego, our moral conscience, which balances the id out. The ego is the conscious part of our personality and shuttles constantly between the id and the super-ego. The ego is your self-image of who you think you are and is driven by a need to be liked, and in achieving this end it will bullshit us all the way to the bank and back. By focusing on past triumphs to make itself feel good – and like a spoilt child it's always thinking of acquiring this or that car, watch, friend etc. – it will make itself look even better to others.

Look back on your life at the times when you've lost the plot and later regretted your behaviour, and you'll probably see that it was either the id that was out of control, or your swollen ego getting in the way. The ego takes you away from your real self and connection with others. It's a diva that left unchecked can take you to a dangerous place where your happiness depends on the recognition and praise of others. If it doesn't get the stroking it needs, it becomes demanding and difficult.

An ego left unchecked finds itself wandering into some very dark territory; look at Jimmy Savile, who at the height of his long-standing fame was feted by politicians, actors, rock stars and royalty. Soaking up all the adoration, his ego seemed to think that it was forgivable to prey on young children. Hitler didn't have a problem murdering millions of Jews and gypsies because his ego was so enormous that everything was driven around satisfying its needs.

The problems of the world are caused by bloated egos wanting more and never being satisfied. Think about Russia invading Ukraine, and it's about one man's ego and the flexing of his muscles because he senses his loss of importance on the world stage; it has nothing to do with the denazification of a neighbouring country. Once we begin to learn when the ego is driving our behaviour, we can start to recognise its voice and how it affects our thinking. For instance, not backing down for an hour from an argument even though you know you're wrong; feeling threatened by others' success because it shines a light on your own lack of it; or the need to judge others in order to make yourself feel better.

Controlling your ego begins with taking more of an interest in other people and being less obsessed with yourself. We're living in a time of unprecedented self-vanity in which the ego is constantly being stroked and enriched by the love hearts of social media. Don't believe the hype. Happiness starts from within, not from exterior things. Once you realise that happiness is generated from within yourself, you don't need to rely on anyone else to make you whole. Just existing in the present moment is the best thing that you can do, because that's where your wisdom grows. The spiritual teacher Eckhart Tolle says, 'Non-reaction to the ego in others is one of the most effective ways not only of going beyond ego in yourself but also of dissolving the collective human ego,' while according to Mahatma Gandhi, 'When the ego dies the soul awakes.'

IT DOESN'T MAKE YOU GO BLIND

I don't know about the ladies but many a boy at around the age of fourteen finds himself multi-tasking between trying to focus on his GCSEs and wanking furiously in the nearest toilet. And I mean *any* toilet, even the 'worst bog in Scotland' where *Trainspotting*'s Mark Renton takes a swim to recover his white suppository pill. We are, if nothing else, devoted masturbators. And with this giant release, something akin to the Hoover dam bursting with testosterone, we explode in zits, body odour, foul temper and lose ourselves in self-orientation. We revolt at home in our desire to break out of the boundaries we perceive around us, while within our friendship bases, we jostle for supremacy and quickly learn who's the *alpha* in the group (the dominant one), and who are the *betas* (the followers). And whether we be geek or jock we keep wanking, as if possessed by an itch we cannot scratch.

No wonder so many religious folk lose the plot and turn to heinous activities. Trying to deny your own biological urges doesn't in fact make you a favourite of the man upstairs, it makes you an idiot and a repressed idiot at that. I would go further and say sexual repression in the name of religion across the world leads to some horrific by-products. Grooming gangs, rapes, honour killings, mutilations, deaths ... you name it, it's being done, when just having a wank or sex would have been way easier. These individuals all starve themselves, pretending to appease a higher power that created you to do the things that religion is now telling you not to do. It's mental, it's like giving someone legs and saying, 'Oh, by the way, you can't use them. God doesn't like it.' Well, God created us so why did he give them to us? 'Mmm, God works in mysterious ways ...' That normally puts an end to any argument.

We are meant to have sex and pleasure ourselves. This may shock you but teenage boys are the worst and prioritise this self-gratification so much that they even start to smell of cheese, the scientific term for which is 'smegma', a build-up of unwashed bacteria, and you guessed it, spunk. This disgusting mix gathers in the region of the foreskin and smells to high heaven. Ever walk into a teenage boy's room? Well, now you know. Enough about these odorous individuals.

If you're a jock, as I guess I was at school, you'll probably find your tribe on the sporting field and base your esteem on your performance. While if you're a geek or emo, you'll express your identity through fashion, music and books. You may find you turn out to be a bit of both, which can be confusing: a bookworm jock, or a bit of a nerd who suddenly discovers he's a brilliant runner, or just a late physical developer. Our identity is constantly shifting, building, being knocked down and rebuilt in fresh form as we reject or accept the values of groups we become part of and then leave for others. For instance, you go to college and fall in with the Cheech & Chong mob, smoke weed until you go green, then after one too many whities you tire of their company because that's all that binds this group, weed; or, having been injured and declared out of action for a while, you no longer feel close to your teammates because you're not regularly practising the same sporting rituals. All of you reading this will have shed multiple skins in order to get where you are now. It's like Mr Benn going into the fancy dress shop and trying on different coats. Eventually, we'll find one that feels just right.

HARRY STOTTLE

Two and a half thousand years ago Aristotle said, 'Young people have exalted notions because they have not been humbled by life or learnt its necessary limitations ... their lives are regulated more by moral feeling than by reasoning – all their mistakes are in the direction of doing things excessively and vehemently. They overdo everything.'

However, Aristotle also believed in something the Greeks called *eudaimonia* (which can roughly be translated today as 'contentment'), and that young people could access it by finding a purpose, realising their potential and by constantly working to be the best version of themselves. They achieve this, he believed, not by thinking about it but rather by *doing* it, so that good behaviour becomes ingrained in us as habit. And that means in the way we treat and react to others and how much self-discipline we apply. He encourages us to practise moderation, be honest with ourselves and get to know our weaknesses. And he also suggests we can help ourselves enormously by planning, not an awful lot, but at least get ourselves sufficiently organised so we are not in our own way. This idea of *eudaimonia* is something that I try to pursue all the time. I have talked about my search for a new identity post my playing career, and all the varied things I have tried. The things that I have ended up doing all give me contentment, they don't feel like work. They test me and allow me constant room to be better. One of the hardest lessons that I had to learn in my journey was the planning ahead. When you are a sports person you are very much in the present; the idea of looking too far ahead is seen as a bad thing. Injury, form, lack of selection, all these affect how far you can look ahead. Basically, you are never in charge of your own destiny; you only ever get your schedule a couple of weeks in advance and that can be subject to change at any moment. Retirement meant that I could now plan ahead, have weekends, decide what I was going to do when I wanted and not at the whim of the coach. It took me a while to master this and it's something I have to work on every day. Routine is essential for me, as it is for most humans. Routine around things that give you contentment is the perfect recipe for life. If you have no routine then add one to your life: it can be as simple as a consistent wake-up time, planning your training, factoring in time for self-development, for friends or for chores. We need structure as humans, and unrelenting freedom and no discipline lead to problems and misery, even though you'd think it would be the opposite.

Childhood trauma robs us of a positive self-identity and leads us to a dark place further down the road in adulthood. Dr Gabor Maté is a Canadian psychiatrist famous for his work with addictive behaviour. He believes that the greater the suffering experienced in childhood the stronger the addiction for the adult in later life. The most crucial ingredient in a very young life is the quality of the parent/child relationship they experience, and if parents are constantly stressed, arguing, unhappy and impatient with their child, it is going to be reflected in the kid's behaviour and his self-identity.

Brain scans of addicts have revealed it is the impulse regulator – which controls desires – that is affected. Hence as an adult the person will struggle to control themselves through no fault of their own. Fortunately, they can find a way back to themselves through support groups and therapy. But to get there they will have to dissect events in order to rebuild their identity.

Those of us blessed enough to have sailed through childhood picking up only a few insecurities are not immune to losing a sense of who we are later in life. We may have been institutionalised so much that we find it stifling and seek to rebel and break out of those shackles. Think Jim Morrison of the Doors, whose father was a harsh disciplinarian and an admiral in the US Navy, or Joe Strummer of the Clash, whose father was a diplomat. I was blessed in many ways with my relationship with my parents and especially my father. Aside from always providing for me and my brother, he was always very present when we needed him, and we are loved by both our parents. My father worked extremely hard as did my mother, and they both still do today. His work ethic is something that I have picked up and carried into my own life. One thing I always reflect on was the support that he gave me while trying to work really hard and provide for us. He came to every sporting event or function; at times he may have been late but he always got there when it mattered.

He was hard on me, and probably too hard at times, not seeing that I didn't always have as much self-belief as I should. This lack of confidence is something I ended up addressing when I saw my first therapist, Dr Jill Owen. She comes up in both my previous books, *What a Flanker* and *Ruck Me*. If I hadn't identified this as an area of weakness and addressed it, I would never have had the career I had or been able to do all the different things that I do. Even now I have to use the tools Jill gave me every day to get over disappointment, to battle my demons and to reframe things in the right way.

I had a pretty disciplined home life – yes, it was full of fun, laughter and mischief, but we knew where the boundaries were, and were robustly told off if we crossed them. While I would say I was from a privileged background, my father and mother worked themselves into the ground to send me and my brother to public school. We never went without, but there was always a lot of tension around money. It taught me the value of money, never to be complacent, but also probably instilled in me a bit of an obsession with working at all costs, so as not to be under the pressure that I saw both my parents experience for most of my childhood.

I learnt two of the most valuable life lessons from my father and they are lessons that I carry with me every day and into every aspect of my life. If you remember only two things from this book, let them be the following:

Life Lesson 1: 'You can lie to everyone else, but you can't lie to yourself.'

I can't remember when he first told me this but it was oft repeated. It's something I think about a lot. When you are unhappy with what's happening in your life, love life, career, you name it, and you ask yourself are you doing all the things you could do to change it, only you really know, and for the most part the answer is always going to be no. There is more you could do. It doesn't matter what you tell your friends or family, or put out on social media. When you are alone at night and all you have is your inner voice and conscience, you can't deny the truth of the situation. You can bitch and moan about things, but underneath all that, only you really know the truth. Yes, you can ignore the voice, but I find that if I know I haven't prepared a DJ set properly, or trained properly, even though I said I had to my trainer, I can't outrun that voice and I have to change it.

I will never forget that the day before I started at Wasps my dad sat me down and said, 'Listen, son, you and I both know you are scared of tackling. You don't like it and if you don't sort it out you are never going to make it.' I was really pissed off and argued with him and said it wasn't true, but deep down I knew it was. I hated it. I was a big softy, all show and no go. So the next day when I started at Wasps, I went up to a senior player, Joe Worsley, who for me was the greatest tackler ever in rugby, and I said, 'I need you to teach me to tackle, please.' He did and I learnt to embrace it, to love it, to become known for my physicality and destructive tackling. All because I faced up to the truth I knew.

Life Lesson 2: 'What you put in is what you get out.'

That was the second piece of sage advice my dad gave me. It seems simple and base, but it goes much deeper than that. I built a career out of working harder than anyone else. I was never the most talented, in fact I was never the most talented in anything that I did, but I was always prepared to work harder and smarter than anyone else. The smarter part took a while to nail as when you are young you always think more is better. My journey in sport started out in failure and I have documented it in *What a Flanker*, so I won't repeat it here, other than to say I essentially didn't work hard enough and didn't commit to what I was supposed to be doing, and ultimately failed. My dad sat me down and said you can either see this as an opportunity to come back better or you can just give up. I chose the former.

Whatever I was doing, whether it was rugby, DJing, speaking, podcasting, fitness, I would apply the same mentality. I would work harder than anyone else. I would find people who do what I wanted to do better than me and get them to help. While others rested I was working. When it was time to give in to that little voice in your head that says, 'It's time to rest, you've done enough', I would say, 'Fuck you' and do more. If you break your life down into manageable chunks that you can affect, you can always make progress. I put more in than most and got more out. It was that simple.

Both these lessons I carry with me always. I regard them as a couple of little tools in my arsenal to re-use or re-visit when required. That's the secret of books like this: it's not about reading what I say and suddenly going, 'Bang, I'm fixed!' or 'That's how you do it!' It's about understanding that life is a constantly movable feast that puts you in very different mental and physical states all the time, which require different weapons to deal with. I don't always get it right or use the right tool at the right time, but I am always able to get back on track by revisiting things that I know work. My father and I don't always agree on everything, but what we can agree on is these bits of advice are world-beaters.

EVERY LOCKDOWN HAS A SILVER LINING

The other reason for writing this book was I needed something to stop me going mad in lockdown. I am a doer bordering on workaholic. I decided to push the 'go' button and start writing it while sitting on a train coming back from Glasgow. Even though the UK was in full pandemic lockdown at the time, filming for TV shows was still allowed for some reason. I guess people imprisoned in their houses needed a distraction from reality during this time and nothing does that better than TV, film and radio.

So, my wife and I are out of the house and on an empty train heading back from Scotland after filming a TV show with Paddy McGuinness. The programme involved catching balls, and despite the fact I've spent my professional career catching an inflatable oval thing I was pretty crap for some reason. Being an incurable competitor I got a bit despondent after the show, as I knew I was going to get the piss ripped out of me by former teammates on social media. Normally, I couldn't give a monkey's about being criticised, but when it comes from former peers it stings a bit, or it does for me at any rate. I was experiencing a moment of self-doubt and existential angst. Which as you know from earlier pages is something I have to work on, and it doesn't matter how much success or progress you make, these things are always there to rear their ugly heads. This was one of those times.

The central problem I was experiencing was my lack of identity. I'd been a professional rugby player for much of my life and prior to retiring a few years ago through injury, I'd always known where I was going, who I was, where I fitted in and what my purpose was day to day. Since I announced my retirement in spring 2019, I'd worn many hats – MMA fighter, DJ, public speaker, TV presenter, podcaster, author and music producer – but what I was going to do long-term was bothering me.

When I have these moments of identity crisis, my wife Chloe is great at giving me perspective. Rumbling through the Scottish Borders we talked about what I should do next, what I liked doing and why. She rightly reminded me I was a performer and a storyteller at heart. The podcasts, the books, the presenting, the DJing and the MMA fighting are all performing or storytelling in equal measure. I am a show-off and love attention, and I wear that badge with pride.

'What's the stuff that people really want to know from you, bar the stories about drinking, shagging and scandal that have all been covered in *What a Flanker* and *Ruck Me?*' she said. 'I bet people want to know how you stay positive, how do you deal with your demons and failures, and ultimately what makes you successful?'

This book is the result of that conversation.

Most self-help books hang their hat on one theme – usually positivity – and it being the key to a happy life. 'Be positive, think of positive things, write all the positive things down in a book and revisit them every day ... blah, blah, blah.' Some books go even further and tell you what you need to eat, how to wipe your bum and what to wear or drink to magic success and happiness into your life. There are myriad so-called influencers online peddling charlatan crap: 'Wear these leggings for a better arse, drink this tea and watch the weight melt away' (they're actually laxatives, so you'll need to be near porcelain). And while admittedly they are not peddling crack cocaine to children and some of this stuff is harmless, the reality is these products are deceptive, disappointing and a waste of time and money. For the most part, it's just faddish fluff. Also a lot of what is being prescribed is unsustainable, meaning that you never actually achieve what you want to, or you do it only to last for a short period before it becomes impossible to maintain. So, instead of making actual permanent change, you flit from one fad, book, scheme or plan to another.

I know it's the most overused adage of all time, but the statement, 'Give a man a fish and he will feed his family for a week, teach a man to fish and he will feed his family for a lifetime' very much applies here. Instead of just following a plan, piece of advice, mantra or false prophet that makes only surface change, understand the mechanics and make proper, legitimate change to your outlook, diet, life or whatever it is you want to upskill and fix. If you aren't quite sure what I am banging on about, let me give you an example. I could help you lose weight in four weeks. I could tell you what to eat and drink. I would cut your calories to a super-low level, up your training and basically crash diet you into shape. It would be horrible, restrictive and would mean that by the end of it you would hate me and yourself, and would probably rebel and go out and eat your body weight in fast food. However, if I explained to you about macros, training, calories, energy expenditure, your non-exercise activity thermogenesis (NEAT), looked at your mentality and why you gained so much weight in the first place, you would be able to lose weight over time in a sustainable way and more importantly learn lessons that you could take forward to maintain your weight or lose more whenever you wanted.

'But James,' I hear you cry, 'you love a pound note ... wouldn't you sell your own mother to human traffickers if the price was high enough?' You are not far off the mark; like most people I love earning cash, and I promote lots of things to do so. However, I only ever promote stuff that I like, use and believe in. Humans are endlessly looking for quick fixes and the path of least resistance, and these dodgy quasi self-help products target lazy and weak-minded people, offering them shortcuts and quick results without putting the work in.

If I told you that you could just take a pill every day, like Bradley Cooper in that film *Limitless*, and you would effort-lessly surpass your inner potential, most of you would jump at the chance without even looking at the fine print. Or what if I told you there was another option: that you could change your life through slow, painstaking work on both mind and body, that you would need to track what you ate, get up early every day and go the gym, that you would need to read around on the subject of your chosen career to develop your skill set, as well as developing self-awareness, seeking feedback and being prepared for harsh criticism? Which one would you take: the one that granted immediate gratification or the option that demanded discipline, patience and application?

I also think there is a caveat to all of this: look at who you are taking the advice from. If it's someone who appears to have done nothing but get naked on a TV show and prance around a bit, perhaps you don't really need to be listening to them about life advice. I would follow and listen to people who have been there and done it. Those who have failed, got back up and failed again are the ones to look out for. Reality TV is not the place to go looking for advice or people to follow. Just as you wouldn't let anyone perform surgery on you, don't allow anyone to suggest how you should live your life and what is right. There are many inspirational people out there who should be followed, but there are plenty of famous people who are famous for little more than being in the right place at the right time. I personally want to know that the advice I take is tried and tested in the fiery crucible of life, not because someone was paid a boat load of cash to tell me that if I take this pill once a day, my knob, maybe, possibly could get bigger.

THE CHEQUE IS IN THE POST

My wife always reminds me that cutting corners, especially with regards to your body, always leads to a future bill in the mail; maybe not tomorrow, maybe not next week but at some point you will have to pay the price for trying to do things the quick and easy way. Fad diets, injecting stuff into your body, not sleeping because The Rock only has four hours' sleep will all have repercussions. Even though in my eyes The Rock can do no wrong, Dwayne starving himself of sleep is no good.

Read some sleep studies – we all need at least a minimum of six with an optimal eight hours to replenish, energise, restore and heal ourselves. If you inject yourself with hormones and steroids, you'll upset your homeostasis. Also, bear in mind that none of this stuff *really* works, except the steroids – besides, who wants a clit the size of a football, or testicles like withered Sun-Maid raisins? I don't want to sound negative or to constantly prophesy doom, but I went to get my own hormone levels checked the other day on Harley Street and was talking to the doctor about testosterone replacement therapy (TRT) and other treatments that a lot of men are using. As unlike the menopause which you hear a lot about, men don't really talk about the fact that they have their own version of the menopause, the 'manopause'. Now before you laugh at me, I know women have it way worse, but men's testosterone can decline after a certain age and can lead to all sort of complications, including disrupted sleep, poor mood, ageing badly, lack of libido, poor sexual performance and weight management. So looking at getting some proper legit treatment can actually really make a difference. Luckily, at 37 my levels, while lower than in my prime, were actually still really good.

What the doctor did tell me was he was getting an incredibly large number of young men coming to see him who had all wanted the bodies of the people they saw on social media or on TV like *Love Island*; and without consulting anyone other than Big Sean down their local gym they had taken testosterone supplements among other things to get big and ripped. However, what had happened was because they were taking synthetic testosterone, their bodies shut off making it naturally. Hence why your balls shrink, by the way: if you are not manufacturing natural testosterone then you don't need your balls. The men didn't follow any proper protocol prescribed by an expert or a doctor and a large proportion of them had become infertile and couldn't get sexually aroused as they had burnt out the receptors in their brains. Now for some this was reversible, but for others it wasn't. That's what I mean by the cheque is in the post. You might look ripped today, but your dick doesn't work further down the line, you can't have kids and you don't really feel aroused. I know which I would choose and it wouldn't be a permanent six-pack. If you mess with the equilibrium of anything, you will always get an equal and opposite reaction.

The fact that most of the recommendations from these non-experts are fads means that round and round you go, from one crap diet to the next easy fix, each time spending more money, ignoring science, common sense and health warnings, in the pursuit of a quick-fix nirvana. So don't trust them. Next time you happen to be on a website with whale music in the background and a wet-eyed, smiling man sporting a man-bun telling you that you are beautiful, the best thing since sliced bread, and that if you write down your dreams on a piece of paper the universe will deliver them (on a side note: how shit things must have been when sliced bread was the best thing?), you know you'll be able to smell bullshit through the tang of joss sticks. There are no shortcuts to success, no instant fixes. In the words of Mario Puzo from *The Godfather*, 'Great men are not born great, they grow great ...'

3

SUCKING THE DEVIL'S TIT FOR A DOPAMINE HIT

NO BLUE TICK? YOU'RE A NOBODY

These days our personal space is constantly intruded upon by demanding emails and mobile calls, and pop-up adverts on our computers that have tracked our browsing habits. The solace of the home as a sanctuary has been defiled; anyone can burglarise your privacy, whether it's that sneaky bitch Alexa listening to you or being tracked through your mobile phone. So how do we turn down all this white noise for a few moments to re-commune with our old self? Maybe we need to make time to recharge ourselves with ourselves, switch off our mobiles, avoid Facebook and set an automatic reply to our emails. We all know that happiness isn't found in virtual friends or through 'likes' and 'comments'. Cyber tendrils drain our precious time and energy: it's hard to believe but the average person spends around two hours and twenty minutes per day on social networking sites.

The unspoken message of Instagram is anyone can be famous, you can all have the supercars, houses abroad, and as many Louis Vuitton bags as you can dream of, and you never get older and there are pink fluffy unicorns dancing on rainbows! It's all within our reach and we deserve it because we are special. Everything is attainable.

Between you and me, let me tell you a few truths. The *Love Island* mansion stinks of self-loathing, fake tan and cheap perfume. Ferraris cost more than a yearly subscription to *TV Quick* and will take a while to save up for even if you cut back on the Tia Maria. To earn real, lasting fame – rather than seven minutes of it for being shagged in a hot tub, and ending up back in obscurity stacking shelves in Romford – you have to actually be good at something and to have grafted like hell to get to that point. Of course there are exceptions to the rule: for every new pretty little thing there are fifty others who get nowhere.

The mirage of social media is as crass and plastic as the hotel in Vegas that goes by the same name. It's bullshit and we need to stop buying into it.

The problem with social media sites is they can make you believe that what you have – the car you drive, the house you've worked so hard to pay for all these years, the holidays you take – are not up to scratch. And if you don't have a blue tick or a million followers, you are a non-event. If you're not careful you can start to base your whole life on what @monkeyblast55 says in your 'comments' section. The fact that @monekyblast55 doesn't know you, lives in his mum's attic and faintly smells of piss is not taken into account. Their words can cut us to the quick, we have our self-confidence dented, then we start to second-guess ourselves. Worst-case scenario: we are scared to be ourselves in case we look tired, boring or unsuccessful; scared of trolls, frightened by our own cyber shadow, and despite this we remain on these sites only to become more anxious, develop mental health issues and from here it can go anywhere. Have you noticed that you often head to social media when you are bored and less than content?

I am guilty of it, too. If I am bored or not focused and feel like I need affirmation, I spend my life in this repeating loop of Instagram, Twitter, the *Daily Mail* app (I know, how shameful, I'd rather admit to running someone over than reading the *Daily Mail*), Sky News, Sky Sports, Facebook, WhatsApp, emails and back again. I honestly have to put the phone in the other room to get anything done. I know it's bullshit, but it becomes a destructive habit. The only way I manage this is to split my day up into chunks: emails first thing, WhatsApps next and then an hour for social media posting and for the aimless trawling that we all go through. I don't let one section bleed into another, otherwise I get nothing done.

THE DARK ART OF SILICON VALLEY

Removing ourselves from social media sites is too much for some of us to even consider for the FOMO (fear of missing out) that would undoubtedly follow. And there's a science to this fearful reaction, a dark art developed with complete intention that is as real as the heavily glassed buildings of Silicon Valley in which it was birthed. That science is called *reward and addiction*. The fact is we are now living in an age where, because we're salivating like Pavlov's dogs in response to getting a *like*, poke or love-heart for a comment or photo, we're turning into little clones with fake tans begging for dopamine hits of endorsement from 'friends' we didn't even talk to at school.

Jaron Lanier, a dreadlocked virtual reality pioneer, former Silicon Valley worker and author of *Ten Arguments for Deleting Your Social Media Accounts Right Now*, believed that making everything free in exchange for advertising would result in people being manipulated and their lives being watched. And he was right. Facebook needed to monetise its service so sold its users' browsing habits to relevant companies who would pay for that information so they could target their marketing with sniper precision. Google was the same. Civil society is now addicted to social media. Facebook and Instagram work because they offer a more intimate view of people's lives as well as the chance to receive endorsement from your friends for something you've done, eaten, visited or said. When they get a 'like', the user experiences a frisson of excitement and starts getting hooked on this reward system of recognition from others.

What we didn't realise when we were participating in each other's virtual lives was that we were being tracked by powerful algorithms that assessed our likes and dislikes, followed our browsing patterns, knew when we felt blue and when we were most active. Facebook became hugely successful because of the power it held: an intimate knowledge of who we are, a failsafe profile that was always being added to with fresh data. It's indisputable that they were aware of the monster they were creating; society was being wilfully addicted to the feel-good recognition of others, a dopamine release in the brain in response to those who liked our posts. We handed over our freewill the moment we signed up for it. There's a term for this process: *social modification*. Lanier says: 'When people get a flattering response in exchange for something they've posted on social media, they get in the habit of posting more. When many people are addicted to manipulative schemes the world gets dark and crazy.'

Sean Parker, the former president of Facebook, admitted, 'It's a social validation feedback loop … God only knows what it's doing to our children's brains.' Another high-ranking player at Facebook whose job was to increase user growth admits he feels guilty that, 'Facebook is eroding the core foundation of how people behave,' namely that we are becoming more isolated and losing our empathy. When you consider the fact that the original architects of social validation sites like Facebook now keep their children away from it, you can imagine how harmful it is.

Google knows everything about you from your browsing adventures on the web: whether you like hairy muffs or Brazilians, milfs or grannies; classic cars or gambling, or that you have a thing about dick-shaped space rockets and ten-gallon hats. Being blithely unaware of this is akin to allowing someone into your house to film you naked or at your most vulnerable, then letting them take the footage away with them. We should be focusing our energy on life experience and collecting stories rather than this virtual world we have come to inhabit. Life is about emotions, loving and being alive.

The promise of Google at the start of the twenty-first century was to bring together all of the world's information and make it accessible to everyone through its search engine. Initially there were no ads on the front page of Google. It all seemed innocent enough and so helpful. They gave you these great search tools, but unknown to you they held onto your data so they could optimise the web.

By developing an operating system called Android, which was used in mobile phones, Google could now see what you were doing even when you weren't online, as the Android operating system gave them this info. Very quickly they were collecting a huge amount of information on their users. Google is a giant compression algorithm that sifts through data and simplifies it through a filtering system. Its free email service Gmail tracks every email you send, even drafts, and this info is put into your profile, which increases the accuracy of the information for targeted advertising. Smart devices like Google's Home Mini and Alexa are always on and listening to your conversations. When you ask Google Chrome a question the answer you get is obviously biased. Google has its own agenda and chooses what it wants you to see. You know things aren't good when the Facebook founder was recently interviewed on TV and you could see in the background his laptop and that he had covered up the camera and the mic with duct tape. If he is worried that people are listening in, what should we be doing?

According to Jaron Lanier, there is plenty of evidence that there has been a rise in suicide among young people in direct correlation with the growth of social media. The more you use it the more depressed you get. Concentration levels are also dropping thanks to people constantly being distracted by these social networking sites. We are gradually becoming more disconnected from our inner self because we are externally focused on how people are responding to our comments and photos. Our minds have become more vulnerable to negativity through our disappointment when we don't elicit the attention we hoped to receive from a post. The reality is that the more time we spend on these sites, the more information they have on our preferences to sell on to third parties. We have given ourselves almost willingly to the social modification empire by unwittingly falling victim to a social validation feedback loop.

PILE-ONS

We talk about kids getting bullied 24 hours a day, but adults are being preyed upon too. There are people online – I wonder what the collective noun is for a bunch of social media bullies? I think a sewer of trolls sounds about right – who delight in ganging up in what's known as a 'pile-on' whereby a sewer of trolls come together to screw things up for someone they have targeted. Imagine a pack of ravenous pitbulls with their teeth sunk into the soft flesh of a puppy; that's what it feels like for someone who is not thick-skinned enough to deal with internet abuse. Even international rugby players get cut to the quick; no-one is completely immune to the cruel remarks of others, it takes practice. Or, like Tyson Fury on Instagram, you exercise the power to turn off your followers' comments, so it becomes more of a place to promote yourself and post but you don't have a dialogue to respond to.

The average human being has not yet evolved to deal with this kind of criticism and hate on such a macro level; no wonder the likes of Caroline Flack took her own life. She is not the first and will most definitely not be the last. Once you're addicted to one of these sites, it's as if it gets into your bloodstream; you become dependent on others' recognition as part of your day-to-day nutrition. And if it turns sour, your thoughts develop into paranoia and you think everybody is after you; when the reality is that firstly so many people will not have even heard about it and most people do not care as they are too busy dealing with their own lives. Yet you feel that it's all-consuming. Due to the 24-hour nature of the internet and social media, it follows you everywhere you go, or that's what it feels like. Is that really what successful evolution in the twenty-first century looks like? I don't know which was the chicken or the egg that started it all: was it media first then social media? Anyway, the media portrayed Caroline Flack as a very damaged person, and social media piled on. She clearly felt there was no way out for her, and everywhere she turned was the mainstream media, fuelling social media with hate. Imagine feeling so trapped and defined by the opinions of others that you sadly end your own life. It's very easy to get caught in an echo chamber of poisonous comments.

What then followed was sickening, as the media created a tragic narrative of what a lovely person she was and how could this happen, when they were the very wolves baying outside her window. They were the ones who hounded her and yet they had the chutzpah to pretend they had nothing to do with it. Quality journalism is quite hard to come by these days, so instead we feed the masses with recycled rubbish akin to the very worst Birds Eye food you can imagine. The problem is the worse the food that you feed them the thicker they get. Nobody seems to hold journalists to account and when they do, well, look what happened to Prince Harry, a red-haired Hamlet exiled in Santa Barbara.

I've had so many pitfalls with social media that it's made me a much angrier person, something I had to have a closer look at during therapy. A while back I had this watershed moment called 'Farmergate'. What happened was I dared to take my dog off his lead during a walk on a public footpath that ran through some fields. There was nobody around at the time, but then an old-timer popped up like a rusty jack-in-the-box and proceeded to admonish me for letting my dog off the lead, whining that it was a danger to livestock. I responded that the fields were empty and therefore there was no threat. I later retold the story on social media, and it whipped up a shit storm of the highest order. My greatest mistake was bringing myself down to their level and getting caught up in a mindless war of words with rural extremists.

I had been told that I was going to get shot, that my dog was going to get shot. I could go on, as there are many more very unpleasant things that have happened to me because of the media and social media, but this is not a therapy session and I think you get my point.

While writing this book, I was recently dragged into another media and social media outcry, this time over something I said to a female rugby player who had made a snide and inflammatory comment on one of our *The Good, The Bad & The Rugby* social media posts. Now I can't be bothered to recount the whole story, needless to say it was utter nonsense and instead of being about what it was – i.e. me telling someone who *GBR* had helped promote to not attack us for not using the word 'men' on our Instagram post about a list of England's most capped front-row players of all time – it became about me versus women, women rugby players and feminism in general.

Now we all know Instagram is a visual platform. So when you post on a page about men's rugby, with a 90 per cent male audience, with two men in the picture, you would think that people would see that it was about men. No, not for those people looking for drama and outrage it wasn't. I've never been that arsed about anything to write in and complain or turn to social media to vent my disgust. However, plenty of people do. Their point was we had left out a female player that had in fact got more caps than any of the men on the list. Now what these outraged women didn't know was that the social post was created by two female rugby players, who are hugely proud feminists continually fighting the good fight for women's rugby, and they didn't notice anything wrong with the post – and there wasn't, unless your diary was clear and you needed a pointless fight, which turns out is the case for many on the internet.

After the female *GBR* team members posted this and the ensuing drama erupted, I could see that once the negativity came pouring in these two ladies were getting pretty upset. So I stepped in and told one of the main attackers to have a day off. Now this person had been on our sister show *Good Scaz Rugby*, which is all about women's rugby (myself, Alex and Mike self-funded *GSR* at the time for no profit to help grow and publicise women's rugby), and knew better than to comment, 'Could you please stop disrespecting the women like this?' Now if she really cared and wasn't doing it just for clout, she would have messaged privately. But if you do that, then you can't be the centre of attention, can you?

I then deleted my 'have a day off' comment and replied in what I thought was a more succinct and mature way, essentially saying we do a lot to support women's rugby, please don't nit-pick over tiny things like this as it waters down your cause and actually polarises opinion and sets you back, you are attacking us when we are already on your side. That's me paraphrasing, but essentially that's what I said. I then went to bed thinking nothing more about it.

What I woke up to was carnage. I was suddenly against women's rugby, a fake male ally, a misogynist, my unborn daughter was getting insulted, I was getting death threats and being called names. All the while the people slagging me off were using the #Dobetter. Which they didn't see the irony of as they were asking me to do better while being rude, negative, sexist and downright despicable themselves. My phone was buzzing with people who work with and for me panicking about what the sponsors were saying, about crisis meetings, members of staff in tears. There were articles in the papers calling me out, opinion pieces from bizarre women; one especially gobby lady had a real vendetta against me that I couldn't understand, but once I saw the incredible eyebrows she had drawn on herself, I was less inclined to be concerned with what she thought of me, as her lack of taste and a clear absence of a mirror anywhere in her house were evident. Her lack of any perspective other than her own agenda was clear for everyone to see. Her sole goal, it looked like to me, was to be a voice for female rugby players, who coincidentally from what I have learnt after the event from a large number of the players themselves, never asked her to be that mouthpiece; she has no qualifications for doing it and they didn't want her anywhere near their sport let alone being a spokesperson for it or them.

This woman is doing irreparable damage to a sport that needs men and their support to help it grow. Why doesn't someone say something? Well, as in most cases, no-one wants to challenge her, for fear that she will turn the mob towards the whistleblower; not everyone can handle a social media pile-on, especially not from someone who makes it their life to be outraged and is primed and ready for the attack. Too many of us have proper jobs and things to be getting on with.

One of her bizarre statements was that women's rugby didn't need male support. When from what I can see all female sport needs male support at this point in time, as women just aren't watching it as much as they should. Men watch men's sport and some women's sport. Women are for the most part not interested. Just look at what women find popular for example on TV. There is a reason the Kardashians are multi-millionaires, and all the *Desperate Housewives* shows are so popular. It's not because men are watching them, it's, you guessed it, what women are watching and frankly want to watch. Do women watch women playing team sports like rugby? I would say no as the numbers don't add up, there is not the appetite. Things are getting way better, and the more exposure they get the bigger the female following, but it's not enough to say you don't need men.

I heard a female footballer call in once to a radio show (this was way before the incredible work done by the England Lionesses). She called in to a male-only football show and said that she felt that women should be paid the same as men across all sports. All the men started looking around for an answer that wouldn't get them cancelled; they knew full well what it was but no-one dared say it. They all ummed and aahed as to why this wasn't the case, when the obvious answer was, 'You don't sell as many tickets and nobody is watching your sport to the level required to get the same money.' This won't be the case forever and in sports like tennis there is a real argument for equal pay, but the likes of soccer and rugby are not quite there yet. I hope they get there one day.

Back to my Instagram post, how did this social media outrage make me feel? Well, I was happy that I had done nothing wrong, except responding in the first place, which, if you've read *Ruck Me* you will know was a promise I had made to myself after 'Farmergate': that I would never, ever respond. I mean at least this time I didn't call any of my attackers 'cunts', which has been my go-to move in the past. So I am learning, albeit at a costly snail's pace. All these social media pile-ons do is make me angry. I don't feel worried, I don't feel scared, I feel just pure anger towards the people coming at me and the power they are afforded by brands and companies. It also makes me realise just how sad the world is and what a terrible thing social media is. What becomes very apparent is that a lot of these people were not female rugby players or had even played the sport. They were the vocal minority who will jump on any cause if they feel they are in a like-minded crowd and will get traction from others for being outspoken. They don't need the facts; they just need some drama.

What really upsets me is how the corporate world reacts to stuff like this. My plan was to ignore it, as frankly I didn't care at all, and just get on with my day. However, if you suckle at the corporate teat like I do, you suddenly have to start bending over and taking it dry as and when you are told. Now I have mentioned this earlier in the book, but companies are why cancel culture exists. If they didn't stand people down, or force people to apologise, or take programmes off air, or edit out anything they don't like from old TV shows, or remove books from shelves, the ranting lunatics on social media would stay powerless and just be making a lot of noise getting nowhere like they used to. Not these days, however, and in 'have-a-day-off-gate', there were probably about a hundred people upset with me, as the rest of the world had better things to do. Now who cares what a hundred people think online? Really, no-one should, but because companies are so worried about standing for nothing but good PR, they run around trying to limit any damage and to be seen to be doing the right thing. Now my personal bugbear when I feel I am not wrong is to be told to apologise, or be told what to do full stop. Throughout my whole life I have been told what to do. That was until the day I retired and suddenly I had no boss, no coach, parent or anyone else. I had freedom. I'm a big boy now and I shouldn't be made to do things, but sadly I have found I still am. If you want to pay the bills, you have to.

Now as you can imagine a lot of people were telling me what I should do, which made me angrier and less likely to do anything. Some brands called me up and were amazing; they said it was all bollocks and they would stick by me. Some didn't care one bit and didn't even acknowledge it. Others, however, wanted a six-point plan and various other corporate mumbo jumbo on how I was going to fix it. I had about thirty phones calls with various people and they got very heated, mainly me telling everyone to fuck off and that I wouldn't bow to pressure. Sadly, when things started to affect other people who I work with, I had to throw myself on my own sword.

The most disappointing thing about this whole incident is that I ended up going against my principles and my own personal credo. I felt so sick about being made to do something I didn't want to do that my skin crawled. By giving in to these people because of money, I have perpetuated cancel culture for another day. I swore that I would never ever do something like that again. What was interesting is everyone around me wanted me to prostrate myself at the feet of the mob but didn't have the balls to stand up and say anything themselves. Corporates who have no public profile are always eager to suggest how those in the public eye should do things. If they get it wrong, their boss might tell them off; if I get it wrong it's in the papers and follows me around every time someone writes about me. This whole saga was a huge life lesson for me on a number of levels.

Never give in to the mob. Never let people put words in your mouth, and if you feel you are right then stick to your guns.

I have been cancelled four times to date, but just like a bad penny I keep turning back up. Now I don't think I have many more lives left, so however noble it might sound to be right but poor, it's not for me. As I like earning money, I am going to have to watch my step. With that in mind, I'm going to really, really try to remember the golden rule. Don't reply on social media, it's no place for opinion or debate. Social media is for work and self-promotion. End of story.

SELLING FARTS

The mind is a muscle that needs to be constantly exercised and strengthened. There has to be a complete mind shift on what social media really is. Yes, it's a useful tool if you've got a business that you want to market to other people, but for any other reason you don't need it and if you value your mental stability you won't go near it. Given that it's full of fair-weather friends we didn't like or speak to when we knew them face to face, ask yourself how much are you going to miss them if you come off Facebook? How much do you get from them as friends, and what do you give back as a friend? Think how much time you would win back to spend and focus on the friends that you do see, the real tangible people in your life. Anybody that I want to speak to, I speak to; I don't need to go on Facebook to converse with them publicly.

The likes of Facebook have caused so much trouble in people's lives, with old flames getting in touch sparking affairs that have broken families, all because of a tool linking you to people that you've long ago left behind. Why invite a thousand strangers that you no longer know into your life? You left them behind for a reason.

Unless you've really got to use these sites to promote your business – which in my case is myself – don't bother with them. Do we really care what somebody is having for dinner?

Is that the sum total of our interest and curiosity that we are now looking at photos of fish and chips or some ******* pizza at Pizza Express for our entertainment? Until you see it as a tool that works for you rather than you working for it, it's tantamount to playing with fire. The negatives definitely outweigh the positives.

Football and newspaper gossip are distractions from the mundane reality that you're born, go to school, get a job, have kids, work endlessly and then die. Some of us do adrenaline sports just to feel like we're alive. Others take drugs for the same reason, while some go to fetish clubs or plunge themselves in freezing cold rivers ... we're all trying to inject adventure into our lives to mark time, to say 'I was here!', like putting a flag on the Moon. At best we are collecting stories like passport stamps of interesting places and things we tried, all so we can look back and say, 'I lived.' That's what life is about, creating times worth remembering.

Social media, though, is a different beast. It's collecting stories all right but these are not real stories, they're fabrications. For me, the likes of Twitter and Facebook and all the other social reward websites are the twenty-first-century's version of the Colosseum: a place where we watch other peoples' lives with envy as we look up from the cheap seats at the royal balcony of the Caesars, a place where we pile on like mindless, ravenous dogs and take delight in other people's misfortune as they are steadily ripped to pieces and pulled down from their throne, or are dragged from their darkened hovels.

Throughout the history of Great Britain we've been engaged in necessary wars that not only defended the island but also trimmed down the population. Conscription to the armed forces – not that I'd necessarily plump for it now – gave young people a sense of purpose at an age when their brains were still developing and they need guiding, instead of wandering around rudderless doing fuck all as is the case today. Technology has not helped our youth; it's corrupted their get up and go.

As I have said a number of times, we are meant to do things with our lives; we are meant to test ourselves both physically and mentally. The much-used expression 'The devil makes work for idle hands' I think is more relevant today than at any time. With the multitude of options available for people it's pretty hard to actually end up doing bugger all. You even get paid to play video games now, or rub things on your body for odd people on Twitch. I even saw a woman selling her farts the other day.

With all the help and free services, advice centres, counsellors and apprenticeship schemes out there, I truly believe if you want it there is work and things to keep you busy. However, if you look at stats for crime and unemployment they are going through the roof, obesity is off the scale, schools are not playing sport, kids are glued to phones and iPads all day long. We are becoming lazier than ever. This is at odds with how we are meant to be as humans and what we are supposed to be doing. Hence an ever-increasing level of mental health issues.

PILLAR I
RECOGNISE

THE LIZARD KING

The more that we understand the automatic ways in which the human brain operates, the better we can learn to make it work with us rather than against us. There are essentially three decision-making areas of the brain; the amygdala (aka the lizard or chimp brain); the hippocampus (the horse or mammal brain) and the prefrontal cortex (the rational part of our brain that assesses right and wrong, risk and reward).

The lizard brain and the horse brain have been around a lot longer than the prefrontal cortex, and often they sideline it. So, if you find yourself in a situation where you feel emotionally let down or heartbroken, and things start to spiral, that's your horse brain panicking and telling the lizard brain it feels upset and threatened; immediately the lizard brain pulls the shutters down, gets irrational and responds excessively.

Interestingly, at the very point we hit puberty, while our hormones are going bonkers, the prefrontal cortex is shut off to us as it's 'under construction'. That lack of access to the logical part of the brain explains why teenagers are moody and often confused, as instead of using the prefrontal cortex, teens have to rely on the amygdala, aka the lizard brain, where raw emotion, instinct and gut reactions come from. Compared with the light-filled house of the prefrontal cortex, which is being prepared and won't be completely ready until we're about 25 years old, the lizard brain is like a dingy bedsit, dark and primal. It doesn't think so much as feel, it is extremely binary, it's either one thing or another – and it can be pig-headed and volatile. It's not just the prefrontal cortex and the amygdala; there's also the horse brain, which is responsible for compassion, empathy and the less hot-blooded emotions like love and affection.

Although the lizard brain is dominant in our teens and well into our twenties, it doesn't lie down and go to sleep for the rest of our lives. Far from it. It's a busy little bugger that means well in its endless quest to help us survive, but is constantly getting us into shit because we allow it to over-react to situations that can easily be becalmed by a brief pause. The term 'take a step back' means before you react, take a deep breath and remove yourself from the worm's-eye view of subjectivity so you can have a more objective bird's-eye view instead.

In his bestselling book *The Chimp Paradox*, Steve Peters suggests the best way to tell if your chimp brain is taking over is to ask questions like, 'Do I want to feel like this?', 'Do I like these thoughts?' or 'Do I like the way I'm behaving?' If the answer is 'no' then your lizard brain/chimp is at the wheel. Thoughts beget feelings, so if you're *feeling* anxious, scared, angry or disappointed, the chimp is in control. Fortunately, there are ways of dethroning him; it's as simple as recognising these thoughts and feelings and rejecting them. People who have accidents or develop a degenerative neurological illness that damages the prefrontal cortex can suffer extreme personality changes and become aggressive, outspoken and impulsive (I am like this and haven't had an accident. Or one I can remember at any rate), whereas they were previously level-headed and responsible. Your chimp is reactive and jumps to conclusions without looking for evidence. It looks at situations in a black and white, binary way and will not listen to others. It's highly paranoid and because it is prone to catastrophising, will often think the worst of situations.

We are all prone to listening to our inner chimp: when we lie awake in the middle of the night and can't sleep because we are letting our mind run away with us, feeling anxious over something that has not happened and most probably won't; or flying off the handle when we think somebody is criticising our work when in fact they are giving helpful feedback; or losing our shit when someone cuts in front of us when we're driving as if life has suddenly become a game of auto gladiators. As we'll see later in the book, the chimp operates our survival mode, better known as fight, flight and freeze.

HUMAN VS CHIMP

The antidote to the chimp is what Steve Peters calls the human (prefrontal cortex). As humans, self-actualisation is hugely important to us, developing our full potential and living as our best self. Maslow's hierarchy of needs is a psychological model that consists of a five-level pyramid, starting with **physiological** needs (food and clothing), **safety** (job security), **love and belonging** needs (friendship), **esteem** and **self-actualisation**. In order to get to the top of this pyramid we must work our way up from the bottom. The chimp isn't interested in fulfilling potential, it lives only in the present focused on surviving, and where your human side would think twice about the consequences of tearing a strip off your boss, the chimp, if it feels threatened, doesn't give a damn.

The inner chimp, like a real chimpanzee, is far stronger than the average human and in really perilous situations, like taking flight and scarpering or taking the fight to a mugger, it cannot be argued with. But in situations where its reactions are overblown and unnecessary, it's possible to acknowledge the chimp's suggestion but then by taking a moment to reflect on the consequences of listening to it, and how extreme its response is, realise you don't have to act on it; you engage the human instead. In this way the human becomes a kind of caretaker to the inner ape.

MONKEYS, TROLLS AND EXTREMISTS

Anyone bare-chested who wears a set of bison horns and screams into a bullhorn is probably not to be trusted; particularly someone inciting a mob to storm a government building. We need to stop listening to the enflamed minority, in fact anyone who embodies extreme views and spouts dogma, and recognise their bullshit for what it is. These idiots are definitely in chimp mode as they base their rhetoric on lurid fantasy rather than fact. There is nothing measured about their polemic, no rationale; they're unreasonable enough to blow innocent people up in the name of religion, or drive a car through a crowd of peaceful protesters just because they vote Democrat.

We're all different, some of us happier than others to let the world know our opinions, while others don't feel the need, or are timid of the ensuing response so remain schtum. Admittedly, I'm the former and if there was a degree in gobshiteology I would probably get an A+. That's probably because I'm more of an extrovert than an introvert, and extroverts speak before they think, like to draw a crowd and feed off the attention. So, my personal challenge is to listen to others and not interrupt and jump right in with my opinion. For the introvert, there is less need to be heard as they draw their energy from within, but they often lose out because they are uncomfortable voicing their views.

Some days are better than others, but from practising a little self-awareness of when my own chimp is running the show, I now recognise when he's on the loose, and it's usually when I'm annoyed, in complete disagreement or over-excited. Like that moment against Harlequins when I grabbed Joe Marler by the neck with both hands. It wasn't the best way to respond, I know, as it got me sin binned and Wasps lost to Quins by three points, but Joe had initiated the incident having trod on me at a ruck, then grabbed my scrum cap and was tugging me around, so I flipped him to the ground and proceeded to try and get him to let go. Once we were separated he squirted water at me, and I then flew at him and grabbed his neck in what I would describe as a Vulcan death grip. My inner chimp was like a silverback on PCP, I was blue with rage. I would say that I must have had some control of the chimp, as I didn't punch him as that would have got me sent off and banned. So there is a modicum of self-control in me, it turns out.

TIME TO START SAYING IT STRAIGHT

Doxaphobia is the fear of voicing an opinion, while allodoxaphobia is the fear of hearing others' opinions about you. Although these are extreme cases, both can be applied to social media in watered-down versions. Like those who dare not express themselves honestly because putting their head over the parapet is too big a risk; they might say something the wrong way, it could be woefully misinterpreted and they could be accused of being this, that and the other, so they stay timid in their foxhole. They are in 'freeze' mode. And then there are those who regularly sound off while living in a state of unconscious anxiety in which they worry whether their tweets or instagrams will be praised, criticised or ignored. There has to be a happy medium between the two, a place where we can voice an opinion without the fear of inviting toxic or over-judgemental recriminations from trolls.

The world right now desperately needs people to speak up and be straight, but to do so in a balanced, non-chimp way. The purpose of this book is to help us be clearer in our opinions when we speak to others, rather than being cowed by political correctness, and to begin a lifelong practice of working to improve ourselves and become happier, more honest people. How can we judge others, when our lives, goals and mental strength are a mess? We need to get our own shit together.

Do you feel like your arsenal of tools for dealing with the modern world is fully stocked, your cannons oiled and ready to fire? When was the last time you judged someone, looked down your nose at them, or worse still, sent them a toxic comment online? When did you last lose control, allowing yourself to become wound-up by a cretin and descend to their level of stupidity? I know for a fact there is stuff I can do better, things that I need to sharpen up and sort out. I review these all the time, almost daily, and try to improve them. We all need this growth mentality.

The simple truth is that this snakes and ladders puzzle we call life is not solved and completed in a day; it's a journey in which we learn new things about ourselves through the mistakes and successes we make. Sometimes we're on our game and on top of things, while at other times we unravel and slide back down that greasy evolutionary ladder. But incrementally, provided we have a growth mindset and are awake enough to reflect on what's happening, we should get wiser with each passing year.

That's the theory, but because a great many of us are passively plodding through life unconscious of our potential, or are too timid about how great we could be, we're not learning lessons at all, we are just repeating mistakes. We're too busy firefighting problems or firing off emails, tweeting or instagramming rather than taking time to consciously sit with ourselves and ask some serious questions. Who the hell am I? What do I want out of life? Am I limiting myself? How can I get better?

Sometimes you go forward and sometimes you go back, but so long as you are constantly putting in the work to improve little by little, it all adds up. Those who stand still or slavishly follow others without using their own grey matter are destined to become bacteria.

We all need a purpose and to develop a deep conviction to stick to it. In professional sport there are those who reach the pinnacle and fulfil their potential, and others who lack the grit to do the hard work to match their talent. They're the ones who lie forgotten, covered in the weeds of what could have been. Hard work beats talent when talent doesn't work hard. Many get distracted on the way to their ultimate goal.

Life will throw you curve balls that can take you off track, and what you need is an iron resolve to remember what you are trying to achieve and why you are trying to achieve it. Equally important is having a process to follow which will get you back on track when – rather than if – you derail. We are all flawed and require constant attention and self-maintenance; that's what makes us human.

EGOMAN VS EVERYMAN

Knowing who you are and what you are made of, the things you stand for and the values you uphold, are all key elements that form your identity. People with a strong sense of self are comfortable and can communicate with anybody. It's very different from a person with a big ego, where you need to put others down to feel good about yourself or get constant re-assurance that you're the man. When a big ego meets an everyman, a person at home in their skin, the big ego feels threatened. After all, the everyman doesn't need to talk about themselves, is curious about hearing others' stories and doesn't seem to need a flash car or to tell everyone how minted they are. You get the impression they could be airdropped into anywhere, from Trenchtown to Tallahassee, and they would thrive.

When you know the way the brain works and how easily the chimp gets frantic and how the ego makes you act, you're well on your way to becoming the everyman. You need to recognise your triggers, what it is that is likely to rile you, and ensure that you make time to consider before you react. It's a practice of taking back control and becoming better versions of ourselves. I wish at the start of my rugby career I'd known what I know now; I wouldn't have spent so much of it crippled with self-doubt or taken negative comments so badly. I had to learn the hard way how to deal with this, and I want to share this with you so maybe you won't have to. Don't get me wrong, I have not always been positive and in control, and

I still have work to do. I'm anything but the finished article. The tools that I give you are not about stopping you ever having doubts; they are all about getting you back on track so you can re-focus and crack on.

Every day I see people making excuses, blaming everything and everyone but themselves for their lack of success or happiness. I read a brilliant article the other day that focused on successful people. Most of them had had tragic things happen to them like a parent dying when they were still kids, or they were ill themselves. Some grew up in abject poverty, some had risen up against their disability and still triumphed. All of them had been in a desperate place but something in them decided they were not going to be a victim, and despite the bad cards life had dealt them they were determined to prevail. And the thing that they were missing became their driver, their engine to succeed.

We can feel sorry for ourselves and the things that have happened to us, but at some stage we have to decide whether we are defined by them and held down or whether we break free and use our hardships as fuel for our fire. They say the universe gives us what we want. I am not sure about that, but what I am convinced about is if you allow the things that have happened to you to define you, you'll never get where you want to be. If you constantly project self-pity it will bring more negatives that we then re-sow to become even more miserable; if it's growth, new challenges and exciting goals, if that's what we decide we want, this is what we will attract to us.

The first thing we must do is start owning our shit. The aim of this book is to help you make the most out of whatever time you have left on this world. I want you to be fulfilled, happy and resilient. I want you to gain some satisfaction in life and look at ways to be better every day. We enter the world all alone, so wouldn't it be great to exit it having given life everything and achieved a sense of wisdom and happiness?

KEY TAKEAWAYS FROM PILLAR I: RECOGNISE

- Life moves in cycles – good AND bad. This is normal and to be embraced.
- Rather than worry about trying to right past wrongs, learn from them and change behaviour. We are not defined by our past.
- Save your outrage for situations where you can make a positive difference. Ineffectual ranting or posturing makes nothing change. Action leads to change.
- You need to get your own shit together first before you judge others.
- Never stop thinking you can do better – there are always marginal gains to be made.
- No shortcuts to success. No instant fixes. Constantly work to be the best version of yourself. You never get there, but the journey and the success and failure of trying to be better are what life is about.
- A strong identity = control.
- Beware of social media – it is for business only, and needs to be managed at all costs. It can derail you as quickly as it can make you flourish.
- Are you too worried about what others are doing over yourself? Are you doing everything you can to avoid having to put the real hard work in?

4

SEXUALITY ALL OVER THE PLACE

GAY? I'M HAPPY!

Society is confused, unhappy and lost. In terms of sexuality London is a very different place to the rest of Great Britain; resembling an ever-evolving reef, bits of it die and fall off as exotic new growth takes its place like colourful graffiti. Buildings come and go, as do micro-communities bound by the same beliefs and sexual similarities. But London is a million miles from the rural world of a farmer in middle England. Can he really be expected to know what is going on with non-binary people in Dalston? In some places in Britain, there are still people who think that 'gay' is another word to describe someone as happy. I am being facetious of course, but there are still some very backward beliefs out there; it's not how life should be or how we would want it to be, but it's the truth and you aren't going to change that any time soon. If everyone accepted everyone else's own personal journey in life then we wouldn't have religious wars, *Roe v. Wade* wouldn't have been overturned in the US (so denying the constitutional right to have an abortion – fucking morons for doing that, by the way), and there wouldn't be racism or hate crimes. You need to understand that just because me and you see the world in a certain way, doesn't mean anyone else does. Sexuality for some is a concept centred around Adam and Eve, not Adam and Steve, or Eve or Jane, let alone the myriad of grey areas on the spectrum of sexuality that exist, always have done, and will only keep increasing.

I don't need to think about being straight or say to myself in the morning, 'This is the way I dress,' or 'This is not the way I dress.' Being 'nothing', neither gay nor straight, must be harder work than being *something*. A lot of people in life want to be part of a thing, a movement, a group. That's what is so interesting about obsessive football fans who go apeshit when their team loses; they are not satisfied with their life and so they look forward to matches like a diabetic in need of insulin. The most unlikely individuals are hooligans, and not just working-class council estate yobs. I know of a barrister back in the eighties who got his kicks by fighting on the terraces, and then there was this well-spoken bloke who worked in marketing who showed me how to make a solid cosh out of a newspaper by bending it in a certain way once he got through the turnstile and past security. Mob behaviour is nothing new. Over two millennia ago the mob was all-powerful in Ancient Rome, and this is where we get the term 'pleb' from, the old Latin word *plebeian* meaning 'common man'.

Adolf Hitler, aside from being the most horrific human to have walked the earth, was a smart little man in so far as he took lessons from the great Caesars of Rome in currying favour with the mob. He played to their dissatisfaction, to the inequality the country was suffering as the poor man of Europe because of crippling war reparations from the First World War. And then he painted vivid, pride-filled alternatives of a new Germany and gave them something to hope for. Isn't that similar to the desperation of the Three Lions bullshit in the Euro 2020 finals? If our footballers had beaten Italy, would it really have ushered in a new Golden Age or Renaissance period? No, it would have lifted the country for a few months until the *Sun* and *Daily Mail* got bored and went back to eviscerating Harry and Meghan or found something new to complain about, like water shortages and global warming, the cost of living, Boris Johnson, immigration, war, the royal family and knife crime.

Football hooligans have always been a minority but their mere presence is all that it takes to ruin things for everybody else. My mate Mike Tindall was there at Wembley for the final. Two guys behind him were scrapping so badly (next to a frightened father and his young son) that their T-shirts and faces were dripping with blood. Tinds decided he'd had enough and grabbed both of them, split them apart and asked them what kind of an example they thought they were setting as adults to the frightened young boy cowering behind his old man a few feet away.

Anyway, I've wandered away from the point. *Completely*. According to Tinder, the dating website, there are 19 different categories of gender and counting. Look at healthline.com and you'll find a helpful list of 'new' vocabulary assigned to explain the ever-expanding panoply of how people are identifying themselves:

- **Aromantic** apparently means someone who has very little sex.
- **Autoromantic** describes someone who's attracted to themselves.
- **Cupiosexual** is someone who is asexual and who doesn't experience sexual attraction but still has the desire to have sex.

Hmm, I'm scratching my head already. Not in a what's-wrong-with-these-people or a judgemental way, more of a how-are-we-supposed-to-be-across-all-this way. But let's push on:

- **Fluidity** refers to the fact that sexuality and sexual behaviour can change in a person according to the situation. Apparently, the term 'homosexual' is now outdated and offensive to gay men.
- **Greyromantic** describes individuals whose romantic attraction exists in the grey area between romantic and aromantic.
- **Libidoist asexual** is a person who wanks (but if they're asexual and not attracted to either girls or boys, what makes them come?).
- **Polysexual** is someone who will shag anyone (I know a few rugby players who fit that description).
- **Sapiosexual** is you're attracted sexually to another based on their intelligence, not their gender.
- **Nonbinary** means you consider your gender identity as falling outside the category of man or woman.
- **FTM** is a female to male transgender person.
- **MTF** is … you got it.

I've not finished the list but we'll leave it there for today. Now, can you imagine a farmer called Bill who grows potatoes in Herefordshire making head or tail of all this? Good luck with that! We should always accommodate others' sexual differences, and we should always be kind. But that doesn't mean we can't hold our hand up and admit to being a bit bewildered. Up until about ten years ago there was no nonbinary in the public consciousness, just transgender – people changing sex and gay people. There were straight transsexuals like Eddie Izzard and Grayson Perry who spoke openly and informed us what their schtick was. We're getting to a point now where it's LGBT plus Q and an infinite number of letters that appear to have no end, and God forbid that you leave one out. The wrath of social media and the media will be on to you.

I had a run-in with Stonewall, the LGBTQ+ charity, back in 2018 when things were slightly less fractious, to put it mildly. I wouldn't dare do this now for fear of never working again and my house being burnt down. Tongue in cheek, I put a funny picture up on my Instagram as a social commentary. There were two pictures in one and the first was of a guy drowning in the sea yelling 'Help!' in a pilot hat and a helicopter above him asking, 'Can I help you, sir?' In the second one, the guy in the water is saying, 'Did you just assume my gender?' and the helicopter is shown flying off into the distance. I put this up on my feed with the comment '2018 in a nutshell'.

No-one batted an eyelid really because they could see the humour and that it was not me passing judgement, more just highlighting a subject matter. I think I got three negative comments out of eight hundred. However, Stonewall took offence, and I was emailed at first and told to take it down and was offered a call with someone. I was still playing rugby then so my afternoons were slightly freer than they are now, so I said I didn't understand what the problem was and I would be happy to speak to someone. I was duly called and basically told that I needed to take it down. When I asked why, they said that nonbinary people would take offence: nonbinary folk don't assign to any gender so the joke would be offensive to them. When I said I still wasn't sure what the problem was and that no-one had seemed to take offence bar three people out of eight hundred and it was a joke reflecting the current state of play in the world, I was then basically threatened. The person on the phone said that if I didn't take it down then they couldn't be responsible for the repercussions I would face.

Now I don't like being threatened by people, especially when I try to support the LGBTQ+ community wherever I can, and have worked with Stonewall a number of times. So, I decided to test the water a bit. I asked the caller, 'What would happen if I likened myself to a cat? Would you defend me if I was discriminated against?' They said, 'Well, that's not the same.' I said, 'I know this sounds like a very Piers Morgan thing to have done and for that I can only apologise, I was only trying to gauge where the line was and what these people would and wouldn't accept. But what happens if I felt that I assigned to being a cat more than anything else? Would you defend me?' There was a pause. 'Yes, if there were enough of you who likened yourselves to cats.'

I asked how many cat people would Stonewall have to have before they started to represent us and defend our rights? He said if there were more than 20,000 they would represent us. I checked for any sarcasm, but he confirmed and said, 'Yes, one hundred per cent. Now are you going to take it down?' I said I wouldn't take it down as I don't like being threatened and it was clearly a joke. The call ended and nothing further came of it. I'm sure if this had happened in 2022, it would have made the papers and I would be out of work and you wouldn't be reading this book.

I walked past a lady with a dog in Soho recently, and said, 'Wow, your doggy is so cute, is it a boy or a girl?' Casting me a coruscating look she snapped, 'Please don't assume my dog's gender!' and she walked off. I would love to say she was joking, but she wasn't.

If I were to walk up to you and say, 'How are you, sir?' and you answer in a pleasant, civil way that you prefer not to be called this and tell me what you want to be called, I will of course happily follow your wish. But don't get upset if society and its people don't understand things as you see them and don't get things right the first time around. We are all on a sharp learning curve.

I fully support a person's right to walk around as themselves, which is why I support gay rights. I don't care who you are, what you call yourself and what you want to be, but you need to be more accommodating to the rest of us who are not on your path. It's about compassion and understanding. You should not repeat the behaviours you have experienced yourself on others. It's ironic that those who feel oppressed now seek to oppress others and those who ask for others to do better don't do better themselves. I have said this before but we are all on a journey, and a lot of what is happening now is asking us to go against science, the things we have learnt and used as parameters for our society. I am not saying we can't change them, but I am saying instead of going mad because you can clearly see the right path, others are going to take time to catch up in an ever-changing landscape.

When I started writing this book, transgender athletes were able to compete in the gender they had transitioned to, Lia Thomas being probably the most famous example of this. The swimmer beating everyone she came up against has sparked a conflict that has led to FINA making a new ruling on transgender athletes. The vote by FINA, which administers international competitions in water sports, prohibits transgender women from competing unless they began medical treatment to suppress production of testosterone before going through one of the early stages of puberty, or by age 12, whichever occurred later. It establishes one of the strictest rules against transgender participation in international sports. Scientists believe and have proved that the onset of male puberty gives transgender women a lasting, irreversible physical advantage over athletes who were female at birth. More than 70 per cent of FINA's member federations voted to adopt the policy.

If those making the rules are struggling to get to grips with this fast-paced landscape, we need to be cognisant of that. This doesn't just go for gender; it covers sexuality, the correct language to use around race and many other subjects that are constantly evolving, some from day to day.

DON'T BE AFRAID TO BE OLD FASHIONED

When I was on *I'm a Celebrity …* back in 2019, every mealtime we had this pointless charade as to who ate first. People said, 'Well, James, since you're the biggest you get to eat first.' The problem is, I consider myself a gentleman and I insisted that ladies goes first – it didn't matter who that lady was but I was not comfortable with eating first. I think we have lost the meaning and practice of chivalry amid all this sexist minefield; it's as if men are now scared to be gentlemen.

Kate Garraway kept telling me to have her bed and I kept saying, 'Look, we are doing a TV show, people would never forget it if I kicked a woman out of her bed so she had to sleep on the floor, and besides, what kind of man would that make me?' After many, many days of this roundabout of you go first, no you go first, I got slightly frustrated and said to Kate could we cut all this crap out please, and as far as I and the other lads were concerned the women ate first in whichever order they chose, but can you stop telling me to eat first? So my tone with Kate was slightly more stern than normal after we'd once more gone through this repetitive charade. This caused a stir on home sofas with the perpetually outraged. According to my wife, I was labelled a bully and a wife-beater, which is a slight leap from saying that women should eat first, but never let the truth get in the way of some social media outrage. The argument they had was that chivalry is not telling a woman what to do but giving her the choice and letting her decide herself.

Following the dinner nonsense with Kate and a couple of other frustrating incidents, culminating in a minor debacle over the dingo dollar challenge, where my camp mates seemed incapable of voting for an A or B answer and took three attempts at it, I finally lost my cool and walked out of camp to the toilets for a respite from the frustration. I was followed by Andrew Maxwell, who asked me what was wrong and said that I seemed a little stressed. Aside from being so hungry, my vision was going and I had to lie down every time I did anything. I snapped back, saying, 'I can't be involved in this circus of stupidity any longer. I'm too clever to stand around debating an undebatable question. I am going to umplode in a minute.' Not my finest moment – not only had I said how clever I was, I had then followed that up by inventing a word and actually coming across as thick as two short planks. Which as you can imagine was manna from heaven for the media and social media. Suddenly, people on social networks were calling me the worst names under the sun because I said women should go first. I thought I was better than everyone, how dare I tell Kate Garraway and the others off? Apparently, I was so far up my own arse all you could see were my feet.

The issues of equality and gender are now becoming intertwined. I think any man worth his salt can agree that sexism is alive and real, and while progress with female equality has come on leaps and bounds, things still need to change. Now you throw the gender debate into the mix, which is dividing women as much as it is dividing the world, things are becoming more complicated. I am about to be the father of a little girl and this is a pretty confusing time to be a girl's dad.

There's a story about a school in England where they told the kids all the different gender options available to them and half of them opted to change. We all know what kids are like. I was in a queue the other day and the woman in front of me said to another woman with a child in front of her what beautiful hair her little girl had. Then the kid turned around and it was a boy and the kid's parent, angered by this other woman's mistake, said, 'So I guess you aren't bringing up your child gender-neutral then?' And the startled woman who had passed comment mumbled something like 'Well no, I'm actually not,' and then pretended she had left something in the car and walked off clutching her own little girl, as people tutted at her and rolled their eyes at the fleeing mother.

I don't believe for one minute that we should foist gender roles onto boys and girls. We shouldn't necessarily give a boy a toy soldier or a calculator to play with, and a girl a pair of pink ballet shoes or a mop and bucket set. I would never put limitations or expectations on my child or any child. You can be free to be whatever you want to be and you need to feel like there are no obstacles to achieving your dreams. However, I do at the same time believe kids need to have some idea of what sex they are at an early age. It's crazy when you think about it. You can't have sex until you're 16 and you can't drink until you're 18, and the reason for this is because you're not mature enough to make those decisions, and yet people are advocating that kids be allowed to change their name and choose their gender designation. If one kid wants to be an elf instead of a male or female, others will immediately jump on the bandwagon. It's batshit crazy. How can we be chastised by these new groups for not being aware when nobody is educating us? Especially them. If you ignore gender in children you then come across some major obstacles – for example, toilets. What do you do about that? You can't have mixed bathrooms for obvious reasons. What about when girls come to the time of their periods and all that that entails? Bathrooms are often places of safety and a sanctuary. Kids flitting between genders at their whim is not constructive for anyone. If you had asked me what I wanted to be when I was younger or what I would have liked to call myself, it would have been a ThunderCat and I would have wanted to be known as the Terminator.

In earlier times we were happy to be in our social lane. People felt they had a place, they fitted in. I am not saying we go back to a class system, but it exists already even though a lot of people want to pretend it doesn't. There is nothing wrong with manual labour. Back in the day, there were those happy to have simple careers. But now because of social media where everyone looks as if they have the perfect car, the perfect body, the perfect wife, the bling house, where everything is perfect, people think, 'Why shouldn't I have that?'

Being a professional sportsman and looking like your archetypical meathead mean that you would expect us/me to be entrenched in gender roles. But actually, the changing room at the professional level was a very different place. I think I have spent a lot of my career either reversing the expectations you would have of male sportsmen or at times reaffirming them. I have always been very vocal around the importance of mental health and the fact that we all have good and bad days. I have always tried to check the bravado and be very honest about how things are. Fans will often come up to you and think that you are going to behave in a certain way; they almost adopt a persona, thinking that's what us 'tough' men want to hear. For example, around sexuality, saying things like 'Oh, that's a bit gay, isn't it, mate?' or 'Don't be such a poof!' if you were to be emotional about something or dress slightly differently. They would tell you outlandish stories of drinking and cavorting. When actually every changing room I have ever been in would have no problem or issue with someone with a different sexual orientation. It wouldn't be a thing and there would certainly be no victimisation. In fact, homophobic language is not really used consciously anymore; it may slip out, but then it will be corrected by someone. We don't spend our lives drinking or going out, as the professional game does not lend itself to that kind of behaviour. We actively encourage the lads to speak about their problems and to address them. We are so far removed from what you would think we are like. Of course, we can all do better but the belief that professional rugby players are all knuckle-dragging Neanderthals is very wrong. Actually, some of the front-row players maybe still are, whereas metrosexual back-rows are ahead of the game.

SEVEN MINUTES OF FAME

Social networks, Twitch and YouTube have made minor stars out of individuals who live with their mums and play computer games from morning till night while recording audio over the top of it. I may be doing them a disservice, but that is the image I have of some of them. Admittedly, this was when things first started out before it became a bona fide job.

The mind boggles at just how popular these online stars are now, with the numbers of followers they attract being staggeringly high.

When *Big Brother* first appeared in the late 1990s, it was a social experiment to see what people would do in a controlled environment. A bunch of young people soon forgot they were being filmed and the results were amusing and sometimes a bit dark – like when Nasty Nick (one of the housemates) claimed someone close to him had just died in a car crash in order to curry favour with the other housemates, then was forced to reveal it was untrue. They were rats in a cage watched by millions. Somehow, this one-off experiment of unknowns spawned two generations of wannabes all craving for their seven minutes of fame. And unbelievably, we have given it to them. Well, the unimaginative TV commissioners have, as they keep feeding the appetite that so many Brits seem to have for dumbed-down television with no narrative or artistry.

Ever since the first *Big Brother*, TV has become steadily more obtuse and cruel. There's *The Undateables*, a fly-on-the-wall dating show about people with special needs struggling to find a partner, or *Neighbours from Hell*, or *Embarrassing Bodies*, or *Love Island*, or *Naked Attraction* in which nakedness is reduced to a row of cocks and fannies on display like raw turkeys strung up in a butcher's window. It's like *Play School* mixed with cheap porn. 'Today we'll be looking at cocks through the round window.' It's cheap-as-chips TV with a huge following, and as long as we keep watching this utter excrement, they will continue to produce it. People fed up with their lives, those who are fooled by the sequined fallacy of Instagram, willingly put themselves forward to be prodded, manipulated and humiliated for a very fleeting glimpse of fame. And let's face it, that ain't fame, baby.

5

DEATH

You're in your physical prime from the age of 25 to 30, and are about as handsome as you'll get (though some look better with age, for example Shaun Ryder). When you're in your mid-teens muscles seem to grow from just tying your shoelace or running to catch a bus; your body is your best friend. To make sure you aren't wasting the gifts of nature, you're randy as hell, loaded with testosterone and have your highest sperm count during this period. It's all part of nature's plan to make you your most attractive so you can tempt a mate and propagate the human race while you're still young.

After that you've served your purpose, and you'll find your looks and body are on an irreversible slide to life's departure lounge. It's quite subtle at first, a grey pube here, a wrinkle there; or worse still, looking in a mirror below an overhead light and spotting your scalp through your hair for the first time and noticing your bonce is starting to thin. These first icy breaths of our mortality can be quite troubling; it's as if for a brief instant we taste the end and realise life is only going one way. You can try and fight it all you want with hair grafts, collagen injections, tummy tucks and Botox, but you'll only end up looking like something from *Misfits* (that game where you can have a knight's helmet, a cowboy's shirt, a wizard's gown etc.), with your old, withered hands and expressionless face.

MORE HOLLYWOOD SMOKE AND MIRRORS

Thanks to advances in plastic surgery some actresses seem to be defiantly staying at forty while the rest of their peers are celebrating their sixtieth birthdays. Some even look younger than their daughters. It's not their fault they have to hide their natural age; Hollywood writes women off when they hit forty-five. If they are to remain 'fuckable' (an industry casting term used by film execs) they have no choice but to re-upholster. And the same goes for men on the A-list roster. How many of them allow themselves to grow bald without visiting the follicle bank? I guarantee you'll run out of Vin Diesels and Jason Stathams in your attempt to name ten baldies. And no, Kojak doesn't count, he died years ago.

I'm not saying we should give up taking care of ourselves, visiting the gym and eating well. I am a big believer in firstly taking care of yourself, doing whatever it takes to be confident within reason, and it might not be too long before I have to personally visit the lid doctor myself and get my hair sorted. Even some minor intervention is okay, but the constant desire to cheat it at all costs, to not even allow yourself to show any signs of ageing, is such a slippery slope. Where do you stop? The answer for most is never, hence why they often look like they fell asleep next to a three-bar fire and their faces melted, or you could fire a starting pistol right next to them and you wouldn't even get a reaction out of their perpetually frozen faces. I believe taking care of yourself physically and mentally is the secret to a longer life. But by trying to keep age at bay with ever increasing levels of extreme intervention, we're missing the point and making life difficult for ourselves as we are always going to be disappointed in our failure to capture the glow of our prime. Like Oscar Wilde said, 'Youth is wasted on the young.' It fucking is, but we can't grow backwards, we can't fight the current of time, we have to accept ageing as a cruel feature of life and flow with it. Wilde wrote a brilliant study of vanity in his creepy masterpiece *The Picture of Dorian Gray*. In it the protagonist, Dorian Gray, retains his youth, while the portrait of himself under lock and key in his attic, ages grotesquely. While his handsome face is preserved on the outside, internally he becomes ugly and evil as the people around him fall into old age. I am pretty sure there is a painting somewhere of a hideous and haggard Tom Cruise, as that man is ageing like a dream.

The point is that growing old on the outside should happen in tandem with growing wiser on the inside. You can still have a washboard stomach at forty-five, and far beyond if you really want to spend that much time in your budgie smugglers, but the truth is that as you get older you need to embrace who you are and accept yourself and the fact you are getting older, focusing on your interior world too. Self-knowledge is something that happens from within you, not on the outside. Socrates, the father of Greek philosophy, said 'know thyself'. To do this we need to take account of where we are in life, our weaknesses as well as our strengths, and to know ourselves intimately. We need to take stock of where we have been, what has worked for us and what continues to get in our way. The stoic philosopher and Roman emperor Marcus Aurelius said, 'Almost nothing material is needed for a happy life for he who has understood existence.' Knowing what makes you tick as a person is a thousand times more useful than owning a Rolex watch. The person who finally finds a home within their skin is the happiest, most confident person in the room, and draws others to them like a magnet, not the guy with the loud voice trying to get everybody's attention.

In moments of fearing death we should ask ourselves: are we scared of losing this life we're plugged into because we are loving it to the full? Or is it because we know we haven't really even started living yet? The more you remind yourself that the Grim Reaper is always with you and lives in your body – rather than waiting on some hairpin bend on a distant horizon – the more you will want to make each day count. Time is our most precious commodity. Fact: you are a little closer to death today than you were yesterday.

Remember the film *Dead Poets Society*, about the teacher who returns to his alma mater and contrary to the starched conservatism of the traditional boarding school, he teaches his pupils to celebrate their free spirits, eat the marrow out of life and *carpe diem* (seize the day)? There's a poem in the film that sums up the irreversible passage of time: 'Gather ye rosebuds while you may, Old time is still a flying, For this flower that smiles today, Tomorrow will be dying.' This was written by Robert Herrick and entitled 'To the Virgins, to Make Much of Time'. In other words, 'Get your kit off, girls, and let's get ready to rumble, we'll all be dead as the flowers soon enough!' I wish I'd known a few chat-up lines like that in my teenage years – combined with a romantic dinner for two at Wimpy, I reckon I could have pulled big time.

THE DEVIL MAKES TIME FOR IDLE MINDS

Death shouldn't be viewed like the sword of Damocles hanging over us. Nor should it be a shrouded man with a scythe. For some reason death comes earlier to men than it does to women, probably because we stress more and waste time getting into situations that could have been avoided if we didn't produce quite as much testosterone as we do. Women also produce testosterone, but to a much lesser extent. I can never understand why people suddenly retire and just stop, especially men. That sudden lull in activity, unless it's replaced with a purpose, passion or hobby, becomes an empty cavity where depression comes to rot from the inside; we end up producing very little testosterone, and become a dried-out husk of a thing, like the flaccid cheek pouches in an alpha male orangutan who has just lost his king status in a fight with an upcoming male. No wonder those huge orange units battle like hell and often bite one another's fingers off; as the reigning alpha knows it will be no sex from here on and he'll lose his harem. Once he's been deposed, the testosterone drains from his bulging cheek pouches as if he's losing an erection.

I segue gently from talk of erections to remembering my great aunt. She was 90-odd when she said, 'I'm tired. I just want to die, not in a negative sense by the way, I want to meet death in an embrace.' Forgive me for being highbrow, fair reader, but that reminds me of a story in *Harry Potter and the Deathly Hallows*, about three brothers who meet death on the road. So death grants each of them a single wish. The first brother asks for the most powerful wand in the world. He gets the wand, can't keep his mouth shut and starts shooting off about it in the pub. Naturally, someone kills him in his sleep and takes the wand. And Death takes him away: one-nil to the Reaper. The next brother is given a stone by Death that can bring back the deceased from the grave, and he uses it to reawaken his recently departed sweetheart. She returns against her will but she's a shadow of her former self and tells him the act is unnatural and wrong. He thinks it's awful and kills himself to be with her. Death takes him to his realm: two-nil.

Now the last brother. He asks for an invisibility cloak and no sooner does he receive it he disappears and for the rest of his life he dodges Death. After all, who wants to live forever; vampires are fucking miserable, are they not? So this third brother, after he's lived a rich long life and is ready to graduate to the next chapter, meets Death as an old friend and the two have a mutual respect. Isn't this the way we should live our lives? Always aware Death is there but keeping him at bay by respectfully making the very best out of the base clay we are given to shape into something wonderful.

I'm not saying death is fun, far from it. For some it's full of suffering and pain, fear and tragedy. Again, context is key here; I am talking about those who have escaped some of the horrific things life can throw at them, and have managed to live very late into their lives. I am also not suggesting that it's easy to make this transfer from fear to understanding, then acceptance, to lastly embracing your natural end. No-one wants to lose anyone, no-one wants to die, but if you can make the mental adjustment to understanding that it is an inevitable part of the journey and part of the tapestry of life, it could be seen as something not to be feared. For those lucky enough to die naturally, it should be a welcome relief if we have lived a full life. Death separates lovers and always leaves one behind: lifelong friends, children from parents and sadly sometimes it's the parents who have to endure their children dying first. We all dream of immortality but really, how terrible to see the people you love all die one by one, the world changing beyond recognition around you as time marches on. Being a vampire or immortal sucks. How do I know? Because of every movie or book ever written about people who can live forever. No need to fact check me on that claim.

MEMENTO MORI

I believe death is not what we think it is. The stoics of Ancient Rome had a saying, *memento mori*, which translates as 'remember you will die'. It sounds morose but the ever-looming shadow of mortality should actually be a war cry against wasting your days, urging you to realise that your days here on earth are not limitless, and pushing you to take action and squeeze the juice out of your life. Most people sleepwalk through their lives on autopilot, occasionally awakening briefly to smell death's Arabica when a loved one dies, only to fall back into the old rhythm and general malaise of experiencing nothing new. And so nothing new happens. The writer Henry Miller once said, 'Being dead while you're alive, that's real death.' Miller spent a life rich in experience, he was fascinated by women and sex and his work was considered obscene and banned in the US. But one thing he couldn't be accused of was leading a boring life.

As we age our bodies sort of dry up from the inside as we produce less collagen (the fatty stuff that makes us look young and smooth-skinned) and other natural oils; our bones grow weaker, our brain cells stop replenishing, as well as all those other lovely things like loss of hearing, loss of 20/20 vision, loss of balance, loss of sex drive. The only thing we make more of is being a nuisance and getting grumpier – something I'm looking forward to immensely.

Truth is each day we die a little bit more; wrinkles appear like contour lines on an Ordnance Survey map, aches and pains spread across our skeletal landscape like a case of the clap in a Blackpool boarding house, and all those things we took for granted like our health and youth suddenly seem so much more precious than we ever realised. As teenagers we think we're imperishable, we challenge injury and taunt death by doing dangerous things. We go through puberty and suddenly we think we're men. But beyond that, the sands of time mean we begin to lose that indestructible cloak of armour.

WHEN I WERE A LAD LIKE OWEN FARRELL

I look back to when I first started playing for Wasps with the big men of the first team. I didn't think twice about punching someone who annoyed me in training, even if it did cost me a hiding. I didn't question hitting someone with a tackle hard enough to break bones. This rashness of youth is, as I explained earlier, because that section of the brain whose function is to make rational decisions and act with caution is not developed until we are in our late twenties, and so there is less of a sense of consequence to all our actions. From the age of around thirteen or whenever puberty arrives, until your mid-twenties, we think life is there to be a challenge and boundaries are there to be pushed as we test ourselves and everybody around us. Everything is a contest with yourself and with others: who's got the biggest cock, who has lost their virginity, who is the quickest runner, who can get away with breaking the rules. Our sense of adventure is endless, we think life owes us a living and everything we want is up for grabs.

We laugh as we put our bodies through hell and trust in the power of youth to magically heal us, and it does but with interest that demands to be paid back further down the road. There is always a price to be paid for what you have put your body through. If you do a load of drugs at the weekend then next week you're going to feel shit. If you balloon to an unnatural size then decide enough is enough and lose loads of weight, suddenly you're going to be left with saggy skin as a reminder. If you take your body for granted and treat your knees and joints with abandon, it always comes back to haunt you later. When I played rugby I constantly had anaesthetic injections in my joints and played on injured for most of my career. I pushed it as much as I could. I'm now in my mid-thirties and would I change it? No. Do I regret it? No, but I now understand that everything has a consequence.

Part of getting older gracefully is acceptance, that as one door closes another opens, and the hardest stage is to step from the last stadium of youth as the athlete in his twilight, into the stately gentleman's club of your forties and fifties. At least it feels that way for me. But really this is the next leg of our evolution; it's about letting those other young bucks with their erect cheek pads come through and do their stuff while we move on to other pastures. So long as we have a purpose and keep managing ourselves with a regimen of exercise, keeping our minds curious and engaged with challenges and always looking for ways we can improve and be better. It's also not about trying to recreate what you used to have, or trying to remember how you used to be, instead of the reality of how you are now. You might think, well, I used to do this and that, so when you can't do them now you feel all deflated and end up chasing shadows of a former you. In fact, addressing your reality and re-setting what you can do, then challenging yourself in that area is equally important. I haven't run since I retired! Do I remember running around on the rugby field like a young buck? Of course I do. Did I love to do running conditioning, shuttles with downs and ups? Yes, absolutely. So I could be all morose and sad or I can say, 'Right, I used to do that, but now I can't.' So why don't I accept that and for example do off-feet conditioning? Why don't I use the rowing machine or the VersaClimber? I reframe the challenge I face and do something different. There is no end of ways to go after things, you just need to see that and evolve. At any age there are always ways to challenge yourself, to get better and reach milestones. You can do it with the you now, not the one you think you still are.

Over the coming chapters, we'll explore these tools that can be applied every day in all that you do to ensure you are getting the most out of yourself and the life you're living. I think it was the American author Annie Dillard who said, 'The way you live your days is the way you live your life.' In other words, if today you put off until tomorrow the start of the journey to your new goal, there's a very good chance you'll keep deferring it.

EVERY DAY HAS THE POTENTIAL TO BE SOMETHING FRESH AND MEMORABLE

I don't want to say, 'Imagine it's your last day on earth,' because if it was your last day you'd get yourself in real trouble – doing stupid, radical things that would probably see you end up dead by lunchtime. What I would suggest, though, is for you to remind yourself *every day* that it's one day less that you're going to be here and ask yourself what was memorable about it. Was it better than yesterday? *Memento mori*, remember you will die. From the moment you're born wet and blood-covered into this world, you are indefatigably, unequivocally – those are all the big words in my dictionary – heading towards death. So you might as well enjoy it.

Remember the film *Groundhog Day* with Bill Murray, about a weatherman caught in a Sisyphean nightmare that begins every day at 6 a.m. with Sonny and Cher singing, 'I've Got You Babe'? Everyone he meets is from the same cast of characters as yesterday. Except it isn't yesterday. Every day is today. After the novelty of killing himself (in order to die of his own volition) wears thin, his character Phil Connors starts looking to spend his eternally recurring day helping people and learning something new: be it ice sculpture, learning poetry, first aid etc. Admittedly, most of these skills are aimed at getting his leg over with Andie MacDowell, but isn't this the way we should all be living?

I think the trick of life is to deeply enjoy the journey, to plan financially, and face fear like it was an opponent in the ring. And if you feel like you are caught in a daily loop of sameness as you push that boulder up the hill, rather than staring at your feet, then pause, take a breath and look around, take in the sights, be grateful, aware, compassionate and curious, and suddenly it's not just a hill with the rock that we're pushing up. Every day has the potential to be something completely new and different. The trick is learning to make yourself look beyond the familiar, thereby waking up your brain, because if it is just presented with the same thoughts and data it will switch into automatic computer mode and run on half power. Make sure you feed it with novelty. Challenge it. And though you may be seeing the same thing all the time, like your route to work, it is not the same; every day is different and full of potential, it's you who is sleep-walking. There are plenty of bunnies in the hat, and fresh tricks at every turn, we just have to look for them. It's a fine balance between over-thinking life and being awake enough to enjoy the present.

The poet Philip Larkin once wrote this on the subject of existence: 'Where can we live but days? Ah, solving that question brings the priest and the doctor in their long coats running across the fields.' The fact is you need to think about days and plan to make the most of them. If they lack meaning then you haven't found your true purpose. And if that means leaving your consultant's job at PwC to go and run a climbing school in the Andes, then go and do it while you still can.

As Mark Twain put it, 'Find a job you love, and you'll never have to work again.' My DJing has become a passion, and when I'm playing to a crowd it feels creative, intuitive and I'm in the flow. Time seems to disappear, it no longer matters, as I'm firmly in the present. The mind has three options: it can allow itself to wallow in nostalgia or obsess over past sadness; it can get swept up with anxiety thinking about the future; or finally, it can delight in following what feeds it and trust in its wisdom, listen to its intuition and seek to do something new. You can drift through the mortal coil and have nothing to show for it but regrets, or you can grab life by the horns and ride that bull like you are Hemingway on amphetamines.

6

MYTH FELLING: THERE ARE NO WHITE KNIGHTS

GET REAL

Unlike the lie propagated on social media that everything is tickety-fucking-boo, the struggles of life are real and nothing comes for free. There is no white knight riding over the hill to save you. Yes, you could try and marry into some cash, rob a bank, or perhaps you are in the 0.1 per cent of the population that have a trust fund, but other than those things, you have to make of this life what you can. It's not easy, not always fun and 99 per cent of it you would definitely not want to post on social media. Can you imagine how refreshing it would be to post true and honest photos, to tell the world when we felt like shit? Some celebrities, like Hugh Jackman, are happy to show what they really look like away from the Hollywood tinsel and I admire them for it. Equally, I can't stand those people who take 'bad' photos of themselves or even videos of themselves crying or having a meltdown, in an attempt to keep it real for their audience. I have never ever thought mid-argument or mid-crying fit, 'Fuck, I'd better take a photo of this and post it.' It's contrived bullshit. If it's not and you are posting photos of yourself crying or having a screaming breakdown, I suggest you seek professional help, instead of prostrating yourself at the hands of social media.

Full lockdown showed us that many of the things we thought about life and the world had changed. All the comfort we took from the status quo has gone. The concept of putting things off until tomorrow or saving for a rainy day are dead. I am not saying you should start living every day as if it's your last, as it's as equally stupid as not doing anything for fear of failure. And you should save, plan and have some direction, but you should not be scared of taking action and changing things you don't like.

The concepts of going all-in or being scared of your own shadow are flawed whichever way you look at them. The overriding point is things have changed and it's been a big wake-up call.

LIFE'S NOT FAIR

Whatever you believe in, the distribution of intelligence, wealth, looks and athletic ability is not equally shared. I don't believe in fate or some pre-determined path for us; I think we make our own luck by being prepared, putting the extra effort in, working smart and looking to the right people for help. It's too easy to blame someone working in mysterious ways for why your life is not panning out the way you hoped it would. I'd love to think that there is a master plan for us all, that when I fail 'it's God guiding me onto the next thing, testing me and questioning my faith'. Looking at the starving faces of children in Yemen beset by war and famine, and at babies being tossed over the walls of Kabul airport into the waiting hands of British Paras (in the hope they will be given safe passage to England), it doesn't strike me as evidence of a god at the top of his game. I mean the number of children dying from cancer and other horrific diseases should be proof enough there is no higher power, or if there is one he is a very deranged and odd one. One thing I have never understood is, if there was a God and he is all-seeing and all-knowing, why doesn't he kill the devil? I mean he can do anything, or so the Bible says. He made heaven and earth, and man, and he must have made the angels, and made the one that fell that became the devil, so surely the first thing would be to get rid of him and all the other fake gods that other people believe in. Now I like the Ancient Greek gods, they were mega, but they also had faults, flaws and frailties. This new God is not the best. He is arrogant and demands that we spend so much time paying homage to him, and that half the things we want to do are sins! How lucky are we that we are born in the Western world and can definitely get into heaven, when according to the Bible all of India for example is going to hell right off the bat for believing in the wrong god/gods? Again, just goes to show you how weird he would be to do that. There is so much to bring up with him were we ever to meet, obviously if he *were* to exist, but he doesn't, so it's all good.

Please don't use the excuse that anything that can't be explained must be down to some intelligent design. We just don't yet have the answers to lots of questions, but why God must be the answer to everything unexplained is beyond me. As things progress we will end up learning more and more and explaining more and more about what still appears out of reach.

DICKHEADS

The truth is, shit happens to good people and often those who exploit them get away with it. Hopefully, you were taught by your parents that honesty is the best policy, that if you are good then good things will happen to you. Hope is a fine thing. But it's simply not true. I am not saying you shouldn't be good and nice to people, as that is one of the things that you can control, and more on that later. Michael McIntyre sums up life quite nicely: picture the scene ... you are on a country road, there is a tractor on the road trundling along at about 35 mph and a line of cars behind it. You are the second or third car in the line and the bloke in front is hesitating to overtake. You're thinking about it, edging out but then panicking. Before you know it, some fucker six cars back has put his foot down – probably in an outdated Audi or BMW – and overtaken all of you as well as the tractor.

The whole time all the other drivers are thinking, 'Die you bastard!' and much as you try to visualise them in a smoking wreck a mile down the road, more often than not this doesn't happen. Your wife, mum or friend looks at you and says, 'Well, they won't get there any faster.' Yes, they will, they already fucking have. That's life in a nutshell: there is always someone who breaks the rules, upsets everyone and still finishes first.

The only way we get through this mess and through future messes is with mental resilience and good mental health. Obviously physical health is key, but that is not what we are talking about this time. You can read all about that in my other books *Perfect Fit* and *Cooking for Fitness*. I want to clear the path with this book in helping you navigate the ever more treacherous waters of life. This book is about mindset and developing some tools to help you fight the good fight and win.

THAT FUCKING MOUSE

Disney has a lot to answer for! Now, before I incite you to fill-in Mickey or punch Donald on the beak, let me clarify. Their heart-warming cartoons and movies have led us to believe that there is a 'happy ever after', that magic exists and that good triumphs over evil every time. Oh, and as we are on the topic, they've done men a disservice for years. Women watch this stuff as children and believe that men will be like these animated heroes: chivalrous, caring and prepared to slay a dragon just to get a kiss of their soft lips. Life is perfect and hermetically sealed like an enchanted snow-globe.

Now, I'm not saying I am not chivalrous, in fact I am the embodiment of chivalry, as my mum hammered it into me as a child. What I am saying is there is an inevitable sense of disappointment when a girl realises, after her perfect white-picket fence wedding, that her man is fallible, and, shock horror – human. This dawns on them when they don't end up marrying their first love and the spell is shattered. Love is not supposed to hurt, or so it appears in every child movie I've ever seen. Love makes birds land on your arms, it makes rainbows come out and melts even the coldest hearts. Doesn't it?

Before you scream, 'You sexist pig!' at me, I know there are millions of women who don't think like this, don't want to get married, and don't need a man to complete them. Who is to say the girl didn't break up with the boy in my hypothetical story? Look at the norms of engagement, men getting down on one knee, women wanting to be swept off their feet, songs about putting a ring on it, every crooner singing about syrupy love. The simple fact is we paint this picture of what life and love should be and we all get our pants pulled down when it isn't. Even men get hammered by Disney and other unrealistic imagery. I too have fallen foul of this fantasy factory. I thought that once you found a partner you never argued. I believed in love at first sight and that you got on with your partner and never had a single cross word or drama. Where did this come from, I wonder?

Some bare universal untruths

- Never argue with your missus/partner.
- It was love at first sight.
- The marriage was plain sailing all the way through.
- Good things will happen to good people.
- Good always triumphs over evil.
- You don't have to work at love.
- Real love is just like the movies, birds sing around you.

Some universal truths

- The birds shit on you.
- The couples who've been married for 85 years are still together because he's deaf and hasn't heard anything she's said for the last 60 years and they sleep in different rooms.
- Couples always argue.
- Men and women are very, very different.
- You have to work at love.
- Bad shit happens to good people.
- Evil often wins.

I learnt these things from seeing couples ride off into the sunset, all smiles and longing looks. What Disney should do is a follow-up episode six months into the relationship, when Prince Charming has put some weight on and Cinderella won't let him go out on the piss with the seven dwarfs, because he spends too much money on alcohol and hasn't paid this month's firewood bill. He is also late on the witch tax repayments and fucking Cinderella insists on singing every five minutes, meaning birds keep flying in the window and shitting all over the kitchen surfaces, especially the new Aga, which she doesn't clean up as it's not her job. That would make for more realistic viewing: *Cinderella 2: The Divorce Years*.

The *Frozen* movies made for a refreshing change; for the first time ever they portrayed some actual real relationship stuff. It turns out that even though Anna and Hans can finish each other's sandwiches (am I revealing myself to be a *Frozen* fan?), their relationship falls apart. Hans is evil and selfish and uses Anna for position. This has never happened before in any Disney movie. Now, while I am not suggesting men are evil and use women by trade, it gives a far more realistic turn of events to the movie; the person you meet on your first date is unlikely to be the person you move in with six months down the line. Relationships typically start and end in a power struggle, and it takes a while to find someone who is compatible with you, and even then, you have to work at it. Nothing in life should be straightforward and effortless.

For once, Disney has shown the realities of life, that people let you down all the time. You have to understand there is no fairy godmother or kindly witch who is going to visit you one day soon and wave her magic wand so you can live your life again minus the mistakes you've made. Nor can she give you the required energy, personal admin skills, self-discipline and inner belief to sort your shit out and do that one thing you've always dreamt of doing – whether it be setting up your own business, or becoming a professional cliff diver in Acapulco. Actually, steer clear of Acapulco; you're more likely to get pushed off a cliff these days by the narcos.

Only you can change your life, and it starts with a clear intention and willingness to transform. However much you think you deserve, or however much you hate your life, you are not going to be able to change it unless you *do* something. You have to be your own source of strength. This is easier said than done, but it's possible. If you are not happy, it's your fault, so change it. We live in a culture where we don't say things like, 'It's your fault.' Instead we try to go around the houses. We sit, listen and say, 'Oh you poor thing!'

Successful people are accountable for their actions. They hold a mirror to themselves and are not scared to identify their weaknesses, examining them so they can rectify them.

Bad shit happens to good people; it's an ineradicable fact of life. What many of us fail to realise only too late is that this is not a dress rehearsal. I am pretty sure it is the only life we have, and while some of you believe you will be happier in the next life when you are reincarnated as a porn star or a flamingo, there is no guarantee. Spoiler alert: it's not going to happen, so you'd better squeeze the juice out of what you've got. We allow our pasts to sit like grizzled monkeys on our shoulders, dictating our responses and seeping into the present. In the next chapter I'll teach you not to be a victim of your past but to focus on the now, while getting your focus clear to achieve your future goal.

There was once a time not so long ago when people were considerably more satisfied than we are now, because they didn't know any better than their sphere of influence. That was often good enough, as the less wild expectation there was, the fewer the disappointments. Not anymore. Because we now think we can all be famous, rich and beautiful, naturally we're going to get let down. Hope is a fine thing. Until it becomes delusion.

PILLAR II
REFLECT

SQUEEZING THE JUICE

The England rugby team have a post-game analysis and UK Special Forces have debriefs immediately after a mission, but how often do we take time to reflect on what's gone well or badly in our day/week and ask ourselves why? We shouldn't be afraid of seeking out feedback from those who are in a position to help us grow. And just like the SF we should invite total honesty. It may be hard to swallow but that single piece of feedback might be a game changer for us. There's no point asking for feedback from somebody who gives you a soft answer; you need to look for it from somebody who will say it to you straight, save you time and go directly to the point in order that you can tackle it and improve. Constructive feedback is essential for self-development.

An old Chinese proverb reads, 'Be not afraid of growing slowly, be afraid only of standing still.' In other words don't rest on your laurels and think it's okay to stop interacting with life, sitting in a chair like a man pondering his end; keep moving, always learning, always doing. An idle mind is the devil's work. Don't worry about your age, even when we were twenty-five we thought we were ancient. Age is just a number after all, and while you might be ageing on the outside, developing as many new lines as Gordon Ramsay on a stressful day in the kitchen, within yourself you can be as young and spirited as you allow yourself to be. Look at Peter O'Toole and Richard Harris: until their demise both of those talented hellraisers were still squeezing the juice out of life, even if their drinks were no longer alcoholic. There's a fantastic clip of them as doddery old men at an Irish rugby international; despite their broken bodies, they're mucking around like teenagers having a good craic as O'Toole tackles Harris to the ground. You're as old as the spirit that resides in you. I'm not saying, 'Sixty is the new forty' and all that bumper sticker bollocks, but if you're feeling old on the inside, make positive changes to feel more alive. Until your last day on Earth, you are still a work in progress.

Unlike Dorian Grey or Peter Pan, we need not resist getting older, trying to hold back time like the kid with his finger in the dyke. And before I go any further, lest my friends at Stonewall misunderstand and start reprimanding me for being anti-gay, I refer to 'dyke' as the flood-barrier type thing, rather than a lesbian. Curiously, the original meaning of dyke according to Wikipedia is a stone wall. How about that for serendipity!

I'm having a senior moment … now where was I? Ah yes, while our bodies may be headed in one direction, we can still maintain our fitness as best we can and respect our bodies for the scrapes they've carried us through. You may not be able to do as many press-ups as you could when you were twenty (it'd be weird if you could) but that's not to say stop doing them; you *should* keep pushing yourself. Admittedly, when Roy Jones Jr and Mike Tyson climbed back in the ring in

2020, with a combined age of 105, it was more of a freak-show draw than a hotly anticipated competition between two fighters in their prime. And though they had slowed down considerably since they last danced on the canvas, they admirably proved they hadn't lost their fighter's spirit and had plenty of juice left in the tank. Don't let anyone tell you that you can't grow older and still maintain a decent level of fitness.

THE MIND IS MASTER OF THE BODY

Of equal importance to keeping in trim, if not more crucial, is ensuring we don't stagnate in our inner selves, becoming set in our ways, hidebound to the same grumpy views as your average *Daily Mail* reader. Instead, we should try to remain open to life's lessons each day, seeking out new hobbies and practising curiosity: reading good biographies, gathering wisdom, travelling, listening to young people's views (however impractical or fanciful we think they may be) and taking time to reflect on our own journey and what we can perhaps offer younger people based on our own misadventures through life.

Self-knowledge is something that starts from within, and it requires the practice of listening to others, reflecting on your actions and getting to make your inner wisdom grow. Unlike Orange Donny, as you get older your ego should become more diluted, you should feel less of the need to big yourself up and outshine others, and more of a generous desire to encourage those coming up through the ranks. That's called gravitas, and it's earnt through developing a quiet belief in yourself and generosity towards others. It's only when you recognise the presence of your ego at work that you can start to become closer to yourself.

KEEP FLOWING AND YOU'LL FEEL LUCKY, PUNK

Now, I know the average reader of this book is more likely to be nineteen than ninety, and sorry to burst your balloon, but we're all headed that way. The level of grace we do it with is entirely up to us and the luck of the genetic draw. Even at ninety-two, Clint Eastwood manages to be cool, and I think he achieves it by doing things that give him a buzz and make him feel alive. In his own words, 'I get up every morning and I go out. And I do not let the old man in.' Like Harris and O'Toole he doesn't allow himself to think he's over the hill. And he knows the best deterrent against ageing for him is to keep moving; despite his advanced years he is still directing, producing and starring in movies. And keeping involved in politics, charity work, listening to jazz … People like him redefine the expectations of age brackets. William Blake, between writing that wonderful hymn 'Jerusalem' and getting arrested for wandering about in his birthday suit, once wrote, 'The cistern contains, the fountain overflows.' In other words, you have a choice – stagnate and sleepwalk through life by doing the same old shit, grow old and die, or flow, grow and glow. That last bit, 'flow, grow and glow' I saw in a shop window and it stuck in my mind. Apologies to whoever's shop it is.

In my last few years as a player, I had to constantly channel my inner Clint Eastwood. I often let the belief sink in that I was getting older, that these young players were going to usurp me. I was told by others that I was getting older. My coach told me during one contract negotiation that I had been playing great, better than ever, but I couldn't expect to keep it going and that I surely didn't think I could get better after becoming another year older. I had to fight to keep the old man out. I had to constantly reframe my thinking and at times

I got it wrong. I started to believe what I was being told and what I believed happened when you got older. But that was all proved wrong. I got back into the England side, I improved in other areas of my game and in life off the field, because I had that growth mindset. I had to work fucking hard in therapy and on the tools I am teaching you in this book to get back on track when the doubt crept in or I had tough days on the training paddock or issues with my body. Never allow other people's beliefs about what they think is possible limit you. Never do things just because they have always been done that way.

Growing old gracefully means accepting you no longer look like you did in your graduation picture and being at peace with your aching joints, the grunts that involuntarily spring from your mouth as you stand up and the possible relocation of the hair on your head to your nostrils, ears and back. Part of the next leg of our evolution is also about letting those young bucks come through and do their stuff while we move on to other pastures. So long as we have a purpose and keep managing ourselves with a regimen of exercise, keeping our minds curious and engaged with challenges and always looking for ways we can improve and be better, we're using our time well. Life is about sweating the small stuff, noticing things and making an effort to stay on the right side of your street.

JUST IN CASE YOU'RE NOT DEPRESSED ENOUGH ALREADY ...

Imagine if we could tap into the experiences of those who've lived before us and ask what, at the close of their lives, they wished they'd done, so that we don't make the same mistakes in ours. Fortunately, we can. And no, I haven't been spectrally sat at the shoulder of multiple people balanced on the precipice of this life and the next – there are lots of lists on ghoulish Google.

Common deathbed regrets

I wish:

- I'd spent less time working and more time with my loved ones.
- I'd got to know my parents properly.
- I'd made more memorable adventures with my kids.
- I'd told people I loved and valued how much they really meant to me.
- I'd been better at saying 'sorry'.
- I'd worried about the future less; the really bad things never actually happened.
- I'd lived in the present and paused more regularly to take in life.
- I'd learnt a second language.
- I'd pushed myself more and achieved my full potential.
- I'd allowed myself to fail more.
- Saved more money for my retirement.
- I'd taken better care of my body.
- I'd faced my fears, e.g. bullies, phobias.
- I'd lived abroad for a time and travelled more.
- I'd learnt to forgive and let go a bit more.
- I'd trusted my instincts more.
- I'd started my own business and been captain of my life more.
- I'd stood up for what I believed in and been less of a wallflower.
- I'd lived life on my own terms.

- I'd had more confidence in myself and my abilities.
- I'd left that abusive marriage years earlier.
- I'd worked harder on my marriage.
- I'd worried less about what others thought and been less of a people-pleaser.
- I'd had more sexual partners.
- I'd learnt from my mistakes.
- I'd followed my dream.

Exercise

Read through the above list of deathbed regrets and ask yourself if you're guilty of currently doing any of these. Whether you find one or ten that really resonate with you, it doesn't matter. What matters is that you make a note of it and carry it/them around in your pocket like a reminder until you are certain you have rectified it or made peace with it. And I hope it's not just 'do more shagging' you've decided on.

It's also a case of balancing your needs so that you get fulfilment without damaging those around you. The ancient stoics constantly took a close look at their attitude and their impact on others. For example, 'following your dream' and becoming an actor at the age of sixty is fair enough if your kids have grown up, your mortgage is paid off and you can afford to do it; but dragging your family into poverty for the chance of being a noddy on *EastEnders* isn't really good judgement. I recommend revisiting this list on a weekly basis.

You need to make the most of what you have now. You should not spend a life in misery, in a relationship you hate, in a job that undermines your true potential, or stopping yourself from doing the things that make you happy.

If you're in a relationship that seems to have lost its way, think about why and consider what you could do to make small, positive changes. When kids come along the dynamic between man and wife, or man and man, or woman and woman, changes. How could it not when you insert this noisy little disruptor of sleep, sexual pleasure and depleter of your bank, into your life? Having kids can be an amazing experience but it alters so many things. If you and your missus are to continue to flourish you need to take date nights and the odd dirty weekend away to keep each other's passion alight. Being a mum for the first time is hard work, and after the trauma of childbirth many women are not interested in sex; they just want to nourish the baby and feel like a good, doting mum. Eventually they will come back to their non-mum body and start feeling horny again. You need to surprise them with weekend breaks, little things that make them feel wanted. Don't take each other for granted. Equally, as a man don't focus on the baby. Someone once told me that when you first come into the house don't go straight for the little one. Go to your partner first and ask how they are, how their day has been. Then lavish attention on the baby.

But what if you're in a relationship that has lost its shine and you no longer get on? If you've been with your partner for a long time you may have now grown in opposite directions, having become very different people than you were when you first met. Having done a lot of therapy in the pursuit of trying to get better and address issues that life throws at you, I have also done therapy on relationships. I will never forgot what one very good practitioner said to me about relationships. If the divorce rate is at 50 per cent then over half of people just can't get on or don't understand how to make a relationship work or they just plain made a mistake for all the obvious reasons. Then you have the other 50 per cent who on the surface appear to be able to make it work. But knowing humans, you have to say that probably at least another 30 per cent are unhappy. They don't really put the work in and are just getting on with things because it's easier than confronting issues or getting divorced, because of financial reasons, shame and all the other stigmas attached to it. Remember, divorces up until only recently still had to be blamed on something. There was no such thing as a blameless divorce.

Then you have another 10 per cent who by sheer luck of the draw have fallen into a pattern that works or who have found a partner that completely complements them and things just work out and they live in bliss, more by accident than design. Then you have the final 10 per cent who work on things, they start looking into how their partners communicate, the different ways men and women use language. They look at how each person displays their languages of love and what's important to them. No-one teaches you this shit. Instead of learning religious studies it would be good to learn how to navigate relationships. How to understand the differences between men and women. How one is practical and one emotional.

If you can honestly say you have gone through it, worked on things, tried your very best to get on, to change yourself for the better, but yet being in their company makes you unhappy and you've already tried to fix things, then you have the right to leave. You have one life, live it. I do think that too many people give in too easily in most areas of life, but relationships are the big one. Nothing comes easy and nothing comes for free. I would never condemn anyone to a life of misery, but before you blame others, or your partner, look at how you conduct yourself and the effort you have put in to self-development. If your side of the street is super-clean then by all means move on with no regrets or fears.

KEY TAKEAWAYS FROM PILLAR II: REFLECT

- Be accommodating to others who are not on your path.
- As you age, embrace who you are and revel in that.
- Instead of fearing the Grim Reaper, make each day count.
- Learn from other people's mistakes and experiences.
- Take a deep breath, look around, be curious and compassionate.
- Bad shit happens to good people. Deal with it.
- Relationships are hard. They need work.
- You are not perfect and neither is your partner. Do not place unrealistic expectations on yourself/them.

7

WHAT WE CAN CONTROL

BEND WITH THE WIND

In Ancient Greece and later Rome, the stoic school of thought believed we could steer ourselves through the worst situations by focusing on what was in our control rather than worrying about things that were beyond our ability to change. In order to separate the two the stoic Epictetus, who was actually an Italian slave, made a list of things that he could have some influence over and things that were beyond his sphere of control. Under 'Not in My Control' he listed: job, parents, body, weather, economy, the past, the future, the fact he was going to die eventually. And under 'In My Control' he simply listed 'my beliefs'. He was surprised to say the least.

Many things that we think we can control, we actually can't. You can strive like hell for that promotion and do everything in your power to make sure it happens, but ultimately the final decision is out of your hands and you may be a victim of nepotism or there may be someone more suited to the role than you. You can take great care of your health and respect your body, but again you have no control over whether you suddenly contract an illness. That's not to say we should give in, roll over and die.

The idea of accepting and focusing on what you can control seems so simple and obvious, but I challenge you the reader to ask yourself how often in you daily life you actually do this. I can tell you I never did for such a long time in my career, and I honestly believe that if I had not understood this concept and worked hard to action it, I would not have had the career I had or the success off the field. I remember my second session with my psychologist Dr Jill Owen, when she talked to me about this concept. I was so hung up on what others thought of me, what coaches thought of me, why I wasn't getting picked, why other players my age were getting further ahead quicker than me, why the media seemed to have it in for me. I worried a lot about others' criticism of me, I took things to heart all the time. She reframed all this and asked me what I could control out of all of these things that I worried about. The answer was none of them. Which was like a light bulb going on. I was like, fuck, you're right, I can't, so why am I wasting physical and emotional energy on them? She then asked what could I control that would possibly have an impact on the things that were outside of my control.

I could control my body, so in rugby terms that would be the following broken down into simple sections that could be easily mastered and managed. You can drill down further again if you want to, but controlling your body looked like this in my case:

- Diet
- Training
- Sleep

- Hydration
- Position-specific work
- Recovery
- Medical

When all around you is falling apart, or you get into an excuse mindset, centring yourself and remembering to focus on what you can control gets you back in the game very quickly. It makes you accountable, it makes you reframe what you need to work on, and gets you to understand what you should be worried about and what you shouldn't. I found this to be one of the most valuable lessons I learnt on my journey in sport. It's the one thing that I revisit almost every day or in any moment of self-doubt.

It's important to note that you can do everything, and people still won't like you, people will still find fault. But at least you can reconcile it with yourself, when you inevitably ask yourself the question, 'Do they have a point?' There are some who say, 'I don't care what people say about me.' The reality is, I think everyone cares but on a sliding scale. When things don't go your way, in whatever form that takes, and you are questioned, you should always ask yourself, 'Am I doing everything that I can do?' If the answer is yes, then ignore them. If the answer is no, then it's a wake-up call to go back to what you can control. I am not saying that changing people's perspective or trying to be liked should ever be the target; it should be about you getting better and finding your own personal level of contentment. Understanding that you will never please everyone, never be everyone's cup of tea and that there will always be naysayers is again liberating. If you are liked by everyone, how fucking vanilla must you be? I am Marmite and I love it.

While we can't control other people's reactions and the flux of what life blindly throws at us, we can have dominion over the way we respond to its challenges; we can bend with the wind, or as Bruce Lee once said, 'Be formless, shapeless like water. You put water into a cup, it becomes the cup. You put water into a bottle, it becomes the bottle ... water can flow or it can crash, be water my friend.' The martial artist was echoing the stoics when he suggested we flow with events rather than try and stand up against them.

Epictetus believed our disappointment and frustration in life arises from thinking we *can* control the things in the 'Not in My Control' list, rather than focusing on what is in the 'In My Control' list. Life is 10 per cent what happens to you and 90 per cent *how* you react. Your power is choosing your reaction. When hard times hit home you can either blindly get lost in the emotion of self-pity and spiral into negativity, or you can reframe the bad as a valuable lesson you are learning, that is making you stronger. Rather than absorbing someone else's shit, choose to let it bounce off you; you can't change how others treat you, but you can render them powerless by not giving them the satisfaction of responding in the way they thought you would.

Viktor Frankl was a respected psychiatrist, who had the misfortune of being Jewish during Hitler's reign of terror, losing most of his immediate family in Nazi concentration and death camps. What he observed during his own incarceration in the camps was that those who chose to react to the inhumanity visited on them by the Nazis by being kind to their fellow inmates and helping them survived longer. It wasn't that they were stronger physically, more that they had chosen to retain their own humanity and react in a way that they controlled. Though stripped of their clothes, hair and personal belongings, the Germans could not take away their freedom to act with kindness to those weaker than themselves.

When we find ourselves in a crisis, we should tell ourselves: 'Okay, so I can't change this, but what am I in a position to do?'

TRIGGERS

Seneca the Younger, a Roman politician and stoic philosopher from the first century CE, wisely remarked, 'Let us take note of what it is that particularly provokes us ... Not all men are wounded in the same place; and so you ought to know what part of you is weak, so you can give it the most protection.' His pointers on anger management are brilliant. 'Let the expression on our faces be relaxed, our voices gentler, our steps more measured; little by little outer features mould inner ones.' It's simple kidology then: put a smile on your face and eventually you reframe the mind to feel better; you tell it what to think, not the other way round. In stoic thought we get to know our triggers intimately, things that can enflame us to lose ourselves in reactive emotional outbursts rather than keeping a clear head and thinking things through beforehand. There are also positive triggers we can use to shift our thinking into a more productive space, just by visualising a time when things were going well and we felt confident, or as I'll talk about in the next chapter, using music with a positive association to lift us into a desired mood.

We are all anxious at times, scared, worried, nervous, or simulate the feelings of being depressed to certain degrees. We're all a bit broken and that's just part of life. We may lose our way from time to time, but like anything there is always a way to deal with this stuff, a lesson to learn and a road back to equilibrium. It just takes practice. Everyone regularly has shit days and wonders what they are doing with their life, everyone has moments of self-doubt and vulnerability. It's okay, it's normal, and anyone who says differently is either crazy, wired very differently, a liar or trying to sell you something.

If on reading this you are thinking, 'I am fulfilled, I am happy,' then good on you. I'm sure there is a 0.2 per cent who have really found what makes them content. They have probably shunned modern technology and are running an owl sanctuary on the side of a mountain somewhere. I say, 'Amazing, well done,' but for the rest of us life battlers we are still struggling through. I wonder whether we need to change our thinking so we're not constantly standing on our mental doorstep sweating for the arrival of trouble and heartache. Yes, life is random and we will probably be thrown a lot of shit, but is there any point waiting for it to happen when we could just get on and try and enjoy ourselves in the meantime, safe in the knowledge that when it does arrive we'll be ready to choose how we react and deal with it?

Now and again when I experience something fresh and life-affirming – usually when I'm outside and invigorated, in a new place, or DJing – the sense of wellbeing is like a new skin. But what if I wanted to be in this skin more often instead of always worrying about the future or the past? What if I were to put my foot down with myself and reject the common assumption that life *has* to be difficult and complicated all the time, and happiness merely a seldom-visiting friend? There may just be an answer for the twenty-first-century's disquieted soul and it doesn't have to cost hundreds of hours on an Eames chair in a psychologist's office to attain. It's called mastering your thoughts and it takes a lot of practice.

Thoughts are like waves rippling across the ocean towards us; some of them are helpful and lead to positive feelings, but many are not. Our experience of life is created by us through our *own* thinking, and not the false presumption we've been brought up with that life happens to us. If we think of ourselves as being purely shaped by events, like ragdolls passive to the whims of fate, that's all we will be.

The epitome of being unhappy is blaming others for our dissatisfaction. Not a day goes by without opening a paper and seeing some person, normally an angry skinhead called Terry from a seaside town, saying, 'These immigrants coming over here are taking our jobs.' Well, Terry, taking automation out of the argument for the moment, as I doubt you know what that is – and no, it's not a ketchup dispenser – let's not forget that you don't want to wash the dishes or clean the floors anyway; you want to start your own business selling hot tubs to footballers so you can go to O Beach in Ibiza wearing next to nothing, with some makeup-doused treacle on your arm who's only with you for the champagne you took six months to raise the funds to pay for. The phrase 'living a champagne lifestyle on a lemonade income' springs to mind. You see, this is the equivalent of nirvana for the modern person. For milk and honey read lukewarm Veuve Clicquot and Fiji Water.

While you can't control or eradicate suffering across the world, what you can do is make yourself the best possible version of you, and by doing so you will end up helping those around you. Only once you have your own shit in order are you best placed to help others.

THIS BOOK ALONE IS NOT GOING TO FIX YOU

Just owning this book and reading it will NOT fix you. However, if you practise the techniques and processes I have already mentioned and those yet to be revealed, you will transform the way in which you deal with things. I am not claiming to have come up with these ideas or concepts, but what I have done is put them into a system that works for me and that will work for you. The 5 Pillars approach amalgamates processes and ideas from some of the most successful and brightest people in the sporting and business world. For the 5 Pillars even to begin to have any positive effect on your life, you have to understand this one inalienable truth. Only you can fix you. Let that sink in for a moment … *only you can fix you*.

It starts with being self-aware enough to learn about how you tick, what worries you, what shortcuts you often take, what excites you, and how you react well or poorly in different situations. If you can become your own observer you will get to know yourself more deeply. Books aside, it's the same with therapy: you are not fixed just because you see a therapist. It takes time to learn the way your mind operates; you analyse yourself and learn what triggers you into negative, self-destructive behaviour. Therapy is amazing, it's so important to wellbeing. Some of you go around saying to yourselves, 'Well, nothing super-bad has ever happened to me, so I'm okay, I don't need therapy, I am okay the way I am.' That's so flawed as we can all improve ourselves, we can all do better, me more than most. The day you think you have nailed life and can't get any better is the day you fail.

But seeing a professional does not make you better. Only you can do that. They don't have a magic wand that fixes you.

144

What they do is they either give you the tools to do it, suggest things to try, or they put things into perspective, allowing you to view the world through different optics. They also listen, which is such an underrated tool. How often do you actually talk to someone with a truly objective view?

The same can be said with close friends. If you want to be told, 'You are right, poor you,' and 'It's everyone else's fault not yours,' you go to certain friends, because they will always agree with you. Therapists have no emotional connection, they aren't trying to be your friend. They listen, and because you open up, you are actually fixing yourself, by either being steered to your own conclusions or naturally talking yourself around into seeing things in a different light. This personal development can happen in so many ways, it's not about just being happier.

Mental strength covers so many areas. Yes, being happy is great, but what if I told you that you could be better at your job, better at dealing with criticisms, maximise your potential on all fronts, be more fulfilled and ultimately mentally prepared for the shit that life throws at you (which at times can be a Greek tragedy in the making)? Those who find success through therapy have gone through a process of fixing themselves, and it's the same with self-help books. The book doesn't fix you. You could read thousands of them, which people do and never get anywhere – they get the affirmation but change nothing. No, the one thing you must do with self-help books or therapy to make either work, is take action, get off that chaise longue and start fixing yourself; it's not just a case of knowing, it's a case of *doing*. I have seen a sports psychologist since the age of 17 and will continue to do so until I die. Not because I have any pressing mental health conditions but because I see it as an area of improvement and it keeps my mental health in a good place. Just as I watch my diet and train my body, I work on my mind. It's that simple. It fits into a checklist of the things that I can control.

Don't get me wrong, I'm not a master at this. I still have shit days where I worry about what people think of me, and I often catch myself still worrying about things I have no control over. I get down, I feel sad and I lose my way. But I also know that I can quickly change my state back to one that is strong and mentally positive where I'm ready to deal with anything. That's what this book is about: giving you some key skills that I think will help you understand how to get the best out of your life, and tricks and thoughts to develop cast-iron mental strength without any of the sugar-coated nonsense that we're fed on a daily basis. I am sure it's going to offend a lot of sensibilities and raise a few eyebrows. To hell with that, 'twas ever thus!

THE BLAMER

You probably know someone like this as they are way more common than they should be. The person whose shambles of a life is not their fault. The reason they have failed in every area is down to the government, husband/wife, boss, trauma that happened to them when they were younger, bad friends, no money, no time, it's the kids, the dog – you name it, it's nothing to do with them, it's always someone else's fault. They are always negative, there is always drama. They have an excuse for everything.

Does this sound like you or a friend? Here is an example just for clarity and it's never so clear as when getting someone in shape. My wife trains hundreds of people online and every round she has a person that says, 'I have been doing this for three weeks now and have lost no body fat, the scales have not moved.'

Okay, let's ask a few questions. 'Have you stuck to the training plan?'

'Well no, I haven't done the training, as the dog ate my gym kit,' or 'the kids got in the way.'

'What about the diet?'

'Well no, I haven't eaten properly as I have been stressed, and I like my food, and I got upset so I ate a birthday cake.'

'Did you then return to a normal diet after you ate the birthday cake?'

'Not exactly. I got depressed because I ate the cake, and my hormones were playing up, so I put it all in the "fuck-it bucket" and kept eating bad and I hate myself blah blah fucking blah.'

Substitute body transformation for anything else and this is what you'll get all the time from this kind of person. My answer would be, 'It's no wonder you are out of shape, it's your fault: you have no discipline, no mental strength, no commitment, you are weak and are blaming everything else for your problems.' Everyone likes to find a crutch to lean on. It's always down to some unknown factor as to why you can't be doing what you want, or getting the results. These people very rarely change, they will turn from one fad to another to another until they give up. They never get the results or life they want. Yet conversely you get the people who just do what they should, they don't ask questions, they just do it. While you are still moaning or trying to negotiate your way out of it, they already have the body and life they want. You see it in professional sport or business. There are those with loads of talent but they just can't put the work in. They have to question everything. The less talented then pass you by because they put the work in. In life as in sport, there is always some-one prepared to do what it takes to make it. Never forget that. We teach kids it's all about the taking part. Is it fuck. Life is a dog-eat-dog battle. When you make it you can be all philo-sophical and generous, and talk about taking part, and why can't we all just get along. But until you are in that rarefied atmosphere, get your head down and do what needs to be done. No excuses.

Luckily my wife Chloe is not me, and that's probably why she has a thriving business, and I don't work in health and fitness anymore. She would be understanding and in a round-about way make this person accountable so they could understand the error of their ways. When you blame it on having no time, or your hormones, or genetics, or the gym being too far away, or the universe doesn't like you, only you will know in that moment when you put your phone down, and switch off the light for sleep, whether you are actually doing all the things you could be. Are you actually doing what needs to be done, or are you bullshitting yourself and those around you? I guarantee you, 9.5 times out of 10 you are lying to everyone and you know deep down you are where you are because you just aren't doing the work. Nothing will ever change because they/you have no self-awareness. If this sounds anything like you, then this book will help you avoid or confront pitfalls to navigate life's curveballs as well as self-limiting habits and behaviours that keep tripping you up. Then you'll be in a better place to achieve your full potential.

GLASS HALF-FULL/HALF-EMPTY

There are different types of people and different ways of dealing with things, but let's look at the two most common examples and how they react when it comes to dealing with a break-up, for example.

First, you have the glass half-empty type of person who pines over their lost love, only looking at what they had and ignoring being in the present and open to opportunities. They do nothing to help themselves out of their heartbroken rut and just wallow. Because they only allow themselves to feel sad and passively allow themselves to be blown along without looking inward, it takes much longer for them to feel better. You probably know that person; maybe you've been them.

Then you have the other type of person, the glass half-full type, who looks inside of themselves and admits they're still sad but decides it's time to rebuild and start fixing their lot by creating a better body, tuning their mind with a fresh challenge or hobby, eating more healthily, and generally trying to become the best version of themselves. They often then find another person when they are not even looking. Do you know why? Because they centred themselves by anchoring their thoughts in the present; they developed more self-esteem having worked on themselves physically and mentally, and finally, having realised that they couldn't control how their ex felt about them, only how they felt about themselves, they let go. Remember the Serenity Prayer used by Alcoholics Anonymous and Narcotics Anonymous: 'God, grant me the serenity to accept the things I cannot change, courage to change the things I can; and the wisdom to know the difference.' I'd rebrand this in light of my atheist ways. 'Insert own name', so in my case 'James, grant me the serenity to accept the things I cannot change, courage to change the things I can; and the wisdom to know the difference.'

Serenity can be translated as calm. It's about being calm and rational enough to look at things objectively and admit a situation is out of your hands. Stress is bad for your health mentally and physically, so by accepting that many situations are beyond your control you release their power over you and minimise your agitation. You can't change another person's behaviour or the way they feel, you can only control your own behaviour through being on top of your thinking, which then creates good, productive feelings rather than negative ones.

Look at the COVID-19 pandemic. Those who got through it relatively mentally unscathed were accepting of what at times were draconian rules; they didn't like them any more than the next person, but they recognised rules were necessary and accepted they had no control over the demands and regulations dished out by Professor Chris Whitty and the PM. What they could control was localised to their own person: whether they took care of themselves, whether they used the time to catch up on a good book, learn a new instrument, take an online class or enjoy time spent with loved ones. They could start running, lose weight, eat healthier, call their friends more often ... The sooner people realised the only thing they could control in the pandemic was themselves and the choices they made to respond to the privations and downright oddness of those lockdowns, the sooner they adapted.

You might have had real hopes that you and your son would use the time available during the lockdown to work on an old wreck of a sports car together or learn Swahili, but unless your son wants to you can't force him. We can only try and influence somebody to feel a certain way but we have no dominion over their feelings, even if we are only trying to help. The reasons you hear the cliched saying at least three times a month (or I certainly do), 'You can take a horse to water but you can't make it drink,' is because never a truer word has been spoken. You can't make people change, you can't make people better. You can give them the tools, the advice, but they have to take action. Remember, talk without action is worthless, listening without action is equally as worthless.

Just like Epictetus earlier in this chapter, you may be very surprised to see how many things there are in the 'not in my control' circle and just how few things are in the 'in my control' circle. In the example above, the one thing that the person has any control over is themself. They can seek to control their gambling, join a Gamblers Anonymous support group, and work with their mental baggage to try and heal the addiction. There's no guarantee they'll succeed but since this depends on their own actions, at least they have a fighting chance.

All the other things listed are beyond their control. Sure, they can influence their kids to work hard and revise for their exams but ultimately it's their kids who have to take the exam. You can try and improve the odds of not getting lung cancer by stopping smoking but ultimately you have no control over other forms of cancer, despite living as healthily as possible, just as the price of fuel is not worth worrying about as it is not decided by you. You can decide not to use it. Your boss deciding to promote you depends on your present performance and if you're right for the job; you can work your arse off to seem like the right pick but ultimately it is down to your boss to decide. You can't make your boss like you. Some bosses like some people better. It's life. Humans are humans. You can only be the best version of yourself, and put the work in. If you don't get the promotion then of course you have every right to be hacked off, and while it is small consolation you can know that the choice was nothing more than personal because you have all of your shit handled at your end.

When we look at what's in our realm of action and what is not, we can then channel our precious energy into *only* that which can be improved, namely us. It's also quite liberating when you realise that the really important things that the news keeps us in a constant lather of panic about, like global warming, are not things we can do much about apart from recycling and spreading the message, not taking too many flights etc. Unless we are going to work for Friends of the Earth and dedicate ourselves to the environment, we need to file these things under 'Not in My Control'.

8

GETTING YOUR SHIT TOGETHER

THE ACT OF PREPARATION

The way you manage yourself and your affairs is paramount. If you split every area of your life into manageable, change-able parts, everything becomes more achievable. A career is something that gives you direction and gets you up in the morning, whereas a job is something you do to keep a roof over your head, feed your kids and pay for holidays. But sometimes you lose the fire for your career and choose to switch to something more appropriate for you at that given time of your life. Like a burnt-out London doctor might have a dream of setting up a business selling motorbikes in Cornwall. If that becomes his passion and if he showers it with attention, it will grow into a reality.

It's never too late to make a change, but there are certain conditions that we have to meet in order to make that change as feasible and as painless as possible. One of those conditions is about being organised and planning ahead: having a goal and breaking that goal down into manageable stages, and not putting your head in the sand but looking at every angle, from finances to logistics. The ancient stoics believed that we should consider all the things that can go wrong in our life. The act of preparing helps take away the fear that comes from blindly worrying about something but doing nothing about it. You can never anticipate every curveball that life will throw at you, but by having a plan of how you will respond to the usual ones allows you to relax into the present and concentrate on what you really want to do with your life.

PERSONAL ADMIN

The first five weeks of the 44-week officers' course at Sandhurst Military Academy is a bootcamp of extreme exercise, drill and the mastering of personal admin, which in other words could be deemed the art of self-presentation and organisation. That, and constant inspections from the colour sergeant. It's a time when new habits are created and the intake of officers have their rough edges smoothed out so they can be team players as well as leaders. The pedantic attention to detail is infamous: such as the way a bed has to be made following a specific system, the obsessive standard to which rooms have to be kept tidy, including equal distances between deodorant can, flannel and toothbrush, and the exactitude of how a bergen (rucksack) must be packed (with the stuff that you'll need most readily at the top).

All this is breaking the civilian down so the staff can build an officer in their place, and it is done by repetition. By making you do what appear to be silly little tasks like shining your boots, scrubbing your clothes and starching your collars, you are learning to take pride in detail, pride in how you look and also pride in yourself. All of this begins to make sense when you apply such fierce attention to detail to your rifle and live rounds; remembering to move your position after firing a burst of rounds, as the enemy will fire back at where the muzzle flash comes from. Sweating the small stuff saves your life, like keeping your rifle clean of dirt and sand so it doesn't end up killing you.

At 5.45 every morning a colour sergeant barks at the Sandhurst recruits to muster behind a black line in the corridor where they sing the national anthem and their uniforms are checked. If they pass muster they start the day with a sense of achievement. At least if the rest of the day turns out badly, they did this one thing right.

When like me you're self-employed, your personal admin has to be very strong otherwise you just don't get things done on time. And where in a regular nine-to-five job you are somewhat protected by the infrastructure and can make excuses, as a freelance public speaker and DJ I'm completely exposed if I forget to turn up to a gig or do so unprepared. One of the easiest ways to improve your personal admin is by embedding positive habits that will stick.

FORMING NEW HABITS

Forty per cent of any individual's day sees them unconsciously following established habits, be it driving a car, making breakfast, wearing a gimp suit (well, only on Tuesday evenings) or driving the same route to work. As we covered earlier, this familiarity allows the brain to go into automatic pilot mode, which is how you can arrive on the other side of London with no recollection of having driven there. I'm not suggesting you've been abducted by extraterrestrial beings in the form of naked four-foot zeta reticulans with lightbulb-shaped foreheads, just that your brain has switched off and guided you and your killing machine past all kinds of obstacles like other cars, pedestrians and cyclists.

Anything repeatedly performed becomes a habit, so it's important to take an inventory of your habits to see which are unhelpful and can be replaced with more useful habits. Perhaps you have a quick temper and are in the habit of losing it too easily; maybe you have got into the habit of not exercising; maybe you're looking at too much porn or covering up depression by constantly buying things from Dr Evil aka Mr Amazon. When you isolate weaknesses or traits that are undoing you, dealt with separately these small improvements can add up to a lot when you put them all together.

I have a habit of speaking my mind and then paying the price for having done so, and following the shit storm of Farmergate or Have-a-day-off-gate (see pages 72 and 74) I now try to think ahead a little more when entering into a battle of words with complete strangers on social media. That one mild adjustment of self-restraint known as moderation or temperance has made my life quite a bit easier and relatively free of death threats. Being honest, I am still working on this and trying not to relapse. I will be nine months sober (holding my tongue) by the time this book is published.

In the book *Stand Up Straight: 10 Life Lessons from the Royal Military Academy Sandhurst* Major General Paul Nanson talks about the ripple effect the smallest positive habits have on the rest of the day; like not sleeping through your alarm, taking an early morning run, carving time out for yourself in the morning to plan your day, and assessing what went well and what didn't at the day's end.

According to James Clear in his book *Atomic Habits*, 'Success is the product of daily habits – not once-in-a-lifetime transformations. Transformations don't occur overnight, we need to chip away at them like a master sculptor. The quality of our life,' argues Clear, 'depends on the quality of our habits. With the same habits, you'll end up with the same results.' Jessie Potter once said, 'If you always do what you've always done, you'll always get what you've always gotten.' Isn't that the case?

If you're not where you want to be you need to review your habits, correct them and keep repeating them so they become embedded as behaviours. Our behaviours reflect our identity, the way we see ourselves. We are what we do. If we're to change long-held views like 'I'm not a morning person,' the only way forward is to practise the habits of a morning person, i.e. getting up early. If we practise the habit regularly it becomes second nature and we have changed our identity.

In order to put everything in place to make an early start happen, write a checklist of what you need for that day. Have you got your trainers or suit (whatever the occasion is) by the front door? Make sure you've slept well, had an energy drink, eaten something healthy, got all your stuff for the day all lined up. Whenever anyone for example starts off in the gym and they do the odd session, they find it hard to commit to regular training and more often than not give up. But if you gave it four weeks and went a minimum of three sessions a week with a good plan, you would get results. Once you see results you commit to it, as you understand firstly what the point of training is and secondly its benefits to body and mind, so you then want more. I used to hate training, and I couldn't ever sit still long enough to get work done. I changed my habits, I put things in place that made my life easier, I paid for people to train me so I had to get up and do it. I split my days into workable chunks, so I would put down, for example, 20 minutes to get emails done. Only emails and no other distractions. I would then put in say an hour of book edits, and again nothing else was touched. I slowly taught myself to switch on and switch off.

For a long time, I also had a problem with self-organisation, probably because everything was done for me, mostly by my parents, who loved me dearly but could see that a young James was just away with the fairies at all times. Also going to boarding school from age nine meant that I was essentially institutionalised until I left at eighteen to play rugby and then went into another institution of professional rugby until I was thirty-five. I was a bit like those animals you see in zoos, who could never be released because as soon as they were, they would either get eaten because they would just walk up to the nearest thing and try and be mates with it, or die of hunger because their natural instinct to hunt had been negated back at the zoo by food that would have been delivered daily by some slightly earthy woman with dyed hair and lots of body piercings.

At school we were told what to do and when and where to do it, so time was not our own, it was organised for us. All we had to do was take the right books to the right lesson. Another reason that I used not to be as organised as I should have been was because I relied on my parents. My dad describes himself as the bloke who walks behind the elephant and sweeps up its shit with a dustpan and brush! I was completely focused on my goal of being a rugby player, but I let everything else get out of hand.

Every now and again I would try and reform myself by buying a new notebook and a new pen in which to write down all the lists that I needed to get myself sorted. There's something so appealing about a fresh start, the aroma of blank pages. There's so much potential within us and it's as if we get a glimpse of it when we take the positive action of going to buy something in which we can keep account of what we want to do. A stationery shop suddenly turns into an Aladdin's cave of possibility. But then two or three pages in, the notebook would be left and forgotten. At least that was the case with me.

When I was a young professional sportsman my mood would fluctuate wildly like the spikes and dips on a cardiograph: one minute I'd be raring to go, the next I would have read something somebody had written about me and my mood would drop and the lack-of-self-confidence demons would rear their ugly head. I might have been trying to put on weight and then I'd weigh myself only to discover I was massively under the perceived bulk required to be an effective rugby player, and then my mood would drop. Obviously, you learn pretty quickly that size has no bearing on ability at all, but in a young, naïve, non-hardened mind it's everything.

In my early career at Wasps my dad used to encourage me to go to anything I was asked to, whether it was to sign something, to officiate at the grand opening of a shop or give a speech, attend an event, or go and have a meeting with anyone who was potentially interested in working with me. I found that because I was training so hard and trying not to miss any of these other opportunities, I was burning myself out completely and would then be scrambling the whole time to get that work/life balance right. I would then underperform in one area, whether that was on or off the pitch. This would then have knock-on effects in how I dealt with things and how I felt. It was only when I took the time to stop, reflect and take account of this that I began to self-organise, rein it in and start to create a proper routine that suited my needs. In organisation I found balance and calm. I found that I had the freedom to do what I needed to. I looked at what my priorities were, the main one of which was of course being the best rugby player that I could be. So I worked back from that. I would only start my off-field work when the job was done with being the best and most professional player I could be. If that took all day then so be it, but I wanted to leave no stone unturned in the pursuit of excellence. Then once that was done, my work day started. It also made me look at my off-field stuff. Could a meeting have been an email? In most cases, yes. So I stopped going and just said right, what do you need, what do you want to pay me and this is what I can do for you. That cut down car time and wheedled out the time wasters. I then looked at what made me happy outside of rugby: speaking, presenting, extra training, writing and DJing. The rest was just not needed. Why would I go and meet an insurance company about getting some work experience? I don't want to work in an office or sell insurance. Why would I do an online study course? I don't want to do that kind of thing, it doesn't serve me as an author, DJ, presenter, or make me money. So sack it off.

SEGMENT YOUR TIME

By the end of my career with Northampton and as a long-time England player, all the wear and tear my body had accumulated after endless hours of rugby training and matches was taking its toll. Back in the day I was known for being a very physical player. But those last few years of my career were very tough and emotional on a number of levels. Having joined Northampton on the cheap to keep my England dream alive, I had started with big hopes. I asked the trainers to look after me and not run me into the ground. They all agreed and then on day one got me running 15k, which was utter madness. I regret not being stronger and telling them no way was I doing mad training like this, but I wanted to be part of a new team and not be seen as being too big-time. Sadly, that entire year was not what I wanted it to be even though I had an amazing time and Northampton were a fantastic club. Then as things progressed I developed an issue with my ankle, which then needed operating on. Every day the seeds of doubt crept in. Was this it for me? I couldn't stay fit, I wasn't able to string games together like I used to. I felt old, people told me I was old. Am I going to have to retire soon?

It was probably the hardest part of my entire career. I was so desperate to play for Saints and to get back into the England squad. At one point I'd just been into hospital for yet another operation, this time on my ankle, which I had tried to avoid for as long as I could, and the night before – in order to make myself as calm and relaxed as possible – I sat down and wrote a list of all the things that I would need while I was away in hospital, the things that I would need to do in recovery, the things that I was going to work on while I was laid up, and the tools I would need to help with recovery. I started to set targets on body-fat goals, size goals and who I needed to talk to about that. I wanted to set goals on other areas of improvement that I could make while my lower body was out of action. I wrote down how I wanted to come out of this period and what I would have to do to get back on the field with both the Saints and England.

There are plenty of different apps that help get you organised, where you can note down what you want to do and it will remind you as the day goes on. Just writing notes on my iPhone, or blocking things out in my iCalendar, was perfectly adequate for me. As humans we love to feel that we're doing *something* useful, and it doesn't take much activity to get us started, but the problem is we so easily fall off the track of intent and endeavour. As a way of combating this, I'm a great list-maker; I break my days down into a 'do or die list' that features the most important things – usually four or five points – that need to be achieved by the end of the day. I then list my moderate goals, which helps refresh my intentions and reminds me what I am trying to do.

Personally, what I find most helpful is not just writing a list for the day but segmenting and organising time so you stipulate exactly what you are going to do in a certain hour and you keep to it. Some people call it 'chunking'. For instance, I'll have breakfast from 7 until 8 and I won't look at my phone; we have a rule in our house that we don't look at phones when we're eating together. The next thing will be emails from 8 until 9. That means no social media, no surfing the net, no distractions; all I'm doing is answering emails and smashing them out. Next up from 9 until 10 will be social media, and that doesn't mean I'm reading comments and disappearing down a rabbit hole, it's more about me making sure that the right content is where it should be and everything is squared up. I have said social media is a business, or it should be. Post what you need to post on all your platforms, reply to any relevant DMs if needed. Perhaps look at a couple of people that inspire you – in my case it's DJs like Fisher, Carl Cox or Nic Fanciulli. I always have this voice in my head that says, is this going to make you better, is this going to make you money? If the answer is no, then stop fucking doing it and do something that will help you meet your goals.

TACKLE LIFE AS YOU WOULD TACKLE AN OPPONENT

When I began to get really organised, one area in which I started to feel the benefits of improved personal admin was before games. Where previously my room would have looked like something out of the post-apocalypse, now I made a point of getting my kit all perfectly in place, packed and ready, as well as ensuring my iPod was charged for my music pre-game and my headphones were there. I had my pre-game notes written out clearly and my focus for the game nailed on. Once that was done I was then able to reward myself with something: it might be allowing myself to watch a Netflix film with a free conscience, or maybe read a book I was enjoying. Organisation and preparation give you confidence that you are prepared for the job in hand. You will never not have a few nerves pre-game, it doesn't matter how long you have been at it, but looking back at your week and knowing you have done everything you could possibly do to prepare almost gives you a suit of armour to don, to then go out there and smash it. I would always split my training into core skills workouts, which every day I would revisit. So I knew I had worked on my tackling, ball carrying, passing, footwork, high balls, lineouts and physical prep. So when any self-doubt or the big occasion started to get to me, I knew I had banked all these bits. I would only ever spend 15 to 20 minutes on these things, but it would be every day. Monday handling, Tuesday tackling, Wednesday running lines, Thursday passing and high balls, Friday – a combo of everything. Saturday game day and Sunday recovery. Rinse and repeat the next week. You can apply this process to anything that you are trying to nail. I do it with DJing now and other skills that I want to perfect. Don't moan that things aren't going well, if you aren't putting the time in.

I had so many tools to put in place before a game. For instance, re-channelling negativity where the coach might have said I was shit that week, so I would make a note to do X, Y and Z, just to either prove him wrong or use the disrespect or negativity to fuel me. It's all well and good being positive, but actually I get more shit done harnessing negativity in my mind than making it all about positivity. Another note to self might be to make sure I tackled low, or to be up quick on my feet after a tackle to compete for a ball. These wouldn't just be little trigger words, these would be reminders of the process. If you hope to get better at something, you firstly need to understand what the best practice is for that thing or skill. Then you need to break it down into a process that you understand, delivers the best execution for you, and is something that can be repeated time and time again. This goes for anything. DJing, writing, lifting, rugby, tennis, cooking, you name it. How can you get better if you don't know where in the process you aren't getting things right?

I am lucky that for most of my life my skill executions were being filmed in training or in games. I would then be able to minutely watch these back. For example, I watched hours of some of the best tacklers in the world including my good mate Joe Worsley, who for me was the very best time and time again. I looked at what he did and realised why he was so good. It was about his mentality but also where he put his feet. If his feet were in close to the person he was going to tackle he would never miss. It was almost like he was putting his feet on their feet so whatever the size of the player or however they ran into him, he would never miss. Then I looked at his tackle height; he was always so low because of his foot placement. Then how he wrapped his arms with his hands open, and where his head went and lastly how he exploded into his opponent. He attacked them, not the other way around. I then translated that into a process that worked for me. I broke this down into firstly locking onto something visually. To set my height and where to aim on the person I wanted to tackle. This was the player's knees or leg strapping. I would then say in my head 'up, up, up!' which would get me off the defensive line and have me attacking the player, which created forward momentum. I would then be thinking about the placement of my feet, which was to step my feet as close to if not onto the opponent's feet, meaning I was not going to miss, and the idea of stepping into the player meant again I was going in with force. I would then think about keeping my feet and tackling with open hands, so if I slid down them I would always catch hold of a flailing leg or a boot. I would then spend a couple of sessions a week practising this process on live opposition. I would also spend four minutes at a time throughout the week, visualising it with my eyes closed.

Visualisation is one of the most powerful tools you have in your arsenal. Your mind does not know whether you are mentally doing it or actually physically doing it. I would close my eyes and run through different scenarios the entire time. I would remember what it felt like to hit people, the physical sensations that went with those hits, like the impact on my shoulder. So while I would actually practise tackling I would do the same amount of mental tackling through visualisation. I would do this for every skill at different times of the week.

The other useful thing about visualisation is you can use it to change negative thoughts. For example, what if you imagine suddenly that you are going to drop a ball, fuck up a speech or crash and burn with a girl? You can close your eyes and turn that negative thinking around. You imagine things going really well. What happens if you leap in the air to catch the ball and make a break, the speech gets a standing ovation or the girl falls head over heels for you? It helps if you have positive experiences to fall back on as it makes it more real. So when you imagine it, you also have the sensations to add to the mix; what it feels like to jump and catch the ball or the emotion you feel when a girl says, 'Yes, you can have my number.' The more real you can make it the better. It takes practice, but it makes a massive difference. Controlling your thoughts and fears and turning them into positive feelings, letting your mind think you have so many positives to recall, all help improve you and prepare you. They chase away your negative voice and only reinforce the good things, meaning you are much more likely to smash the challenge. Having done this all week, by the time I got to game day my notes pre-match might only have said tackle height, up step and bounce (bounce off the floor to compete for the ball), but that was all I needed to trigger confidence and reassurance. You can apply this same mentality to whatever you need to do.

If you have entrenched positive habits, and they are now a part of you, the voice of doom has to work much harder to get in your way. It's about practice and repetition, and the more that you get used to doing these little rituals, which when set in place give you a sense of control, the more confident you are in yourself.

The more successful I became as a player the more these positive habits and routines became necessary. Just before I retired, Chloe flagged up to me that I was going to need to have a routine set in place, a reason to get out of bed once I stopped playing rugby. For the first time from the age of 16 to 35, I was suddenly not required to get out of bed at a certain time. It soon lost its novelty; not being compelled to get up, shower, dress and get to work became a dangerous freedom. One thing I don't like is 'drift time', when I've not nailed down anything that I need to do, and I have a sense that time is wasted. The more organised I am the more I can relax. Some people can just sit there and do nothing. Sadly, I'm not one of them. I need to fill time up with *doing*.

Contrary to what some people might say these days about being more relaxed with punctuality, even the most airy-fairy musician or artist will not thrive without some level of discipline or timeline, whether it's getting to rehearsal or having a deadline for getting your paintings ready for an exhibition. We are all apt to come off the rails occasionally and that's fine; the question is, how long does it take for us to rectify ourselves and get moving again? That's the most important thing. I'm sure Wim Hof and Tim Robbins have off-days; like everybody they are just human. Beware of anyone who says, 'No days off': it's neither smart nor sensible. You don't have to lie on the couch but you do need some down time. I always watch movies when I eat meals, I read a lot of fiction, I take the dog for a walk, I see friends and I love a good night out. Doing extremes, either an all-night piss-up or a 12-hour working day, is far worse for you than a good work/play balance. Once you have balance you can do what you want, when you want. It's a bit like dieting. Every time my wife and I do an interview together they always say the same thing – 'So as everyone knows, you and James love the gym. Do you ever let your hair down, do you ever have something naughty like a pizza or chocolate?' – as if Chloe and I are a couple of off-the-wall people who eat boiled chicken and rice all day. The fact is we eat what we want, when we want, along with being disciplined. We have more balance than those who shun dieting or the die-hard restrictive eaters. If you understand what you put in your body, understand calories, if you have discipline, you know when to enjoy yourself and when to tighten things up. I always tell the journo, 'Of course we let our hair down.' They always look so shocked. 'Do you really?' 'Of course, we do.' I say to them, 'Do you train and eat healthily?' and they go, 'Oh no, not really.' So who has balance? Those of us who do it all but at the right times and in the right way, or those who go from extreme to extreme? There is so much bollocks out there about what's good and what's bad for you. Everyone is missing the point: there are no good or bad foods. It's about understanding moderation, discipline, your activity levels, how your body reacts to food, calories, your genetics, and then the world is your oyster. It seems hard, but it's not. You have to work at balance. Just like you have to work at everything.

REWARDS AND PENALTIES

It's said that you learn habits depending on how rewarding a behaviour is. Find a reward that is genuinely pleasing to you and something that doesn't self-defeat you – if you're tracking calories all week and you want to reward yourself with an untracked meal, that's fine. You just don't need to go on a binge and smash five thousand calories in one go. Most people forget it's about your weekly calorific intake, not your daily count. So if you have one untracked meal then all good, but if you go off the rails from that meal on then you will negate any calorie deficit you are aiming for and poor results will follow. Falling off the wagon and treating yourself once is no issue at all in the grand scheme of things, it's just about not going mad and throwing the whole diet in the fuck-it bucket and giving up because you lost your way a little. If you tighten things back up straightaway then it's not a problem at all. Moderation is key, but if you can't handle it don't do it; find another way to reward yourself.

You also can't live like a saint all week and get out on the smash all weekend, drinking and eating crap, and hope to get the good results you want. You would still get some improvements, if you kept your diet and training spot-on in the week, but it wouldn't be what you wanted if you want very low body fat. If you are happy with that lifestyle and it makes you happy then do it. You need to find goals that work for you. Don't try to live a life that doesn't work for you; accept how you are, what works, and cut your cloth accordingly. If you like to train and eat perfectly all week and go hard at the weekends then that's fine. Just understand what's possible and what's not.

Equally important is that we understand *why* we're cultivating a specific habit and what the reward is for doing it. Ask yourself, what is its purpose? If your new habit is running, what do you get out of it? Maybe it's a clear head, the pleasure of feeling more active, the ability to get into your old 32-inch Levi's, or to feel good in a pair of trunks on holiday. You should have some kind of reward system that recognises your efforts as you reach each milestone. The flip side to this is imagine that if you give in, you have some negative forfeit. So, for example, if I was to lose my temper and reply to some troll online, I would imagine that I have to give my worst enemies three grand, or worse still, pay the troll. The idea of having to do something you don't want to do is a psychological tool that often works. If you don't stick to your diet you have to buy your two best mates cakes and watch them eat them without you touching them or getting any. It sounds silly, but if you can catch yourself in the moment, this idea of having to do something you don't want to do as a penalty is powerful. I have used it myself many times.

Of course, the penalty for not fulfilling your task is up to you. You can go from the hypothetical to a real physical penalty. Maybe it's a financial penalty whereby you give money to a charity or to a friend and get them to agree with this. After I retired from professional rugby, I had no imperatives to train and I kept making excuses for not going to the gym. In the end, I found that the only way I could increase my visits and establish a really strong habit of training was by finding a personal trainer, telling them of my weakness and then paying them in advance so that if I didn't turn up to our session I immediately lost the money I was investing in myself. Of course, I never missed a session and I got back into the old habit. The idea of wasting money so flagrantly just because you're too lazy to go to the gym is so repellent to me that in the end I just went, and I felt a lot better for it afterwards. I am not saying that you should waste money but if it gets you up and out and makes you accountable then it's working for you. You could of course find a training partner or convince someone to undertake the same challenge with you, so when you don't turn up you are not just letting yourself down, but your friend too.

HABIT STACKING

The idea of habit stacking is that by clustering habits we want to develop alongside existing established habits, we stand more chance of cementing them. First of all, we break down our day into chunks: morning, lunchtime, coming home and evening. So, your first stack will be in the morning when you're getting up and getting ready for work. At the moment maybe all you do is brush your teeth and then get changed after a shower, but what if you want to add some new package like drinking a glass of water, taking a vitamin pill and then flossing for one minute? What you do is cluster these additions around your existing habits like brushing your teeth.

In order to make the new habit stick as easily as possible, keep a glass of water next to your bed so there's no effort and no excuses for not executing it. Next, take the vitamin pill that you've purposefully placed next to your toothbrush. Also, beside your toothpaste is your floss. So long as you follow the same pattern every day, four weeks is all the time your brain requires to make this an established habit. This is going to sound a bit odd but I always have a bag of tooth-pluckers in the car. I was never good at flossing and just wasn't getting it done. So what I did was to use a plucker on my teeth whenever I was in the car. Sounds a bit rank, I know, but it's not. It means I was flossing three times a day, and I also always brush my teeth in the shower. So when you shower three times a day, you end up brushing your teeth three times. It's the perfect plan and means I don't have to go out of way to nail something simple. I have introduced things that I claimed I didn't have time for into my daily routine.

Your second stack might be your commute to work, but don't work on this until you have completely cemented the habit stack for the first part of your day. The science behind it is that your prefrontal cortex, where data is processed, has to create a new neural pathway in order to make these habits stick, but once they've become established that neural pathway is like a sealed road passing through jungle, and so long as it is maintained it becomes automatic, entrenched behaviour. Linking habits is great for getting more done in less time.

Try to think of the first routine habit stack as just one habit rather than lots of little ones, so that you don't get over-whelmed.

Ask yourself what small habits you could adopt to support a major habit. It could be packing your clothes ready for the gym the night before and placing the kit bag beside the front door. In order to make the new habit stick, if it is exercise-related don't try and be David Goggins in the first attempt; instead start with really small expectations – for instance even if you can't do 20 push-ups, start with 5 or 10, so you build your muscle memory of completing the task, and *then* grad-ually build up the difficulty. If you have never trained, then don't buy all the gear, just start slowly. Try and take some time to understand what your goal is. What training do you actually need to do? What would be an easy win? Why don't you try and just get in 6,000 steps? Or if that's too easy, try 10,000. If you have never been to a gym, why not get a PT to show you what to do or use YouTube as guide. Try just doing ten minutes and building from there. Make your life easier by nailing simple goals and gradually building up. It sounds simple, but you'd be surprised by the number of people who go in so hard having never trained before; they buy all the gear, go running twice on consecutive days in the morning, realise it's cold, dull as shit and hard – so they give up. They also miss the massive point that running will not give you the body you want, unless you want to look like Mo Farah. Engage in something that will get you the results relevant to your goal.

SMALL STEPS, BIG PROGRESS

So many people sit around and don't understand how to get going. For them, getting into shape is such a massive task they don't know where to begin. It seems so far off. Where to start? It's actually quite simple when you split it up into chunks you can manage. For example, I have included here all the factors that affect you getting into shape. There are always things you can do if you take it piece by piece, step by step. It's never about the end goal; it's about what you can do *now*.

To change your body or get the body you want, you can easily find five or six things under each category to be getting on with. So if you look at your training and you nail your goal and how you want to train, that is a start. Next you get a training plan from, say, a personal trainer. Then you could move on to nutrition and watch a video on protein and its importance. Suddenly, you have started and you are already ahead of where you were. Meaning that you may only be making a 1 or 2 per cent improvement every day, but it all adds up and what initially feels like slow progress gradually becomes a lot of cumulative success. Action is always better than sitting there and saying, 'I just don't know how to start.' I have talked a few times already about trying to be better today than I was yesterday. This is how you do it – slowly chipping away on all fronts for all your goals. You may not make big leaps to begin with, but you will get there. Live in the present and never look too far ahead. Remind yourself of the goal, but work on what you can in the present.

- **Training** – what's your goal? – type of training you need to do – get a plan online or get a PT to help you start – book in sessions, start working out, develop your technique, track your progress – if your goal is size gain then get a gym membership – purchase some equipment for home if just starting out.

- **Nutrition** – what's your goal? – start tracking – understand your protein, carb and fat intake – get a plan – book a session with a nutritionist – follow a meal plan if tracking doesn't work for you – get some healthy recipes.
- **Recovery** – massage – physio – days off – ice baths – recovery tights – sauna – sleep, naps, electro stimulation.
- **Sleep** – what's your routine before bed? – choose a good mattress for your needs – a cool room temperature – lighting situation (ideally pitch black) – pillows – tog level of your duvet – what you do before bed, reading a book to help you relax – does your partner snore, can it be managed to help you sleep? – hydration during the night.
- **Accountability** – training partner – paying for training – making time – daily goal setting – posting about your progress – film your sessions – photograph your training.

All of the above are just the things that could get you ready to change your body. So when you say you don't know how to do it, you have 30 things you could be doing and making a start on. You can then split these down further and further again after that. It's all about execution, seeing what the small steps are and not looking at the bigger, scarier, out-of-reach picture all the time.

DECLUTTERING: HOW TO LET GO

Decluttering is defined as the act of clearing away unnecessary crap and paring down to the essentials, making your existence less about superfluous possessions and energy-sapping clutter, and more about the important things like your life vision and happiness. We can learn to travel much lighter through life, freeing ourselves up so we are more able to seize opportunities when they present themselves. Each morning I open my inbox to see that while I was asleep my laptop has been bullied with random emails hoping to sell me products, and more worry-ingly, *not*-so random emails from brands that have stealthily been following my browsing habits and formed a troublingly accurate profile of my tastes. This stuff doesn't just accumu-late in our inbox, but also in our wardrobes, bookshelves, attics and our minds. Books we've never read and never will; instruments we abandoned after a few lessons but hang on to in case there's a pandemic (which we never play during said pandemic); gadgets we grew quickly tired of but insist on keeping, again to perhaps use later.

'Stuff' even extends to people in our lives who are not good for us, but out of habit or fear we keep them anyway. How much of our time is taken with adding stuff that we think will fill gaps in our lives? Shopping online, collecting Facebook friends, buying overly expensive things that we don't need and will just get us more into debt? We all need possessions, of course we do. After all, it's a pleasure to live in a beautiful house, create a nice garden, collect the odd bit of art, and own a dependable car. But having more than we need and not using it? If we place the accumulation of stuff too highly in our prior-ities, it clouds our way towards a simpler, clearer life. Chinese philosopher Lao Tzu said, 'He who knows that enough is enough will always have enough.' It makes you wonder why you buy shit you don't need when all it does is weigh you down.

How many hoarders do you know fiercely holding onto possessions from their past as if they were a lifejacket they can never let go of; even if it means their garage and cupboards are crammed with letters that will never be reread, or chairs that will never be repaired (and are steadily rotting in the damp)? I appreciate that many of us are sentimental creatures, and we think stuff defines us and connects us to ourselves, but does it? And when does it become a negative?

Ryan Nicodemus and Joshua Fields Millburn are the Minimalists, a pair of public speakers, podcasters, authors and radical free-thinkers. At their TED Talk entitled 'The Art of Letting Go', they invited the audience to 'Imagine a life with less: less clutter, less debt, a life with fewer distractions. Imagine a life with more: more time, more meaningful relationships, more growth, a life of passion unencumbered by the trappings of the world around you. What you're imagining is a rich life that has nothing to do with wealth.'

Ryan's life appeared to others to be highly successful: he had a six-figure income, a three-bedroom condo, a nice car. But with all these exterior tokens of wealth came a shitload of debt and a mountain of anxiety and stress. That and the emptiness of overconsuming; a void he tried to fill with more stuff – new cars, electronic gadgets. In this self-perpetuating state he forgot about his health, relationships and passion; he was just on a treadmill, earning to spend, all the time bombarded by ads and soaking them up like a sponge, and believing he needed it all. Josh Fields, the other half of the Minimalists, introduced Ryan to a group of people who seemed much happier than him, and they all had something in common: minimalism.

There and then Ryan set about having a packing party, putting everything he owned into boxes and thereafter living with only the basic possessions he'd need on any given day: toothbrush, toolkit, bed sheets, the furniture he used, kitchenware, clothes and computer. After three weeks, 80 per cent of his stuff was still sitting in their boxes. Unbelievably, he decided to donate and sell all of it, and started to feel 'richer' almost immediately. Next Ryan started a blog to tell of his experience. Three years later more than two million people a year read his words and simple message: get the clutter out of your life to make way for what is more important.

A cluttered environment causes stress, whether conscious or not, every time you come home and look at it. When you clear this distraction, your mind immediately becomes more open to dreaming about bigger and better things. But to achieve this mental space we need to be ruthless and remember that people and memories are not synonymous with possessions. Money spent on hobbies, travel or your passion is more likely to bring you lasting happiness than material possessions that soon become a thing of the past, having lost their sparkle.

9

STEERING YOUR OWN SHIP

MONEY IS ENERGY

Money is often the stumbling block that can hold you back before you've even got started. Depending on your parents' relationship with it when you were growing up, you might have a healthy or unhealthy view of it. Personally, because my parents always seemed to be struggling to earn enough, and it was hand to mouth at times, I think that affected me in a way which means I'm always trying to fortress myself financially, probably explaining why I'm a workaholic. That and the fact that everything I do is all about performing, so it never really feels like work. The way that you treat money says an awful lot about yourself.

What you *can* control is the extent to which you are prepared for the inevitable. For instance, are you saving for later life, or as many young people are doing, just living for the day and making the most of what you've got now? To hell with that old spinster called Prudence, I want a lap dance with Providence. While the latter might be a great idea for seizing the day – after all we never know when our time's up – the reality is that if we don't plan our finances so there's enough for us to fend off poverty when we're old, possess less energy, and are far less employable, then our twilight years will not exactly be something to look forward to. Without having made provision for ourselves, our wife and our kids (if they're still living at home!), the more anxious we will become the closer we get to retirement.

In her book *The Energy of Money*, Maria Nemeth suggests, 'Your money is your life,' that the way you manage your money is itself a reflection of the way you treat your life. Here are a couple of juxtapositions: 'Do you waste money? Do you fritter away time?' Or 'Do you know how much you have in your bank account/your savings? Do you have an accurate picture of your physical health?'

Money, suggests Nemeth, is simply a form of energy. Hold a pound coin in your hand. It's not just a lump of metal, it has passed through many hands, perhaps on its journey contributing towards a present, building a house, buying a bike, a wheelchair. It's helped change lives. It's not static and dead, but a moving thing that flows with us or against us depending on how we view it.

THREE DIFFERENT KINDS OF BACON SARNIE

So, with this notion of money being an extension of ourselves, I'd like to suggest three states of individual financial evolution. Meet the straw debtor. He's accrued debts, not to the point they're suffocating him but he's become oblivious to those monthly payments, despite the fact he's only paying off the interest. The credit card company is milking him every month and he's aware of it, but he's in denial. And denial will only lead him to further debt. His debt has been wilfully put on the back burner, to be dealt with at a later date; but he knows that while he's in debt he will never make provision for retirement, and it constantly nags away at him.

Despite his bank account being in a relatively healthy place, he spends as if those debts weren't lurking in the shadows, as if he's in a safe place. If he was one of the Three Little Pigs, his house would be made of straw. His wealth will never mature because he has no plans to do anything useful with it; he doesn't allow himself to visualise becoming financially organised because he can't start to grow beyond these debts. In short, he's fucked.

Our next little piggy is the saver. Recently, he put his big boy pants (or knickers) on and finally faced up to how much he owed, and what his incomings were versus his outgoings. Having rushed to the toilet to vomit, appalled at how easily and quickly his finances had unravelled – did his son really watch so much pay per view pornography or was it him? – he makes a firm decision to change things with immediate effect.

It's not easy breaking those spending habits, but the fear he harboured of facing these figures was far more intimidating than the reality. He sits down and decides to tackle the punishing high-interest debts first. He takes an honest look at his lifestyle to see what has to change and what isn't needed, like that swish car on HP. Instead, he now knows what to pay per month and how long it would take him to be financially free again. Almost immediately that his intention to clear debts and save is set, he feels a kind of purging of his old self; a new clarity emerging, a sense of fresh potential as he strides from the consumerist swamp of denial into the possibilities of tomorrow. Despite his temporary skin of austerity, of having to be careful over the next couple of months/years, he feels liquid with new ideas and so much lighter in himself. He's learnt to temper his spending habits, mindful of the fact they kept him in stasis, never moving him forward beyond a brief gratification.

Meet the last little piggy. This annoying little porker exudes calm and ease. He doesn't seem to rush, as if time is on his side. When he talks of doing things, be it raising money for a charity by walking the Andes on his front trotters, or getting fit for a marathon, these ideas always seem to be realised. There's a sense of congruence about him, things are in symphony, all his ducks in a row. Like a farmer carefully planting and tending his crop, he's now able to appreciate the fruits of his efforts. He takes his family to inspiring places, thinks with excitement of learning to sail in the Aegean once he's retired, and of the college fund he's been growing for the last fifteen years that his children will soon need. Life doesn't faze him, his nights are not riven with anxiety, there is nothing to fear of the future. Like that guy in *The Purge* who designs security systems to keep the wolves out, our third piggy has worked hard to secure his family in the brick walls of their castle.

Don't you just fucking hate him! Where are you on your financial journey? Giving blowjobs to the interest men just to keep your boat afloat? Or have you got the seats with a decent view of the watering hole watching the animals scrap for a glug while you drink from your ice-chilled glass of Evian? We can be the architect of our finances; all it requires is taking that first step in changing the way we view money and our relationship with it.

If I was about to set off on a voyage, one of the first things I'd do would be to create an inventory of everything I needed on board as well as another list of everything I needed to do beforehand.

HOT TUB EUREKA!

We all have turning points in our life we look back on, something that changed the game a little and maybe shook us up, like a few choice words from someone we respect. I remember the time that my dad walked in on me playing Xbox. He was stressed with work, impatient and said, 'You can either sit on your arse all day playing Xbox, or you can get the fuck up and make something happen with your life.'

Of all the things my dad taught me over the years, and there is so much to thank him for, this moment of subtle candour seems to have resonated the most, so much so that as a reminder of it I had a distilled version tattooed on my foot. While Einstein came up with $E = mc^2$ during a sabbatical in the studious alpine city of Bern, my best friend and I came up with the following work of minimalist genius while steaming in a Vegas hot tub (in the excellent company of a couple of porn stars, I might add, but they're another story). So here it is, sports fans! Can you hear the gentle caress of velvet on cold, smooth marble as I pull back the drape to reveal the plaque upon which this priceless formula is engraved? Oh, and a small drumroll if you will. The tattoo on my foot reads …

$$E + M = D$$

In other words, Embrace and Maximise and you will Dominate. Life really is about embracing and maximising every situation that you are presented with, choosing to explore it with curiosity rather than closing up like a short-sighted clam.

Every day of our lives is full of opportunities and it's up to you whether to embrace and maximise each one or not. It's about being open to abundance, treating each invitation as an opportunity; maybe you'll be asked to write a book, maybe you'll be invited to dinner, maybe somebody gives you their card and says, 'Let's meet for lunch …' Any one of these might lead to something life-changing appearing on your radar, a break that propels you to the next stage of your life's purpose.

If somebody invited me to a school to give a talk to the kids, I'd do my best to prepare for it and get business cards printed to give out. If I was asked to open a new shop, I'd go because you never know who you're going to meet. The only downside of accepting every invitation is you end up not being able to say 'no' to people and you run around like a blue-arsed fly trying to do everything. And that's when you start dropping balls. It took me a while to realise that quality wins over quantity and that it was a case of me needing to be more selective with that precious commodity we call time. Manically trying to do four hundred things at once spreads you too thin, so it's about being savvy to which opportunities you envisage a door opening, as some of them will be dead ends. As you get more experienced you will know when to say no, when to embrace and when to maximise. You can spot the bullshitters and the time wasters from a mile away. Once you have been to a few film premieres you have been to them all. You will also understand what is going to help the things you are into and what is a distraction on the way to your goal.

I went to a prestigious boarding school and as you can imagine it cost an arm and a leg to send me there, so I thought I might as well throw myself into everything. At Wellington College I did football, hockey, tennis, chess and field gun. Field gun was something you may have caught if you ever watched the Royal Tournament. The Royal Navy's field gun competition is a contest between teams from various Royal Navy commands, in which teams of sailors compete to transport a field gun and its equipment over and through a series of obstacles in the shortest time. It's pretty badass when you see it being done between say Portsmouth and Southampton. It's a bit niche to say the least to do at school, but I loved it.

I joined the Marines while in the Combined Cadet Force, I did school plays, school radio; I even did cooking, for fuck's sake! Everything that was available to me I embraced because I knew that I was there for a limited amount of time and maximised as much as I could. You can easily pass through a school without leaving a mark if you want, but I wanted to have a go at everything.

The thing is, and this isn't false modesty, I'm actually not naturally talented at anything; all of these things I had to work at. For a long time, and probably still now (and if you ask my wife, definitely still now) I suffered from Attention Deficit Hyperactivity Disorder (ADHD) and at age ten they put me on something called Ritalin, a drug that allowed me to really focus intensely on any one thing, and so I became much more excited about work in general. It also had other properties that controlled your behaviour and a lot is written about it now, but it certainly helped me concentrate better, something I have carried into later life.

I talked to my wife Chloe about this the other day (that has to be my favourite saying) and she said, 'Why do you get really intense sometimes about work?' It's not that I have bipolar, but it's like a mania I get occasionally whereby I'll sit down and fire off dozens of emails or write 6,000 words of my new book in one sitting, or I'll tidy up my office from top to bottom. I haven't taken Ritalin since I was sixteen, but its effects of making me feel very energised and switched on have never left me. Its possible side-effects of paranoia and being easily agitated thankfully passed me by, but the by-product of increased aggression maybe explains my errant fists in those early days at Wasps. Then again, that doesn't excuse my predilection for fisticuffs in the rest of my rugby career. I'll come back to you on that.

E + M = D – Embrace and Maximise and you'll Dominate. That was the basis of my philosophy. It has served me well over the years.

ESTABLISHING A ROUTINE

If it hadn't been for rugby keeping me on track and giving me a singular purpose, I'm not sure what I would have done. But then came retirement. Suddenly, you had to plan ahead, block things out in your diary, you had weekends, you didn't have to be anywhere, no-one was going to chase you up. Where you had been paid to train, look after your body, that wasn't there anymore. There was no more free medical care, no more team doctor. So, I had to take control of my life by the scruff to get into shape. But that's what everyone has to do, James, I hear you cry. Yes, but when this has been the case for you since age ten, it's not easy to get things back on track. At boarding school you had everything laid out, three square meals a day and a routine. Move onto professional rugby and it's the same thing.

Don't get me wrong, I was resilient and self-reliant outside this structured framework. I took charge of my career, and never just suckled from the teat of the mothership. England coach Eddie Jones has a big thing about players not taking charge of their own careers and because they are spoon-fed so much by their clubs and they lack life experience, it doesn't make for self-reliant individuals. I was one of only a couple of lads when we started who could confidently say they were self-reliant. I saw every area of my career as a way to improve. I never stood still or accepted what was provided as the only way. I paid for my own medical care outside of the club if I didn't think it was good enough, I would see specialist trainers outside of hours to rehab injuries. I was seeing a psychologist from the age of 17 all paid for with my own money. If there was an edge to be had or a better way of doing things, I would seek it out. I even approached legendary All Black Zinzan Brooke to help me with my No 8 play.

If self-reliance is the brain of the body, then having a routine is like the spinal vertebrae supporting it, it helps you organise your life around it. Within a routine are touchstones that keep you on point. Whether it's howling at the moon on a Tuesday, using the same locker in your local gym every visit or having a big glass of redders at the end of the day, they are all habits and to change our behaviour we need only to make changes to our habits to formulate our routines.

Former Navy SEAL, Admiral William H. McRaven says, 'If you want to change the world, start off by making your bed. If you make your bed every morning, you will have accomplished the first task of the day. It will give you a small sense of pride, and it will encourage you to do another task, and another, and another.'

Since reading this I make my bed every day and some days that's the best thing I've done, but at least I can just come back and flop into that bed knowing I did just one thing right that day. During lockdown, routine went out the window for me, and probably for you until you created one. As a rugby player, barring injury, I knew exactly where I was going and what I was doing for the next six months.

Mason Currey, author of *Daily Rituals: How Artists Work*, researched over 161 artists to explore their daily routines.

From people as varied as Carl Jung to Stephen King, they all had a wide variety of habits, which formed very different routines. Some were schedule fiends, others were workaholics, some worked for very small periods but when they did they super-focused. Two familiar constants in all 161 are that they all had rituals and established routines they followed obsessively. A routine might be defined as a series of choices made consciously, based on a person's available resources – time, willpower, other work.

A routine is a kind of safety net. Without one to hold us to task, the day steals itself away from us and we end up rudderless and depressed. What is your routine like? Create your own routine and make it work for you. Not someone else's routine. There's no one size fits all, it has to be tailor-made like a Savile Row suit; it's something that needs modifying and finessing to fit your temperament and natural focus span, your available time and energy levels. Only you know your body, so learn to get in tune with it rather than punish it endlessly. I look back on what I put myself through on the pitch, the absolute commitment and ridiculously high standards I expected from myself, and the physical damage wreaked as a result, and it's something I could have handled much better.

One point that I should have mentioned earlier is that I don't want you to read this book and try to retrofit my life onto yours. Like I say above, this is about taking ideas and concepts and making them work for you. If you try to copy someone else's approach letter by letter and word for word you will fall short, it just won't work for you. You need to get an understanding of self and what you can cherry-pick to enhance your life goals. Yes, of course there are some universal lessons within these pages, and equally I am not going all wanky and ethereal by telling you things like 'You will find the routine when it's the right time' or some other nondescript, irrelevant advice that is hard to decipher. What I have told you works but needs to be made relevant to you.

To be honest, when I first tried to get into the music and DJ world all I was met with was people giving me these wise looks and what sounded like sage advice but was actually useless. 'You need to find your sound.' What the fuck does that mean? Can you tell me what will work please so I can get on with it? Or another gem was, 'Play the right gigs and you will get the success.' What gigs are these? 'Well, they will be the right ones for your sound.' Thanks for nothing. I will not full into that trap with this book.

As far as your routine is concerned, the earlier in the day that you start it the more you get done, rather than working the same hours later in the day. An early start also creates momentum for the rest of the day. We were biologically programmed to rise with the light and go to bed with the dark.

Scientists suggest morning people are happier, but nights owls might be more intelligent. Who cares? At the end of the day the saying 'The early bird gets the worm' always wins because you get more done. The best way to become an early bird is to get up at the same time each day but to go to bed *only* when you're really tired, rather than at the same time every night. If you don't have the time to focus on your goal because of other work commitments, you have to find it in slivers and just make sure those moments are doubly focused. William Faulkner used to write in the afternoon before his nightshift, while Ernest Hemingway rose at 5.30 a.m. even if he'd been drinking the night before. The old man of the sea said, 'There is no-one to disturb you, and it is cool or cold and you come to your work and warm as you write.'

A BIT OF PRESSURE CAN HELP YOU FOCUS

Separate real work from buggering about at your desk. I know it's difficult, because let's face it, given the choice between filling an Excel spreadsheet in or playing with your Action Man that you've had since you were ten, there's no contest. Even the ones that don't have the 'eagle eyes' switch at the back of the head are boss. Just as somebody who's trying to give up smoking walks a different route to work avoiding a newsagent or a garage, you need to remove all sense of distraction from your desk. It's not about lining everything up and creating the perfect environment to work in, lighting candles and finding the right Spotify playlist – though that's rather nice, and there's a great DJ's playlist I could recommend in 'Backrow Beats' or 'Backrow Radio' (thank me later) – it's about *doing* rather than *thinking* of doing. Using your time rather than letting time use you.

If you can reprogram yourself to work flexibly, be it on a plane, train, ferry or in an airport, you can convert that dead time into something productive. I had to write and edit this book in cars and planes on the way to my other work jobs. I had no free days like I had with my first two books. The time I was trying to finish this book was the busiest of my life. I moved house twice in a short period, started a new podcast, launched a gin (Blackeye) and became a dad for the first time. If I wasn't able to adapt and work on the fly or compartmentalise I would never have completed it.

There's nothing like a bit of pressure to help you work smarter with more focus. In 1975 Paul Schrader was broke, freshly divorced, destitute and surfing friends' sofas and sleeping in cars. With the last of their money he and his brother rented a motel for a week, procured two breeze blocks and a long piece of wood to create a desk, and for the next seven days, fuelled by caffeine and stronger substances, they worked through the nights sitting opposite one another, hammering out the screenplay of *Taxi Driver* on their typewriters. The next year it won the Palme d'Or at Cannes.

Then there's the story of Samuel Johnson, author of the seminal work *A Dictionary of the English Language* in 1755. He wrote the classic *Rasselas* in just a week to pay for his mother's medicine. Sadly, she died before the end of the week. My co-writer wrote up most of his travel books for Lonely Planet in a noisy Starbucks in Brighton. Background noise is something you learn to cancel out when you need to get down to it. I have written all of my books to the sound of house music, often techno as it helps me focus. Once you've decided to do something, just do it, don't prevaricate further.

DISCIPLINE

The most crucial raw material required to power the wheels of your routine is discipline. There really is no greater propellant to get you where you want to go. Discipline enhances self-respect and helps you grow and learn. It's the bridge between a goal and its successful realisation. Aristotle once said, 'What lies in our power to do, lies in our power not to do.' Meaning we have the resources within us to do whatever we like, but ultimately, it's up to us whether we choose to stick to our purpose and make it happen. Plato, Aristotle's tutor, also said, 'For a man to conquer himself is the first and noblest of all victories,' while *Vincit qui se vincit* is an old Roman saying meaning 'He conquers who conquers himself.'

For us to do anything well in life we have to take command of ourselves, silence the resistances within us and steer our own ship, rather than let it be blown around by blind winds. This is what self-discipline is all about. There are plenty of things that want to push you off your course: your inner voice, your own self-doubt but also those around you. You were always warned by your parents not to hang around with certain people as they would be a bad influence on you. Of course, for the most part you ignored them. What do your parents know anyway? They are old and out of touch. Well, it turns out you should have heeded their warnings as you are often surrounded by people who won't help you succeed; in fact, the complete opposite. They won't support you, they won't help you achieve the level of discipline required to be successful, they will be cheerleaders of mediocrity. Also it's fair to say that for some being average is fine. They work all week, they get fucked up on the weekends and that's all they want. They are happy with the nine-to-five grind and the subpar body. They will tell you to chill out, stop being boring. Drink this, snort this, have a day off etc. They will criticise you for trying to do something different. In some extreme cases your progress shines a light on their inferior approach to life, so they may be consciously sabotaging you. In 2022, we now have the added issue of social media and all the things that it offers in ways to blow you off your course.

If you're emotionally attached to what you're doing, you will accept the discipline and pain required to reach your goal. We'll talk about the power of having a super-strong purpose in a later chapter. The stronger the purpose the more discipline you are prepared to submit to.

When I was pursuing an MMA career and preparing for my first fight, I knew from my experience as a professional rugby player that the harder I trained the more relaxed, stronger and focused I would be on the night. It takes a lot of courage to climb into a cage and face another person who wants to smash your face in, and one of the ways of dealing with the natural fear of getting hurt is by being fully prepared; so you work on defence moves, blocks, counter-punches, all of which are part of your arsenal to attack your opponent and protect yourself. You also go to places in training that you may never reach in the ring, so the task does not seem so daunting. Training at times above the required level means that come fight night you are ready. At London Shootfighters, one of the leading MMA gyms, they very much believe in that mentality. You may get beaten with a lucky punch or by a superior fighter, but you will never be outworked and you will never be under-prepared. You have to have discipline in fighting sports or it could be your life that is taken, not just your pride.

Remember Mike Tyson in his prime? There was nothing like him before or after his reign. The world of boxing shuddered as he became the youngest world champion ever at the age of 20. He literally exploded onto the heavyweight division like a wrecking ball, tearing one opponent down after another. Iron Mike trained in the Catskill Mountains, New York with his old mentor Cus D'Amato. Arguably the old trainer saved him from a life of thuggery and crime, as Tyson was a petty criminal when he first discovered him, and his red-hot temper was getting him into all kinds of trouble. Cus recognised the raw potential and awesome power in his young ward, and applied an iron discipline to his training, channelling the rage while giving the young boxer self-respect.

Tyson shortly found himself winning gold at the Olympics but that was just the start of his meteoric rise. In boxing there are very few happy endings, and when Cus died Tyson was left rudderless, lost and angry. Without somebody to discipline him he lost all self-governance, and his life imploded when he was imprisoned for rape. On release, he was a different fighter. When he faced a talented, more disciplined boxer in the form of Evander Holyfield, and the lighter man was clearly getting the better of him, Tyson expressed his frustrations in one of the darkest chapters of the sport of kings, biting a huge chunk of Holyfield's ear off. It was pathetic, a desperate act and a woeful finale.

Luck and talent are not the architects of success, but application, sacrifice and self-discipline are. Hard work beats talent when talent doesn't work hard. As I mentioned earlier, even though I was determined to do well, I had serious self-confidence issues when I was younger. What saved me were the psychological methods I learnt from my therapist, but to make them work I had to practise them and that took a lot of self-discipline. The dividends of self-application are many: improved self-esteem, greater self-belief, respect from others and a sense of momentum and progress in your life. I would say hand on heart the reason for any success I have had in any field is the discipline that I have to get it done, to work when others won't and to go to some dark places to get what I want.

'Discipline is the enabler for anything in life that requires determined effort to make it happen,' says Darren Hardy, ultra-runner, endurance athlete, multiple Guinness World Record Holder and ex-soldier. Discharged from the British Army in 2017 after being diagnosed with PTSD, instead of letting it finish him off he channelled his energies into taking on the most ridiculously punishing challenges to raise money for charities, using brutal exercise as a form of self-exorcism. In 2021 alone he ran five marathons back-to-back, and gained an entry into the new *Guinness Book of Records* for pulling a car non-stop for 53 km. He doesn't just beat records; with a steely determination and mindset that places him in a very select, rarefied group of humans, he utterly smashes them.

'Discipline is needed for self-control and self-control is needed for discipline,' he says. 'You only have one thing you can control in your life/body/environment and that is your mind. To use your mind to its full advantage you must have a mind-to-muscle connection; once you can master this, the circle is complete.' Among his followers on Instagram are the regular staff faces from TV's *SAS: Who Dares Wins*, while there are Special Forces soldiers who aren't known to the public who hold him in high regard. This is the man even the fighting elite look up to.

'My legs are tired, I'm injured …' he recounts in his story of his marathons. 'I have massive blood blisters on my toes and I can't walk anymore. Because I am three marathons into a five-marathon challenge, I can't stop, so I tell my mind to instruct my muscles to walk and take one more step, and even run if I can, just get to it over and done with.'

Discipline and determination are not the same, but they are happy bedfellows, and when one is alloyed to the other, they make a formidable team. I have said time and time again that I was never the most talented player in the world but my discipline got me through. While other players were walking off the training field I would be starting my extras. I would be focusing on my core skills and getting my work done. I'd then be onto my recovery and rehab. I would often be the last one to depart at the end of the day as I wanted to leave no stone unturned in the pursuit of being the best. Holidays were never really holidays; I laugh now at memories of me driving around sunny locations abroad trying to find training pitches or running tracks just to get extra sessions in.

I'd like to say I started late to this, but even at 17 I was on holiday with my mate James and we had been on the smash the night before but said we had to get up and train as we both wanted so badly to get into the Wasps team. We found this piece of grass in Majorca and were doing sprints and down and ups until we were spewing. It was mental and probably not the right way to do things, but I had to get it done. The voice in my head would not let me quit. At one point in my career I was training before training started with Wasps because I didn't rate the conditioning I was getting. Then I was doing a full day and going off to see Margot Wells (the famous sprint coach whose husband Allan won gold at the Olympics) three times a week. I was also doing extra wrestling and conditioning sessions with Shootfighters to improve my tackling and conditioning. This went on for a number of years until I realised that I was probably not doing my body any favours. I think one of the hardest things was never going out with your friends, never going travelling or having weekends free. I would go out at times but I would never really drink. I will never forget Chloe telling me off after I had invited people out for a party and then tried to leave after a couple of hours. She was like, 'You can't do that.' I was like, 'Why? I always have. I have training tomorrow and I need to get it done.' She said it was beyond rude and she was right, but I was so single-minded and selfish in those days.

Even with the DJing, I wanted to learn how to do it and spent time getting little bits of help from DJs who were rugby fans like Seb Fontaine, Jaguar Skills and Simon Dunmore. However, I needed to learn in a set format way so I went and did a course. At the end of it, if you were any good you got to DJ at London's Ministry of Sound on the balcony. I got to do this and it was amazing, and it got me addicted. I then got a DJ agent, who was a bit of prick if I am honest. He asked me why I wanted to DJ, I said because I love it. He said good because you won't earn any money from it. Then he booked me to do a university set for three grand for an hour. To me, that was amazing money. He then told me that to become a celeb DJ, to get to play at venues like Hi Ibiza, Tomorrowland and Amnesia, I needed to get a radio show and podcast going and break the mould. So I started recording one and it began to fly; we were getting 40–60,000 listeners per month and over a million average digital radio listeners from around the world (and I still do on 'Backrow Radio'). That didn't really have the effect I wanted but did create some loyal following.

I pressed those in the know and I was told that if I really wanted to make it, I had to start making music. So, I signed up for the Toolroom Academy production course and spent 12 weeks learning to make music. It coincided with me being on holiday in the off season in Greece. Chloe was not best pleased that after every dinner I would be sitting for three hours at night on my laptop to make the track, with my iPad set up next to it to watch the webinar back on what you needed to do. She is super-supportive, but I do test her patience, let's be honest. Obviously learning to make dance music is very hard, so it was another four years until I managed to get my first track released on D4Dance, a sub-label of Defected. I teamed up with Alex Grover who himself is a badass DJ and producer under the moniker Because of Art, and he translated my ideas into a mega track called 'Make You Feel', which even the legend Carl Cox loved. Did it change my DJ life? Sadly, no. But it started me on a journey. I am now on my seventh release and I hope that it is bringing me slowly away from the Z-list celeb DJ arena and into the more underground scene that I crave. I think a few more releases and people may start to take me seriously.

I have to say, even my determination gets tested when I turn up to well-paid gigs and there are only a few hundred people and some of them are wearing rugby stash and start trying to get my attention for a photo while I am DJing, thinking that it's some sort of meet and greet. Or the nauses who hold up their phones with clips of me playing rugby and committing fouls. They are normally young men who must think that if they get a reaction from me they are somehow supercool instead of the very sad and odd people they are. The worst are the red trousers and Barbour brigade who have turned up for whatever reason and stand arms folded just watching me while holding an undrunk glass of red wine. However, the more this happens the more I want success. Don't get me wrong, there are some mega-gigs in between all the crap ones, as there are in any line of work, but I am never satisfied until I nail some landmark sets. I will never give up until I get what I want.

It takes discipline and selfishness to get this done, and I have that in spades. The following represents the pathway to achieving your own personal goals:

DETERMINATION	DISCIPLINE
Persistence	Control
Tenacity	Restraint
Backbone	Direction
Strong-mindedness	Selfishness

REST AND RECOVERY

Nobody runs on fresh air. We need to refuel in order to do our best work, to carve out dedicated rest time otherwise the wheels soon come off the vehicle and the crash or burnout follows quickly after. It's the quality not the quantity of our rest time that counts; how quickly we are able to access a place of calm and our inner self where we can switch off and allow the brain to unwind and idle in neutral.

Walking in the great outdoors is associated with increased productivity and proficiency at creative tasks. It helps reset our thinking. The desk is not a place for insights to occur, but the place you note those insights down; it's during the walking that the best ideas arise. There's no distraction and you are removed from all the man-made interferences that place anxiety on you (unless of course you run into that man I met in the field, or a bunch of female farmers start sending you gore). Tyson Fury is a big walker. Hang on, I'll double-check I spelt that correctly. He finds inner peace for his manic depression through long walks and strenuous exercise twice per day. Adam Peaty is another one that subscribes to walking in nature to reset his mind and blank out the stuff that doesn't matter.

How often do you give yourself a break from the coalface of work and have some 'you time'? If you're anything like me, probably very rarely. No-one would think poorly of you for occasionally having the chutzpah to take yourself off to watch a film or read a book in a café over a lazy cappuccino. Sometimes I think we martyr ourselves, nailed to the cross of ambition and self-flagellation. Truth is, nobody fucking notices anyway. We've become so caught up in the treadmill of work we forget who we were before we had all these responsibilities, before we had kids and careers. Like me, Chloe is an experience collector, and because we didn't have any kids when I started this book (but we will do by the time it's published) we're able to make the best of our independence. There's something much more magnetic about a person who lives their life not just as a good father or husband but also as an individual who has their own interests and a sense of adventure. Many of us forget to indulge ourselves with our own hobbies and that's just sad.

Tools of Titans, written by Tim Ferriss, is a brilliant book about the tactics, routines and habits of billionaires, icons and world-class performers. When it comes to the subject of learning to take rest periods between work and play, Ferriss noticed a pattern in those he interviewed: '80 per cent of all the guests profiled in this book have a daily mindfulness practice of some type.'

In other words, rest is as much a part of success as working your nuts off. Ask yourself, 'How do I allow my mind free rein to wander – so it can wonder – rather than keeping it tied down like a battery hen.' Time to go free-range.

Carl Jung, the eminent Swiss psychiatrist, lived parts of his year in a simple house by Lake Zurich, known as Bollingen Tower. At his practice in Zurich, he was a workaholic who worked nine-hour days seeing patients. He came to the tower, a place with no floorboards, no carpets or electricity, as a place to unwind, as a sanctuary for writing and to regather his considerable energy. Jung said, 'I've realised that someone who's tired and needs a rest but who goes on working all the same, is a fool.'

Ferriss relates Arnold Schwarzenegger's first venture into meditation when his movie career began to blossom; for the first time in his life the actor felt worried and anxious by all the opportunities flying at him and pressured in a way he'd never been before. Arnie took a course in transcendental meditation and in his own words he says, 'I went up there, took a class and I went home after that and tried it. I said to myself I've got to give it a shot. I did 20 minutes in the morning and 20 minutes at night, and I would say within 14 days I got to the point where I could really disconnect my mind for a few seconds and learn how to focus more and calm down.'

Arnie makes another great point about meditation having taught him not to bunch all his worries together but to learn to separate them. 'Even today, I still benefit from it because I don't merge and bring things together and see everything as one big problem. I take them one challenge at a time.'

SLEEP

Get this: men who live to an average age of 79 years, spend 25 years of their lives asleep. That's a lot of time spent elsewhere. Like something out of a 1950s sci-fi film, humans submit to sleep without demur. Imagine an alien race explaining the concept of sleep after a visit to earth. 'These earthlings are fucking weird. They create elaborate nests to lie down in at night, then they turn out the lights and leave their windows ajar to help them sleep. They put wax things in their ears to stop them hearing, some of them place masks across their eyes, then they lie down in their billions as if they're in a collective trance, unguarded, still breathing, and they disappear into a place that makes some scream, smile or spurt (reticulan-speak for a wet dream) while they dream. Sometimes they grow erections in their pyjamas in the middle of the night, and if there are two humans in the bed, they bounce on top of each other and fall asleep again. Sleep is their vital medicine as without it they change character, become aggressive or ineffective.'

For many of us, getting to sleep is no big deal, it's staying asleep that is the problem. Insomnia isn't purely defined by the inability to get to sleep, it's about not being able to regain sleep once you've woken up or waking too early in the morning. Around 58 per cent of people in the UK complain of any one of these symptoms every year. If you're an eight hours' sleep person and you miss a few hours each night and neglect to pay back the sleep bank, your body will be more prone to illness, as the correlation between sleep deficit and disease is now well known in the scientific community. Sleep is the great replenisher: during its spell the mind relaxes, the body heals, and the brain sorts through its admin for the day and files away experiences.

There are lots of ways to ensure we get the rest we need so we can enjoy our days with both eyes open. If you're someone who finds it tricky to get to sleep, begin to be aware of the average time of night when your body is telling you it's tired. Yes, you're yawning and nodding off in the middle of a Netflix film and it's only half nine in the evening, but when the Sandman cometh you'd better be ready to sail to the land of nod, otherwise you'll be carried off by the second wind and marooned on the shores of second insomnia. Many of us fight our bodies telling us it's time to sleep because we've only just got back from work, had our dinner and don't want to cut the evening short. It's *our* time. I have no problem going to bed at 7.30 if I am tired. Sleep and recovery are essential, especially with the hectic life I have. I am only able to do all the things with the level of energy I give them because I get my sleep. I try to plan when I am going to have a late one so I am able to recover properly. If I burn the candle at both ends, I feel it the following days. In the early days of retirement when I wasn't nailing my schedule, I would be getting home at 4 a.m. from a DJ gig, then having to get up at 8 a.m. to do something else, then speaking at a dinner that same night and getting home at 12.30 p.m. I still haven't nailed it all of the time, but I am much better at prioritising sleep.

Interestingly, mankind is the only living thing that willingly resists sleep. Plonkers, the lot of us.

PILLAR III
RESIST

THE BLAME GAME

How often do we blame our shortcomings on someone else instead of owning our contribution to the shit hitting the proverbial fan? Don't throw someone else under the bus, be big enough to hold your hand up and admit it when you're wrong. The quickest way to get your canoe afloat and running in harmony with life's currents is fessing up to the person you've wronged, acknowledging where you screwed up and explaining what you are going to do to correct it so it doesn't happen again. Only when you take complete responsibility for your actions can you really begin to grow in yourself.

You are where you are in life because of the actions you've taken so far. If things are not working the way you want them to, only you can change them. When you begin to face this truth and take responsibility for the impact you have on yourself and others, things quickly begin to change for the better. It's very empowering to feel like you're on top of things, being transparent, upfront and honest with people. When we try and accommodate people by telling them a softer version of the truth it just blows up in our face and we end up looking like a bullshitter. It's so much better to just be completely straight and consistent, then people know where they are with you. I will just say that you often see people come out and say I am who I am and I say it how it is, and if you don't like it that's your problem. These people are normally socially disabled and just say stupid things in a stupid way and can't understand why everyone thinks they are a fuckhead.

You need some tact and you need to understand the person you are talking about. Just going around saying the first thing that comes into your head in the most direct way possible is not the answer anyway. You can still be honest and direct but without causing offence. Sometimes you do need to drop some bombshells, but again understand who you are talking to and do it in a way to cause minimum damage. Also, be aware that some people have no self-awareness, they are never going to change and no amount of you talking to them is going to fix it. I often don't bother as it's just going to cause conflict so instead, I just handle my shit, make sure I can honestly say I have done all I can, and it's up to this person to see it and change it themselves.

IT'S NOT WHO YOU ARE THAT HOLDS YOU BACK, IT'S WHO YOU THINK YOU ARE NOT

The worst thing you can do is sit around and wait for life to happen, thinking it owes you a living, while you distract yourself with mindless activities like social media. We're all afraid of reaching the great heights that we are capable of, so we pretend we are not interested in doing so. Nietzsche says we should stop being passive spectators and take our lives in our own hands. You can start by watching less TV, removing toxic friendships from your life and avoiding social media as much as possible. Ask yourself the hard questions: what do I want to get out of life? What do I need to do to stop blocking myself?

If we want to be something more than we currently are, we need to practise self-awareness. Thoughts precede and give rise to feelings, and it is feelings that make us happy or sad. So we need to become more attuned to when we're feeling negative and stop that train of thought simply by remembering that the nature of thought is that it passes. Our feelings are like a barometer that gives us immediate feedback about the quality of our thinking in any moment. Inbuilt in us are default settings of compassion, ease, resilience, creativity and common sense, but we can't access these if our thoughts are constantly allowed to roll towards an anxious place. If we are in a low mood, our awareness is like a clouded filter in a camera, letting in less light and clarity of what is happening to us.

Exercise 1: Understanding your feelings

Imagine a time when you were challenged or humiliated by someone. Now notice how a feeling immediately follows corresponding to that thought. Maybe you've got a knot of nerves in your stomach or you feel angry?

This time, think of a moment when you were congratulated or valued, or when you won something. Maybe a standout moment that you're proud of. What did you feel in your gut this time?

When we are able to quieten our over-magnified spiralling thoughts like a surfer rejecting a set of poor waves, the panic drains away, returning us to a place of buoyancy where we're in a better state to creatively think our way out of a problem. When we take control of our choices and stop blaming others for what is wrong with our lives, we start to realise who we are capable of being. Despite years of therapy, I still find myself falling victim at times to old modes of thought, self-doubt and sometimes self-destructive actions. In the end it's a simple question: do I want a calm mind or a distracted one?

I have tried hypnotherapists and more. If it wasn't for them, I would not have had the career that I've had. I couldn't have done what I've done without the mental strength they helped me develop. They didn't magically fix me, they gave me the tools and understanding, and I did the rest. I saw and learnt how to deal with things better, and I came to the conclusion that so much of life comes down to control and accepting how little control we have except over ourselves and the way in which we respond to situations.

Exercise 2: The circle of influence

To figure out what you can and can't control, first draw a circle on a sheet of A4. Inside this circle write down everything you are worried about at the moment or in general, e.g. your job, the cost of living, your health, your gambling, England losing on penalties. Then draw another circle with a circle within it, listing all the things above that you can't control in the outer circle, **the circle of concern**, and all that you can control in the inner circle, **the circle of influence**, e.g. your gambling, your consumption, your lifestyle or your job and performance at work.

SOLO-TASKING

These days I find the best way to get something done is to allow myself to do just that one thing – not three or four things, just that one. There's a new term for it and that's

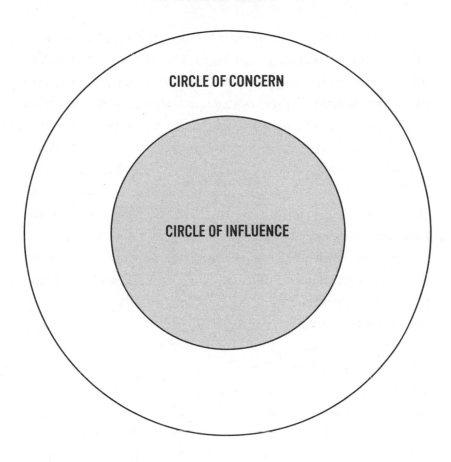

solo-tasking, the polar opposite of multi-tasking. Multi-tasking causes stress and not many of us are very adept at it. The problem is when you're balancing too many plates you're always going to drop a few. Let's face it, when you sit down and get online with your laptop it presents an alluring world of disruption; you have to contend with pop-up ads that are now very good at being relevant to your browsing patterns; your email is giving you notifications onscreen; and then there's your phone flashing. It's an absolute Eden of distraction. Do you type emails really quietly while talking to a friend on the phone? Do you listen to podcasts while writing? Do you send text messages while watching a film, or check your Twitter feed while someone is talking to you? In moments like these are we giving our best, are we focused or really listening to the other person? Multi-tasking waters down our effectiveness and quality, and it actually takes longer to do tasks than if we were to solely address each one independently. A study into multi-tasking at the University of Michigan discovered that multi-tasking contributes to the release of stress hormones, making us feel on edge. It also affects our short-term memory. But for many of us, multi-tasking is a deeply entrenched habit and way of living.

When we overtask we make mistakes; like that WhatsApp picture of your cock standing proudly to attention which you intended for your girlfriend, but mistakenly sent to your mother-in-law because you were in such a rush you pressed the wrong recipient. (This is just an example: it never happened. But if it did, lucky Judy, I'd say.) The more mental bandwidth we give ourselves for a task, the quicker and more effectively it gets completed.

First of all we need to remove all distractions: phone-ringing, social media notifications, open web browsers etc. Next, we prioritise the most important task that needs completing. Set a time for how long you'll work on it. If you're easily distracted, set your alarm for 20 minutes then take a short break after each 20-minute slot. Taking regular breaks keeps your mind fresh.

When we solo-task, we are calmer and more connected with ourselves.

WATCH OUT FOR THE SHITTY COMMITTEE

Like everybody I have good days and bad days, and if I'm feeling a little bit flat it's harder to get myself organised than on other days when I'm feeling pukka and ready to seize life and accomplish things. That's because on flat days it's often easier to listen to negative thoughts if you have them, but it's also easier to listen to that inner voice that whispers to us, saying take it easy, no need for discipline today. Why not take a day off? Why don't you just rest up? You have been working so hard, no need to train or get that work done.

There is nothing better to disrupt a day than laziness. Of course, your personal inner voice could be way more severe than just getting you to take some time off and derail your fitness, health or work journey. Your head could also be filled with more negative things.

A friend of mine who's an alcoholic but twenty-five years sober, knows his inner critic only too well. He calls it the 'shitty committee'. 'The shitty committee,' he says, 'gets up twenty minutes earlier than me and is ready to go at me as soon as I wake up, feeding me over-judgemental scorn about myself, giving me reasons to believe I'm a failure, and telling me that I may as well give up and have a drink. It's then I remind myself that I'm grateful to be alive, and what's more important than getting smashed is being there for my son.'

DON'T BE DEFINED BY *THINGS*

Adam Baker, a minimalist guru who you can find on TED Talks, says: 'As we get rid of stuff we feel lighter, less complicated, less defined by what we own, and freer to move, with more of a sense of who we are. Identity should be based on experience not possessions, a richness of life rather than inanimate possessions.'

He suggests a three-step programme:

- **Step 1:** Decide what you want to achieve by paring down. What's your purpose? Perhaps to create some cash, feel less burdened by stuff; to donate to charity, or have a penis extension. Once you're clear about your end goal, it will make it easier to chuck.
- **Step 2:** The 30-day minimalism game. On day one, throw out one thing, on day two, two things, and so on. After 30 days your house, and mind, will be lighter after decluttering 564 items! And no, you can't declutter your mother-in-law, unless she lives with you.
- **Step 3:** You're allowed a 'just-in-case' box (or boxes) – for things you don't know if you can bear to throw out or not, so you'll keep them just in case. Put these undecided possessions in a box, tape it up and leave it somewhere for 30 days. If after this time you haven't thought about it or used whatever is in there … bin it!

So, step one, look at your finances. Decide to start putting some money away and consider how much you'll need to save each month. Take a really hard look at your bank accounts, and on credit cards if you have them; are you carrying debts that are bringing you down with high interest rates? Do you feel like you're weighed down by hire purchase loans, like Atlas holding up the sky? Seek out debt consolidation companies to advise you, people in the know who can turn the fear of the unknown into manageables. The first step in creating bandwidth for your mind, giving it the space to roam without the usual anxiety, is getting your ship in order. I have found that a lot of people don't realise that especially in the Western world there is help out there, if you want to look and ask for it. I personally know people whose pride has stopped them from reaching out for help and getting their debts consolidated or declaring for bankruptcy. They couldn't face the shame so live this ridiculous charade. I also always hear the same thing, that 'My problems are different' and 'There is no help' or 'I don't know where to begin.' There is always a way if you are prepared to work for it.

I have also had people reach out to me on social media asking for money because they had got themselves into so much debt and couldn't tell their partner due to the shame and embarrassment. So they were looking at others to fix it and give them money. When I pointed out it was surely more shameful to ask a person you have never met for money, they said perhaps I was right. I said that if your partner loves you then you need to come clean and get help. Begging for money is never the right thing to do, not when there are ways of asking for help. All it takes is a bit of time and research online and you can find ways out of most predicaments. If you don't fix the problem at source, papering over cracks with borrowed money is never going to work. It will just happen again and again.

Imagine you're going on a long voyage by boat. What would you need to do with your affairs before you left land? First up, get your finances in order. Next, plan your course: what's your destination and how long do you think it will take to get there? What resources will you need to help you and who are you taking with you? Are they positive or negative people? How useful are they going to be in a crisis? What experience do they have on the open seas when a storm comes? How can you plan for a storm? What spare equipment will you need take with you? How much food will you take? How prepared are you to leave land? Are there any things that you can upskill on before you leave?

For us to do anything well in life, we have to take command of ourselves, silence the resistances within us and steer our own ship to its destination. This is what self-discipline is all about.

How do we ritualise rest periods into our routine? Some of us work well in long blocks of focus, while others need to split short periods of super-focus with small breaks to recover. And this is where meditation can help. Tim Ferriss says, 'Meditation is a skill that improves everything else, you're starting your day by practising focus when it doesn't matter (like sitting on the couch for 10 minutes) so that you can focus better later when it does matter ... Meditation acts as a warm bath for the mind.'

HOW TO SWITCH OFF AND REST MENTALLY

There are some useful apps like 'Calm', which asks you every day how you're feeling, and depending on the given response will find a suitable short or long guided meditation to lead you back to the place in yourself where you're ready to be productive or to relax. Again, it might sound all a bit New Age with whale songs, but meditation is really useful for resetting the anxious mind. Another good app is 'Headspace', where you get ten minutes free for ten days but after that you have to put your hand in your pocket. Narrated by an ex-Buddhist monk, there are no whale songs and it's a lot more stripped down.

Learning to meditate is like developing a muscle: it takes time, you get there incrementally and the results are brilliant. Its purpose is to still the mind; when you're at rest it either races around like an excited dog or scurries around like a frightened rat as it jumps onto self-sabotaging thoughts. It's about being aware of this happening and then returning to focus on your breathing. And the more you do it, the easier it gets. I have also found that trying to clear your mind is nigh-on impossible. If I say stop thinking, all you will do is focus on things you shouldn't, or you think even more. If I said don't think of red elephants, what are you now thinking of? I find the best form of visualisation/meditation is one where you focus on the positives, you focus on doing things well, or changing thoughts you have to the way you want them. You aim to relax, and let drama and stress flow away. I was wound pretty tight post-retirement, training my arse off for MMA, running around DJing, speaking, podcasting and doing sponsorship work every day of the week. My routine had gone out the window. I found that the only time I could really be mindful was when I made myself a coffee, sat in the garden with a cigar and just chilled out. Looking at the world going by, no phone, no distractions, just chilling and not speaking to anyone. I utilised the hour or so it took to smoke the cigar to just be mindful. It didn't mean I found inner piece, but I became mindful of my surroundings and disconnected from the craziness. Now I am not saying take up cigar smoking, but find something that allows you to switch off. It could be something as simple as taking the dog out for a walk.

KEY TAKEAWAYS FROM PILLAR III: RESIST

- We can't control other people's reactions. But we can control our own.
- Bend with the wind, or in the words of Bruce Lee, be like water.
- Stop that negative feeling and remember that every cloud passes.
- Change the narrative in your head, visualise yourself doing things well.
- This book won't fix you. Only YOU can fix yourself.
- Don't be disorganised. Plan ahead.
- Get yourself into a routine.
- Worry about the things you can control: how you treat your body and mind, how hard you work and how you treat others.
- Let positive habits entrench themselves in your mind.
- Don't be a hoarder. A cleared environment is a cleared mind.
- Embrace + Maximise = Domination.
- Luck and talent are not the architects of success; application, sacrifice and self-discipline are.
- Learn to meditate and switch off mentally.

10

SCREW YOUR COURAGE TO THE STICKING PLACE

It's time for me to arm you with the vital tools to help you make lasting changes to your life. In my own life, if I begin to go off the rails when trying to action my personal goals, or I'm feeling uninspired or a little lost in myself, I need to be able to refocus and zone back in. With regard to work, some weeks it's utter carnage, others it's quieter. Sometimes I am making good money, other times not so much. Whatever I am doing, when I need to get things firing again, I always return to the four principles of life, which I address later in this chapter, that have become my touchstones to success.

STOP FOCUSING ON NEGATIVES

The problem with humans is that we tend to focus on one piece of criticism rather than allow ourselves to enjoy praise; it's always the negative that attracts us. Like on social media somebody writes one cruel comment and that's the one that you are compelled to focus on and obsess about. When you're judgmental about yourself you feel an accompanying emotional response. So what we have to do is pause right there and say to ourselves, 'Actually, that comment/feedback is not true, what I know to be true are these facts, so I'm not going to believe the emotion that I'm feeling right now.' For some people, they are so mentally strong that they can move on from this. For others, this one comment out of, say, one hundred can really affect them. You can't see the wood for the trees. You start believing what they are saying is true or at the very minimum it has merit. You need to check the facts. Say someone says you are shit at what you do. Look back at your personal inventory. In my case, I played professional club rugby across the world, from the UK and France to Japan and New Zealand, was capped 77 times for England, and was a British and Irish Lion. So, the statement can't be true. It's just an opinion. An opinion from someone who you have never met. An opinion from someone who more often than not when you look at their profile has bigger issues than you ever will. Also, you have to ask yourself who goes around slagging people off, anyway? I am not suggesting you have to do this every time, but it's good practice for those who really struggle with this kind of thing.

It's vital we visualise the true statements in place of the negative ones. So for instance, if it's somebody telling me that I'm a terrible writer or terrible DJ, I just focus on a moment, a career highlight, a real memory, then I can qualify that shitty statement as not being true.

Recently, I was DJing in Cafe Mambo in Ibiza alongside Simon Dunmore, the legendary house DJ, and Bob Sinclar, the famous French Casanova DJ. I mixed really well and had a good time but then I made a mistake. I was putting a big build together and at the last minute stopped the wrong track and it went quiet for a second before I started again. I stupidly looked online and saw the negative comments; I might be 37 but I have certain vulnerabilities, especially when it comes to

DJing, which is something I want to do really well. I want to be considered as a good DJ, but seeing those comments online was really upsetting to me. This was a big moment for me, mixing with two proper legends of the music scene and I made one small mistake. None of the important people cared, Bob just laughed it off and we all carried on. However, when you want to be taken seriously, making a mistake during your big moment with the big boys is always going to bum you out.

What was interesting was that I physically felt the whole chemical change in my body as I read a less than kind comment about my set; I felt hot and red with embarrassment, almost ashamed. I was thinking of giving up DJing, but then I said to myself, 'Hask, you didn't do badly at all, in fact you nailed a really good set, and you did your best ...' And then I went back through all the evidence of the things that I did well during the set, just to ensure that my mind knew what had happened and I could get rid of this horrible feeling in my gut. I looked at my process and why I made the mistake, and I looked at how I had mixed using two decks next to each other instead of mixing on one player, on one side of the mixer, and then the other like I would normally. I asked myself had I prepared enough for the set, and the answer was yes, I had. I was able to shrug things off in a couple of hours where back in the day with rugby it would have taken a couple of days.

I also decided to go one step further and reach out to someone who does what I do but way better to see if I could get any tools to help me deal with the pressure of DJing. It's a technique I always use when I know there are things that I can do better or I need advice. The upshot of this was that I reached out to a DJ called Alan Fitzpatrick, a world-class guy in the field. I told him about this stuff I was carrying around and what had happened, and he said, 'Look, don't be too hard on yourself. The DJ thinks the audience knows when they make a mistake, but they don't, and even if they do it doesn't matter. We all do it all of the time.'

What he said wasn't rocket science, but because it came from somebody who's at the top of his game and somebody that I respect, it made me feel so much better and it put things into perspective. When I next did some DJing, I felt so much more confident. And if I ever thought back to that mistake, I just flipped my thinking so I imagined myself doing it right and smashing it. Mistakes shouldn't deter you, they should make you more hungry; after all, you're learning from them, improving all the time. Don't watch your performance straight after, give it a little time for things to settle and then in context you'll see a very different picture.

One thing my psychologist Jill Owen taught me was not only the importance of making mistakes to improve but also to never be worried about making them. She said that when a painter, for example, has their work displayed in a gallery you only ever see the finished product; you never see all the crumpled-up sketches in the bin or littering the artist's studio. You never see all the failed attempts; all you see is the final piece of art. If you extrapolate this, it works for anything. There will always be mistakes; a game of rugby would never flow if there weren't mistakes. Embrace making mistakes, they help us learn. Critics are everywhere but they are only ever on the sidelines passing comment. Ernest Hemingway nailed it in one line.

'Critics are men who watch a battle from a high place then come down and shoot the survivors.'

Looking for feedback is essential for our growth. I have talked about this a few times already, but it's where you look that is important. You shouldn't go to 'yes' men who will give you what you want to hear. If I want to hear I did really well regardless of what happened, I will ask my mum what she thinks. Equally you shouldn't go online to people you have never met to ask for advice. You want to find people who know what they are talking about. There is no point going to someone who knows fuck all about mixing to ask them how you were DJing. I try to find good people in the areas of life I am interested in doing well in, and ask them for advice. I choose people I know who will tell me how it is but whose opinion I value.

These days pre-performance – be it DJing, doing a public-speaking gig, podcasting, being interviewed as a rugby pundit – I close my eyes and picture what I'm about to do. I show my mind very clear images of me executing the task elegantly, and it gives it a kind of waypoint to get to, a very clear coordinate. As I do this, I'm also visualising how I will feel while executing the task. Your mind cannot tell whether you're physically doing it or whether you're just visualising it. This means that if we identify really vulnerable areas and weaknesses and catch those negative thoughts that always lead us back to these places where we feel most threatened, and if we can reprogram these places with positive thoughts, flipping the situation in our mind and imagining the absolute positive outcome, we can utilise them to our benefit. One trick I have is that I will make sure where possible that I have either recorded or filmed what I did so I can get it reviewed. Failing that, I will always reach out to co-hosts or event organisers and ask them how they think it went. All this information is important to help you get better at what you do.

AFFIRMATIONS

An affirmation is a positive statement that you say to yourself regularly to help you challenge and overcome negative thinking or to change unhelpful self-sabotaging views of yourself. Again, your brain, bless it, on hearing the affirmation, does not know the difference between fact and fiction. An affirmation is a statement that helps the brain create a fresh neural pathway through all the jungle of neurons and grey matter.

The stories of people who have got themselves out of difficult situations – physically and mentally – by choosing the right affirmation(s) are myriad. Bruce Lee was bedbound for a year after screwing his back up by not warming up properly. The doctor told him he'd be lucky to walk again, never mind practise kung fu. So Lee, ever the master of self-will, wrote a letter to himself on Post-it notes and got his wife to stick them all over the ceiling, so as he looked up at them he was constantly seeing what he wanted to achieve. During this period in his life, while he ran his own fight school and counted among his students the likes of Steve McQueen and James Coburn, Lee's acting career had hit the skids, so these words to himself couldn't have been more timely. 'I, Bruce Lee, will be the first highest paid oriental superstar in the United States. Starting in 1970, I will have in my possession $10,000,000. I will live the way I please and achieve inner harmony and happiness.'

Bruce Lee not only walked again but went on to achieve all and more of the above before his untimely death in 1980.

So maybe the universe will give you what you want if you Post-it note everywhere? Sadly, where a lot of people go wrong is failing to match affirmations with actions, directed by those who know what they are doing. Affirmations are one tool in your arsenal, along with:

- Visualisation
- Routine
- Seeking feedback
- Having goals
- Worrying about what you can control
- Being disciplined
- Asking for help

If you only take care of the mind, your body will fail. To achieve amazing success, all of these things have to be linked up together to create an unstoppable force. Never buy into the dogmatism of those who pronounce their way to be the best. There is never one single thing that is better than all others that will make you have the life that you want, however much they sell it to you or however much you want the same life you perceive them to have. If they guarantee you results, run the other way. What you quickly realise about success is it takes time and is made up of lots of moving parts, and that not one singular thing works. You may have to take a few steps back to go forward again. You will be tested; your discipline and mental fortitude will be assayed. It's also horribly hard work that never gets easier. Those who utilise all the facets we have discussed in this book and stick to them will make the biggest changes to their lives. It won't be easy and it won't always be fun – in fact it's going to be pretty bloody hard at times – but you know what? More often than not you never reach the goals you set yourself, as you will keep changing them the more you develop and manage what you can control.

YOU ARE WHAT YOU THINK

Negative thoughts about ourselves become self-fulfilling prophecies, but when we consciously flip them and say the opposite to ourselves, it's amazing the changes that we can create in a short space of time. A typical affirmation might be, 'Today I'm feeling open to all the good things that come my way,' or 'I am healthy, I am wealthy and I am happy.' Before you get to writing down your affirmation, you need to zero in on the area of your life you want to develop. So if it's to be a better friend you might say, 'I'm a great listener and make time for my friends.'

Back in the day, I'd write three or four affirmations on my rugby strapping: words or sentences to remind me of what was important to me during the 80 minutes. The shorter the affirmation the easier it is to say. My favourite affirmation remains to this day: 'The best revenge is living well.' I liked it so much I bought the company. Actually, I had it tattooed on me, and since it was a bit too wordy to fit on my toe, it's inscribed on my inner left bicep. What does the quote mean? Focusing on improving yourself and embracing life is the best revenge; while your critics are scratching their balls and lambasting you, you are getting stronger and living to your max. Whenever people question me about what I am doing or pass judgement, I always just go back to focusing on me. I have said it before while others are making nasty comments online or worrying about what others are doing, I am too busy getting shit done and living my best life. Doing this is the best way to shut up all the doubters and the trolls, and keeps you focused. You can sometimes look over the garden fence for inspiration but you should be 95 per cent of the time focused on tending to your own garden.

Next, make sure that your affirmation is credible and realistic. We all have aspirations. Some of them we believe in, others are mere fantasies, and with the help of a frequently spoken affirmation at the start of the day and during it when our thinking blackens, we can realise them. But if you don't believe them and you cannot see yourself being what you are telling yourself, it can't happen. Even if you are not sure how you are going to get there, what is important is for you to believe it's possible. You may not be able to say I am going to do this, but you can say it's possible. It's possible for me to become a professional rugby player, a top DJ or a bestselling author. Then you take the collective tools within these pages and match these affirmations with concerted and planned action.

DON'T BE A SHEEP, BE AN AGENT OF CHANGE

I am many things to many men, women and non-binary people: a joker, a talented performer, a Casanova, a living legend, a renegade master, an intellectual, a natural-born killer, an international man of mystery, a Pulitzer Prize winner. What? Oh, you want the real version?

Okay, take two: I'm a compulsive performer, I love being the centre of attention and I can't stop talking; I love pranking – though I confess, I prefer to be the architect of a prank rather than the receiver; I often put my foot in it, but one thing you can't accuse me of is not being true to myself. I'm neither a sheep nor am I a clone like the Borg (the nickname we gave Leicester Tigers players). I've always had the courage to stand by my convictions and I believe the standards you walk by are the standards you live by. So, if you're prepared to watch someone being bullied on a street, in a tube station or wherever it may be and are in a position to help but choose to pass them by, you're no better than the person/people causing the trouble.

'It's alright for you, Hask, you're as big as the Honey Monster,' I hear you say. 'It's different when you are five feet tall.' I'm not suggesting you get involved physically, just do *something*: if it's someone being robbed or beaten up call a policeman; if it's a work thing and you see someone being passively aggressed go to your HR dept – but call the person out. Be an agent of change. Whatever you do, whatever action you take, it shouldn't be to stand there doing fuck all with your phone out recording it. That seems to be the default setting of the average person in the street. I will always say something, or intervene where I can. I am not a vigilante nor am I that good a person. I just believe strongly that you have to maintain personal standards. I am not like one of those wankers driving round trying to catch people on their phones and then report them to the police on some bizarre crusade. I am not that morally righteous, I just draw the line at what I feel is important. Everyone now is so worried about trying to cancel someone and be the first to pass judgement, but if you look at your own personal standards, and look at how you live your life, can you say it's up to scratch? Should you be so worried about what others are doing when yours is a mess? Do you have manners, do you stand up for what is right on the right occasion?

My mate Dozza – who many of you will know from my first two books as my Wasps teammate and partner-in-crime Paul Doran-Jones – was in a nightclub and saw a man slapping a woman. He flew in and belted the bloke before being bottled by another one of the lad's mates. A huge brawl kicked off. He came back the next day to lunch with his ex-partner and some of her family and their friends. One bloke sitting next to his wife at the table started to pass judgement and said something when Dozza walked in. He said, 'Doz, trouble seems to follow you around like a bad smell.' Dozza responded, 'So you would turn a blind eye if you saw a woman getting hit, would you? That's the kind of man you are, is it?' The bloke tried to mumble his way out of it, but it's true. You either want to do the right thing, or make out your shit doesn't stink and spend all your time looking at what others do. I know which one I would be. If we don't walk our talk every day, then who we think we are is just bullshit. Muhammad Ali said, 'Service to others is the rent you pay for your room here on earth', and I agree. You have to do your bit and not leave it to others.

THE BYSTANDER EFFECT

Maybe you've heard of the 'bystander effect', the phenomenon whereby the more people there are present the less likely they are to help someone who's clearly in trouble. So long as they've seen others walk by, they're able to justify their indifference to themselves, 'Well, they didn't stop so it must be okay,' they comfort themselves. For every Good Samaritan there are a thousand cowards. We really are sheep. But take the numbers away, so it's you and the person in trouble, and your body reacts in a completely different way; it's as if it knows you are being tested. Suddenly, that frozen, terrified shape becomes a human being you need to help.

Tap in 'bystander effect' on YouTube and you'll find loads of examples of experiments that highlight our ability to selectively see what best suits us. In one scene, a blob of a commuter stands in a queue and watches on as a thief (who's actually an actor) sidles up next to him and brazenly removes the wallet from the rucksack on the back of a woman a few feet away. The man observing the theft can choose to help or be a frightened robot. He does nothing. His life could have changed in that moment, he could have evolved himself by taking charge, but instead he remains in indifferent mode.

In another set-up, a guy is collapsed on the rain-soaked steps outside Liverpool Street station, beer in hand. Everyone ignores him and it's twenty minutes before anyone shows the least bit of concern. Next, the same guy dresses as a smart city gent and lies collapsed in the same place (no beer this time); it takes only six seconds before a black lady calls him 'sir' and asks if he's okay. Shortly, other commuters are flocking around him. Because he's in a suit the passers-by feel he's one of them, that he deserves their care. Next a woman lies prostrate on the steps. She is casually dressed and it's four minutes before anyone chooses to notice her. In the next stage, the casually dressed actor is writhing on the floor doubled up and pleading for help. Nobody stops. How you look affects how you're treated, and the more attractive you are the more likely you are able to get what you want.

In another experiment a plain-looking girl is trying to haul a huge suitcase up some stairs at a London train station. Nobody stops to help her. Next, an attractive, bubbly blonde struggles with the same bag – it takes just four seconds for a white knight to appear. In fact, there's about four men with their mouths hanging open. One of them, having helped, says, 'I'm a sucker for a pretty girl who needs help ... just like my grandfather.'

Sometimes I wish we were more like our great- and great-great-grandfathers, those generations who lost and gave so much of themselves in war. I wonder what they would have thought of what British society has become today. I think they'd be rather disappointed we've become a bunch of whingers. I know it's wrong to compare eras as they are non-relative, but I think that they'd agree we've not only lost the art of being honest and upfront, but we've also lost a bit of heart when faced with the dilemma of taking a chance and helping someone or not. We possess the choice to be a better version of ourselves and each time we stretch to it, I believe we grow stronger and become better people for it.

I think we have lost a bit of toughness. We used to have leaders and those who decided what we do. We didn't have a platform like social media to question everything. Now, because everyone has a voice, we have to pander to everyone. I couldn't believe the fuss that was made over a heatwave in July 2022 in the UK. They closed schools, people just didn't go to work. It's not like it was raining fire or lava streams were flowing down the streets. It was hot, like Dubai hot, Bahrain hot, not you will die if you go outside hot. What a lot of people forgot is the next football World Cup is in Qatar and it's going to be that hot all the time. So the travelling British fans might need to toughen up.

We live in a Western country with air-conditioning, and water on tap. This isn't a developing country. This is the UK. I was shocked when I was asked if I was going to come in for our *GBR* work meeting by our MD, and if all the others were going to be able to travel in, some from their regional home starting points into central London. I replied with the following: 'I'm fine because I am not a massive fanny 😂. You have been working too long in the corporate world. Tell them to get the fuck in, we have work to do.'

Now I'm sure you are not surprised to hear that I don't work in HR, but my point stands. Why are we even asking the question? There will always be someone who is keen to get shit done, who will deal with rain, hail and fire to put the effort in to be a success. I believe if you can't hack it, fuck off and we will find someone who can. That's what I truly believe. I am sick of hearing all about the problems everyone has and how we have to accommodate everyone. There are 8 billion people in the world and that number is climbing. If you can't deal with the heat then stay at home. If you aren't hungry, don't like working weekends, feel that because someone dumped you, we all need to run around after you and dry your eyes, then success is not for you. For every one person who won't work, there is someone to take your place and do everything you won't to be a star. Luckily all the *GBR* team rolled in and smashed a full day of work without a hint of a problem.

It turns out that I might not be the only one who thinks like this and it's definitely born out of my years as a sportsman. If you weren't good enough, you didn't train, you didn't turn up, or you wanted to be bringing your baggage into the mix then you were gone. It's that simple. Your teammates would call you out on it as well. There is nothing more potent than your peers giving you feedback and policing the standards of the business/team.

Netflix have a ruthless policy that shares much of this approach, which in the corporate world is pretty surprising. Netflix's company culture is often cited as one that start-ups would do well to emulate. The now famous document 'Netflix Culture: Freedom & Responsibility' – which emphasises self-directed decision-making, being candid and transparent, keeping only the most effective employees and doing their best to 'avoid rules' – was created by Netflix's then-Chief Talent Officer Patty McCord. In 2013 in a *GQ* magazine piece about the rise of the company, Facebook's Sheryl Sandberg even said of McCord's work, 'It may well be the most important document ever to come out of the Valley.'

According to a *Wall Street Journal* report, after people are fired at Netflix, the next step, in keeping with the company's modus operandi of transparency, is to explain why on a broad scale, leading to emails that can be received by hundreds of employees detailing what led to someone's dismissal. These post-mortems can also be in-person. A former VP named Sean Carey told the *Wall Street Journal* that he was asked to be at the meeting following his layoff to provide continuity for his team. 'It was certainly awkward for some, but was also consistent with the culture – there is sometimes a cost to transparency,' Carey said. 'In the end I felt it was beneficial.'

WE CAN BE HEROES

I was disgusted to read about what happened on a train in Philadelphia in October 2021 when ten people, to their shame, pretended not to notice as a woman had her clothes ripped off by her attacker, a 35-year-old homeless man, and she was raped right in front of them. Nobody called 911. Instead the passengers seemed to think it would be more useful to film the event with their phones. CCTV footage shows the woman trying to fight back, initially pushing her attacker away as first he gropes her and then rapes her. Finally, one person, an off-duty rail employee, made the call and transit police boarded the train and stopped the assault.

What the hell was going through these people's minds? How could they sit there and watch it happen? All it required was one person to have the backbone to do what was right and then appeal to the others to join them. Of the ten who were present in the carriage, excluding the woman on the floor and the man on top of her, not one single fucker was capable of finding the courage within themselves to do the right thing. This really disturbs me.

I don't care how dangerous it is, if someone is being attacked you should help them! We live in a society where it's deemed okay to be soft as shit, where the idea of risking your skin to help a complete stranger seems to be only something heroes do. In 2017, in a spate of terrorist attacks that shook the nation, three nutters on a mission to meet 72 virgins in the next life, resorted to hacking innocent people with 12-inch kitchen knives in Borough Market after they'd knocked over and killed two innocent bystanders in their van shortly before crashing it. Eleven people were killed in total and almost 50 injured, but unlike the bystander effect on the train in Philadelphia, people fought back, throwing chairs at the knife-wielding assailants. Two years later a knifeman wearing a fake suicide vest killed two people in their mid-twenties in a building beside London Bridge. It took a Polish guy, a South African and an ex-burglar to contain him long enough for a police officer to shoot him dead. The South African-born Londoner heard the commotion, ran to the scene and then in a brilliant stroke of improvisation grabbed the five-foot horn of a narwhal framed on the wall and used this to keep the jihadist with a knife in each hand at bay.

The message? We can all be heroes.

I remember being on the Paris Metro and the whole carriage tried not to notice as this drunk guy selected choice members of those gathered and started pressing their buttons; sadly, one of them was me. First, he started flicking my headphones then took them off me at one point. I asked him politely to stop. I mean there is no need to go to DEFCON-4 straightaway. He eventually moved on to another person, this time a lady. Instead of touching headphones he was touching her, getting very close to her, singing to her and basically groping her. She looked very uncomfortable and was asking him to stop. Nobody did anything, they just sat there mute with their heads buried in *Le Figaro*. I'd had enough by then and got up and told the guy to stop. He did, but then his pervy compulsions got the better of him and he resumed his oily harassment. This time I waited until the train pulled into a station and I grabbed him, picked him up by his trousers and collar, giving him a wedgie in the process, screaming, 'Ouvrez la fucking porte!' at the commuters standing by the door, and lobbed him with all my might onto the platform, then threw his bag of toot after him. Some commuters cheered and clapped, some shook their heads at me in distaste. What made matters worse, the French woman who was being toyed with didn't say anything. But in the end that was irrelevant; very much like a lawyer will always defend even the worst criminals because everyone deserves a fair trial, I will always do what's right, even if it was for some ungrateful person.

'Freeze mode' is the lesser-known sibling of fight and flight, the rabbit in the headlights. Unless you have been a student of the martial arts or a boxer, one of the first things your body does to protect you in the face of a threat, as we know, is it pumps you up to fight or helps you escape with added speed to flight. Since there's nowhere to run in a train travelling through a tunnel, and you can't escape out the window, all you can do is freeze. Or fight back. Cowardice is infectious, but so is courage. It takes one person to stand up and act, then others will follow. Gingerly! Personally, I'd rather get arrested for helping somebody, even if that means I have to clobber some wanker to do it. The problem with turning the other cheek is it lets us off the hook too easily.

THE FOUR PRINCIPLES OF LIFE BY MARCUS AURELIUS

I mentioned at the start of this chapter the four principles that I use to guide my life. According to the stoics of Athens and Rome, the following are all you need to live by: Justice, Moderation, Wisdom and Courage. Perhaps the most famous exponent of stoicism is Marcus Aurelius, one of the five great emperors of Rome. You might never have heard of him before, but most likely if you've seen the movie *Gladiator* you'll remember him as the wise old man murdered by Commodus, his son, by suffocation.

The father and son were like day and night. While Marcus practised careful governance on a personal and state level, Commodus had no self-restraint whatsoever. At the age of 12, it is said that on finding his bath lukewarm, he had the servant responsible for its temperature thrown into the furnace that heated it. Although he was obsessed with blood and fighting, he was a born coward and would only do battle with carefully selected gladiators who were sworn not to harm him. He would charge for his cameo appearances in the Colosseum, the odds always heavily stacked in his favour, i.e. taking on dwarf gladiators or disabled or malformed people dressed up as monsters armed with rocks, which were actually painted sponges. On inheriting the empire from his father at the age of 16, Rome was the wealthiest country in the world, but by the time Commodus was finished with it the world's greatest country was on its knees on an irreversible slide to its end days.

What a shame that the character of Maximus, played by Russell Crowe, is a work of fiction; he could have whooped some ass. Marcus was emperor of Rome between 161 and 180 CE, and his reign was not an easy one; beset by the constant challenges of natural disasters like floods and earth-quakes, and the continual threat of uprisings in different corners of the Roman Empire, he was increasingly on the road. He would have loved nothing more than to have stayed in Rome in the last years of his life, spending time with his family – but obviously not Commodus – instead of overseeing winter campaigns in freezing European countries, dealing with an endless stream of hairy fuckers who looked a little like the England rugby squad when they all grew hipster beards. Those winter battles claimed the last ten years of his life, and to while away the lonely freezing evenings Marcus kept himself company with a journal.

His entries were never intended for anyone else's consumption but his own, and published long after his death under the title of *Meditations*, they have since become a kind of moral companion and compass to some of the world's greatest leaders and politicians. Marcus used his diaries as a means of self-tracking and holding himself to account according to the four principles of Justice, Wisdom, Moderation and Courage, capturing and analysing his thoughts and behaviours during the day, and considering which of those values he had followed or neglected.

Self-tracking is the process of keeping a record of our actions to self-improve and become familiar with the way we react to certain situations. When we keep a diary, we hold a mirror to our actions, quickly establishing patterns in our behaviour and identifying weaknesses that we can then focus on and start making improvements. All the four principles are equally important, but the ones that stick out to me the most are those I could improve upon – Moderation, closely followed by Wisdom. Moderation is the skill of self-restraint. Congenitally defective in this area, I seem unable to get this one right. Arguably, you wouldn't be reading this if it was something I'd already perfected. Moderating James Haskell is something James Haskell finds challenging.

I know I don't lack courage or a sense of justice, as you can see from my story of what happened on the Paris Metro. As regards Wisdom, well, I am slowly learning from my mistakes; if you'll excuse the pun, Rome wasn't built in a day. But it is temperance, otherwise known as Moderation, that I really struggle with sometimes. Let me give you an example. The problem with being a celebrity, or in my case a Z-list celebrity, is that the public think they either own you like a piece of property, or they feel they know you because they've seen you on TV so many times. Sometimes they just panic and say the weirdest thing; it's almost like something takes them over. I remember one guy who said to me, 'Can I have a photo, you cunt?'

'What?!'

'You know you're a cunt, Hask,' he said. 'You fucking love it.'

'I don't even know you and you've called me a cunt.'

'Do you prefer being called a cock?' he said.

Another stranger said to me, 'Good to see your hair's falling out.' Then there was the little man who offered me outside, and the bloke who put me in a headlock. But the worst was when I was guest speaking at an event and taking pictures post-talk with people who wanted them when this bloke came up to me from behind, licked his finger and put it in my ear (it's called a 'wet willy'). I grabbed hold of him, his mate stepped in and I pushed him over a table and proceeded to choke the fingerer until he was down on the floor. I then got up, turned around and carried on having my picture taken with people as if nothing had happened. Imagine a room full of blazer-wearing poshos, all agog at this show of anger that they had never seen before and did not expect at a smart London eating establishment during lunchtime. After about ten minutes, when the bloke had been helped up and the vibe was not quite back to normal, one of the ladies working on the event suggested it might be time to move on and ushered me out of the room.

Ordinarily, I wouldn't allow myself to lose it like this. Moderation is something I try to practise, though I have a few blind-spots with it. Now and then I revert to old behaviour and I need to reassess, recalibrate. And then TERMINATE!

I'm kidding. I was, however, in the middle of my MMA training, so to say I was pretty fired up and in that mode of confrontation would be an understatement. When I told my coaches the next day what happened, they were like, 'Fuck, James, you got penetrated in public!' which, while only in the ear, is still true. They were disappointed I didn't knock the guy out.

There's an old saying, 'If something feels wrong, it probably is.' Given that our stomach is full of neurons that communicate directly to the brain and central nervous system, it's no great surprise where the term 'gut instinct' comes from. We should therefore listen to it. You know when you're out of order. Unless you lack empathy and sympathy, in which case you're a psychopath (don't worry, there are loads of them around), you know when enough is enough and you or someone else has crossed the line of what is acceptable. Cometh the hour, cometh the man. Your life is made up of these little tests, and who you are is not decided at the end of your life but how you are living your days right now.

THERAPY

I knew that I was mentally struggling with self-confidence, but I didn't realise how deep it ran, and how my dad's criticism along with others over a long period had affected me. He wasn't like one of those ruthless dads you see in movies, he just wanted me to do better. He was very supportive and complimentary but he never sugar-coated my mistakes and would tell me what I had done wrong. I don't think he realised that I wasn't a tough love person; I'm more an arm around me kind of person. By the time this book is published, I am going to be a dad. I will try to remember that different people react in different ways. I have no idea what my daughter will be like and I am sure I will get things wrong and fuck things up, like all parents do. You can't live like every interaction is going to define your child and their view on life, but it does more often than not.

My godfather's wife is an amazing therapist and my godfather kept saying to me, 'You should talk to her.' This was when I was still playing rugby. As a sportsman I was of the belief that unless you were crying all the time or seriously mentally damaged by an experience, there was no need to go and see a therapist. But that's a bit like waiting for a building to fall down until the cracks are all over it. I wondered, would I have to lie on a chaise longue and go back through different stages of my childhood? How could she make me a more consistent professional? You could play eight games a season on emotion but not 35 games. So how do you consistently prepare before a game?

Therapists have no emotional connection to you, and they aren't trying to be your friend. They listen, and because you open up you are actually fixing yourself, by either being steered to your own conclusions or naturally talking yourself around into seeing things in a different light. This personal development can happen in so many ways; it's not about just being happier. By going through this process of self-analysis, what I discovered was that behind the bravura and joker mask I was a lot more sensitive than I gave myself credit for, especially to the opinions of others. Now, I'm not suggesting that we all go through life overthinking everything that we say, but parents and coaches need to remember that sometimes the smallest, least relevant things they think they're saying are actually having a massive impact on the other person, and some of this they will carry forward with them for the rest of their life. I really struggled with old schoolstyle coaches who made flippant remarks that they thought were motivating me but were in fact utterly crushing. With the therapist's help I was able to develop a kind of armour to protect myself and not suffer from these jibes and negative criticism.

How did I make a start managing all this? Well, through all the methods I have mentioned, but one of the ways I found that worked quicker than anything was using emotive music as a trigger to instantly alter my mood. It was something I put in place straightaway. Whereas you see everyone wearing headphones now, back then I was the only one on the Wasps or England bus listening to music. If I was down after training or a game after making a mistake, I would put on music that made me feel good. We all have a song that makes us smile or changes our mood. That's why when feeling low or during a breakup you shouldn't ever listen to Magic FM, especially when in your car, as you will end up driving into a wall, tears streaming down your face, screaming, 'Why doesn't she love me?!' Or maybe that's just me.

Therapy opened up my mind and I thought, 'Wow, if I didn't know this before, what else is there that I may be missing? What else is in my power to control for the better?' Then I thought, 'Right, let's go see a physiotherapist, a nutritionist, the best rugby coach, let's find a coach of a different discipline like boxing or wrestling who can help me.' Therapy was one of the best things I've ever done.

11

KEEPING YOUR SIDE OF THE STREET CLEAN

FILTERING OUT THE CRAP

There's an old saying that goes, 'Treat people the way you would like to be treated.' I'm sorry, but that's bullshit. Let's face it, my predilection might be to be urinated on, whipped within an inch of my life or dressed as a baby. (Note to press – I do not wish to be treated like any of the above.) The phrase needs a gentle re-upholster so it should read, 'Treat people the way they want to be treated.'

Regarding the way people communicate with you, it's up to you to tell them how you wish to be treated and spoken to. You also have to spend some time working to understand what works best for you. Lots of people complain that bosses, teachers, partners don't communicate properly with them. Have you asked them to change things? Do you even know the best way for you to learn, or to be communicated with? I spent some time looking at firstly, how did I want to be spoken to, and secondly, how did I want to receive feedback. I then shared this with some coaches. The old school ones freaked out and then thought I was emotionally damaged and needed to be treated with kid gloves; the younger, more progressive coaches got it and understood that all I wanted to do was get better. I then took some time to realise how I learnt. I need to visually see it and then walk through it. Just telling me how to do something never works. Again, I shared this with the people who mattered or those in a teaching/coaching role; some decided I was hard work and slightly damaged and then others worked with me to help me learn.

Eddie Jones was a prime example of someone just getting me. He coached and talked to me in the right way and, shock horror, he got the best out of me. Most people are so immersed in their own worlds that they aren't even aware of how they are talking to people. You need to know yourself to help them then help you. You have to communicate this to people; they aren't mind readers. Don't be worried if you are met with confusion or eye rolls. Fuck 'em, I say. You are on your own journey making the most of your time on this mortal sphere. Don't take what they say to heart, just make a note of it and then apply filters. Take the bits you need and bin the rest. It takes time, but you will get there. I spend my entire life filtering out the crap from what people say to get what I need.

GETTING TO KNOW HOW PEOPLE TICK

Carl Jung coined the words 'introvert' and 'extrovert' as a way of understanding people's natural preferences for either being inward or outward in the way their energy met the world. That's to say introverts generate their own energy from within, while extroverts generate it from others. Introverts tend to listen to others better because they absorb and think about what's being said before they respond. Extroverts can find this infuriating as they move at a quicker pace and respond without thinking – and often regret it later. It's very

240

rare that you find a complete introvert or extrovert; most of us exist in the space between the two, accessing extroversion and introversion in equal measures.

Introverts where necessary have to learn the behaviours of an extrovert; for instance when their jobs require them to communicate with others. Given the choice, however, they'd much rather speak to people in small groups or one-to-one. While they can address a crowd just as efficiently as the extrovert, the difference is they feel relieved when it's over and need a bit of alone time to recharge themselves as it has required more effort than if an extrovert was doing it. If you're able to switch between both equally easily, you're what would be described as an 'ambivert'.

On the flipside, the extrovert thrives on team experiences, talking to big crowds and having the limelight. Imagine a work conference: these social bunnies are the first to the bar after it's over – they are usually the ones telling the stories and jokes. At their best they're the life and soul of the party. We need them for dull Monday mornings to cheer us up.

There's one more classification and that's an 'omnivert', someone who can go to the extreme of both extroversion and introversion and inhabit them both. They can be full of beans one day and quiet and withdrawn the next. They need the company of others, but they also need alone time to recharge.

To extroversion and introversion Jung added 'thinker' and 'feeler', to describe how we respond to the world around us; through feeling or through thinking. If you imagine a quadrant with the extrovert and introvert on the horizontal – oh fuck it, I'll draw it instead.

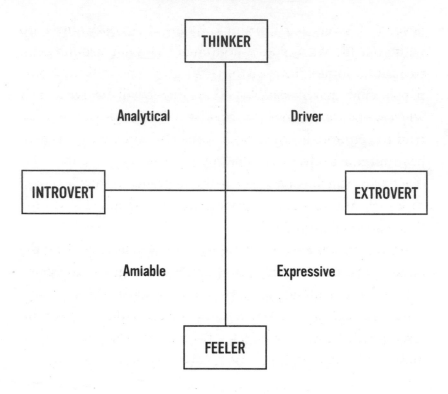

GIVING THE MIND A BREAK

What do we mean by 'keeping your side of the street clean'? What we're saying is, make sure that your life is as good as it can be, that you are making the best of yourself and maximising your potential. So how do you maximise your potential? Certainly not by working 80 hours a week like Elon Musk. Maybe he is a bad example, as let's face it there aren't too many Elon Musks knocking around and interestingly, he doesn't have a dick-shaped rocket (you probably have guessed by now I was not a fan of that rocket). If working an 80-hour week is your idea of heaven and you manage within that time to get regular exercise, eat well and find some mental bandwidth then good luck to you. But for most of us, overworking means you're not making enough time for yourself in order to develop. It's very hard to think about what you want to do with your life when you're continually running around on a treadmill; sometimes you have to stop and reflect. Some people think that like sharks, if we stop we will die, but in fact when we pause and give our brain a chance to slow down, we tend to get more in touch with ourselves and we can start to hear our inner selves a little bit more clearly. For me that was one of the benefits of therapy as it taught me to start listening to myself and to start observing how I functioned and how things worked inside my brain.

All this means exercising regularly as well as exercising the mind – your mind is a muscle that requires regular workouts, whether it's reading to improve and sharpen the way you think, absorbing a decent newspaper every day to keep up with what's happening in the world, or even if it just means making a daily practice of doing a crossword or Sudoku.

CHANGE IS HEALTHY

According to Dante's *Inferno*, you have to go through hell to get out of hell. Illness, relationship breakups and getting sacked are all unpleasant and a shock to our system, but each carries a positive in that it wakes us up and forces us to reassess our life, rather than being on autopilot and low battery mode. Humans don't like change, it makes them feel vulnerable. We don't understand the benefits of short-term discomfort for long-term gain. We're so wired to opt for short-term comfort that we stray into situations that only cause long-term pain.

Imagine being in a relationship that doesn't feed you as a person anymore, and whatever it was that first attracted you to your partner, that's now long gone. You silently resent each other but you're too scared to leave for fear of what lies in the unknown; after all, it's better the devil you know than the one you don't. If you separate you might then have a chance to meet the right person; however, like most of us you are probably too stuck in the habit of being uncomfortable in your comfort zone. To extrapolate from Dante, if you can bear the initial hell of loneliness that comes with being single, after a while you will begin to rediscover yourself and will start to feel stronger and more comfortable in your skin, wide awake and open to what the present brings.

We are programmed to feel threatened at the prospect of anything new that might damage us. It's that fucking lizard brain again, trying to protect us. So, as we go through life most of us are change resistant. Leaving primary school to go on to secondary education, we think, 'Oh no, there may be big boys or girls who'll bully me … I'll get lost in all those huge buildings …' etc etc.

The trauma of moving house is the same as our ancestors leaving one cave to find another, abandoning the familiar for the unknown. Even though your present cave is now unsuitable for you – it's too small and every day an 11-foot cave bear has got into the habit of crapping at the entrance – you are prepared to tolerate it because it's a comfort zone. But comfort zones are not places where we develop, they are places where we stagnate. There's an old saying in Alcoholics Anonymous, 'Shit smells, but it's warm.' In other words, we can be doing, living or working at something that isn't good for us but because it's familiar we stick with it, be it a dysfunctional relationship or an abusive boss. In preference to breaking free and taking a leap of faith into the new unknown, we'd rather be unhappy. We need to realise that change is healthy.

FIGHT OR FLIGHT

Humans have been around in some form or other for 2.8 million years, and as little as 15,000 years ago we were still being hunted by carnivores. As such we remain programmed to be on the lookout for something that's going to eat us. If you're living in the African bush this is a great survival mechanism; however if it's Battersea where you keep your cave it's unlikely that you're going to get a smilodon scratching at your door. Because we're hard-wired to expect danger we can become easily stressed, and when we're stressed it's because we feel in some way threatened; maybe it's a looming deadline at work or a stack of unread emails. Well, these might not seem too alarming but it's what lies beneath them: the threat that if we don't sort them out we'll lose our job, and what happens then …? We'll be on the street, destitute!

Our problem is that we catastrophise constantly, blowing things out of proportion, and just as we can use our imagination to visualise something good, when left in automatic mode that same imagination will work against us in the opposite direction. It's the old 'fight, flight or freeze mode', an automatic reaction whereby the body releases either cortisol and adrenaline, which aid us in our escape and for a short time help us run away quicker, or it releases testosterone, which allows us to become braver and stronger for a very limited time, in order that we can put up a good fight.

If you watch a wildlife documentary when a predator chases its prey, the pursued – if it gets away – visibly shakes off the stress of the experience, then settles down to grazing again, while the lion, or whatever, skulks off knackered to recharge for another attempt. The problem with humans is we don't shake off our stress and reset, but instead we carry it around with us, and it festers and creates yet more anxiety. The demands of modern-day living and the continual noise in our minds through social media and mobile phones are placing us in a constant state of low-level stress. I noticed that after particularly hard training sessions where I had been doing cardio and my heart rate was going through the roof, that if I didn't take some time to calm my breathing and go from my fight/flight mode sympathetic state to a parasympathetic state, I was carrying that into a stressful and busy day. I would then become even more stressed and need to rest. Equally, after a tough seventeen-hour day, if I didn't take some time to breathe and be mindful and to read before bed and decompress, I would not sleep well. We need to learn to change states and manage ourselves. I am someone who is in fight stress mode a lot. I have had to manage that and still do now. I do this through switching off and watching a movie, reading, listening to music or taking the dog for a walk. Post-training, I will lie on the floor and belly breathe until my heart rate drops back down, then get up, grab a protein shake and shower, ready for the day ahead.

FEAR

Ever since the prehistoric cave paintings of Lascaux, stories passed down through the centuries have taught us that facing our fears is a part of our evolution as individuals – Theseus and the Minotaur, Luke Skywalker and Darth Vader, Martin Luther King and racism, Muhammad Ali and George Foreman, Noddy and Big Ears; fiction and history are bursting with courageous feats. To become whole we must confront our inner fears, learning who we really are and growing as a result of it. It's also about knowing what is worth worrying about and what isn't, picking our battles and channelling our energy in the right direction. Fear left untreated creates a monster, and that monster gets bigger the longer you leave it. It's only when you turn around and look into its eyes that your monster shrinks.

Habituation is a technique used by psychologists to treat people with phobias. The way it works is if you have arachnophobia (fear of spiders) for instance, the first step is to get you looking at pictures of spiders without squealing and then introduce you to a physical fluffy toy spider, and finally getting you to touch a real one. So by exploring our fear more intimately, we start to habituate ourselves to it and it loses its sorcery over us.

There are so many shades of fear: fear of failure, fear of the unknown, fear of being alone, fear of the new, fear of violence, fear of being cancelled, fear of being found out, fear of death, fear of missing out ... but as wise Yoda says to Luke Skywalker in *Star Wars: The Empire Strikes Back*, 'Named must your fear be before banish it you can.' So you need to sit with your fear and examine it. Mark Twain once said, 'I'm an old man and have known a great many troubles, but most of them never happened.'

Envisage your absolute worst fear then in great detail imagine how you would deal with it. The more work we do around preparing for a situation that might result in stress and higher fear levels, the less anxious we are because it becomes familiar territory. Astronauts prepare for nightmare situations in space so *if* it happens they know what to do, just as Special Forces operatives plan and train for every contingency so that when the shit hits the fan they fall back on their training.

Often, we are faced with a challenge that frightens us but could at the same time send our life into a more positive trajectory. This is when our fear of success or fear we might fail at something new kicks in. In his book *The Hero with a Thousand Faces*, Joseph Campbell believes we all have an inner purpose that calls to us at some time or other in our lives: 'If you follow your bliss [calling],' he says, 'you put yourselves on a kind of track that has been there all the while, waiting for you ... don't be afraid, and doors will open where you didn't know they were going to be.'

If we can embrace the unknown and keep moving through fear, we become stronger, fuller versions of ourselves, for it is in the darkness we create something new. To change anything in our lives we have to step away from the predictable when the call comes. As Nietzsche says, 'The secret of reaping the greatest fruitfulness and the greatest enjoyment from life is to live dangerously.'

Do you ever get an unsettled feeling in your gut or a sense of hopelessness after watching the news? From a stoic's perspective, there's little you can do to change the bad news stories newscasters rattle on about – floods, storms and polar ice melt, jihadist attacks, rising knife crime and the alt-right – and unless you're going to actively try to make a difference, why allow yourself to over-fret about them?

Thought begets feeling, and feeling begets action – we are quite simply a product of our thoughts. Plato, the Athenian philosopher, believed that like a charioteer our mind is drawn by two horses: a positive one with a natural wisdom of where it needs to go, the other undisciplined and lazy, bent upon sabotaging the first horse. If we can learn to be aware of when the bad horse is biting, says Plato, we can reject the fear and anxiety it produces and let the good one take us to contented pastures. With practice comes wisdom. Or self-awareness. Once you get wise to spotting where the fake fear comes from, you can choose to sidestep it. If you are a what-if thinker, you need to understand there is a big difference between making plans to prepare for outcomes out of your control, and thinking with no filter or sense of likelihood, and then only dwelling on the negatives. You need to get the balance right between thinking about what could go wrong and what could go right. What happens if you turn up to the party and everyone likes you, instead of hates you? What happens if the journey is all good and you and your partner get on really well, as opposed to there being loads of delays and you argue the whole time? By all means bring a raincoat in case the holiday is a wet one, but also what happens if it's sunny every day and you have a blast? It's about being aware of how you think and being practical as well as managing the fear. Who knew that just being you took so much management? That's the shit they don't tell you when they say just be positive and stop worrying.

But how do you stop yourself going down a bad rabbit hole? How do you save yourself from self-sabotage? You need a plan/process to follow to get you out of the fog of anxiety created by constant streams of negativity in the news. The techniques I use to this day were originally employed by me to help boost my self-confidence. I use them daily to remain positive, to believe in myself, for dealing with criticism, to pick myself up from failure and to drive me towards success. They allow me to take back control of my life. The following tools in this chapter matched with specific behaviours will help you achieve what you want out of life. Accept that you will have plenty of failures en route to your goal, but so long as you are clear about your purpose, have a specific end point so you know when you have achieved it, plus a process – a check list of questions to keep you on track – you have a very good chance of realising your hopes, dreams, ambitions or whatever you like to call them.

WHERE FOCUS GOES, ENERGY FLOWS

With the therapy I've had and the experts I have worked with, I definitely believe in the saying, 'Where focus goes, energy flows.' Saying to yourself, 'I want to be happier,' is vague. Ask yourself what you are uncomfortable with and then, having identified it, unpick it. Perhaps it is your body and you would like to feel more comfortable in yourself. Define first of all what you mean by being more comfortable. If *comfortable* in yourself means being energised or looking great, you know you need to eat better food and take some exercise. And if it means happy in your skin, the inner you, then it's a very different set of actions you will have to take. The clearer you are with your intention, the more attention you can give it. This calls for self-awareness. But by taking care of the minutiae, and by addressing what requires attention in a short space of time, you will actually be happier.

How hard you apply yourself has a massive effect on your level of success in life. If you give up at the first failure and lack motivation, you're never going to get anywhere, but if your work rate is consistently high and if you're determined, apply yourself and have high standards, you're well on your way to success. A person can be motivated to go and exercise once, but what happens on the days when it's pissing it down, when it's cold and you're sleepy, or you're hungover? That's the difference: those who can pull themselves out of bed when they don't want to are the people who consistently apply themselves, and it's no great surprise that they are the most successful too. Cheerleading mediocrity is something that society has got itself into now, where being average or even shit is deemed okay.

You want to avoid relying on motivation from other people where you can because it comes and goes. If you constantly need spurring on by others, you are doomed. I get messages online all the time being asked to respond to people who want to change things but need a little bit of motivation from me to really get them going. After rolling my eyes and shaking my head, I then just delete the message, because my motivation would be to tell them to shut the fuck up and get on with it. You have only one life, and if you don't like it change it. No-one is going to do it for you.

Maybe that's not the kind of transformational moment they wanted, but if you need motivation then I can't help you. I never need motivation because I understand that if I don't make myself do it, it's not getting done. Imagine you have lots of buckets to draw from; if your motivation bucket is empty, why not draw from your competitive bucket? You want to be better than your mate or that person at work? Good, get it done. How about your negativity bucket? They said you were shit and you couldn't do it, so fuck 'em, and prove them wrong. Why not use your positive bucket? I am the best so I am going to smash this; or your resilience bucket – I want to be the best and I will not take second best. There are more, but you get the point. Avoid motivation, it's like the weather, it comes and goes. The super-motivated fly one day and fold like tissue paper in a fire the next.

I once read that the king of cool Paul Newman in his younger days could hold his drink and would get hammered some nights after filming with his fellow actors. But knowing that his meal ticket was his looks – after all this was the guy who famously predicted for his epitaph, 'Here lies Paul

APPROACH WITH(OUT) CAUTION

Newman who died a failure because his eyes turned brown' – he possessed the discipline to get up a few hours earlier despite a foul hangover, to work out before a 6 a.m. shoot and arrive on set word-perfect and clear-headed. People who are massively successful aren't successful by accident. It doesn't matter how many books you read, they all say the same things, just in different ways. No-one will do it for you; if you fail you have to get up, enjoy failure, learn from it; but instead of doing any of that we try to find the path of least resistance and choose some wanky option like injecting ourselves with skinny jabs, or drawing a Ferrari in a notebook every day. Please don't be one of those people. Success is never a given and the journey to making it often sucks. That's why everyone isn't successful. I haven't even started to achieve the things I want, and I am hungrier than ever. Hence writing and editing this book in the back of taxis between other work jobs, and sitting up all night to get it done. I probably shouldn't have started another book when about to become a dad, moving house two times, running a business and being busier than I have ever been with DJing and speaking engagements. However, if I don't, someone else will. If the opportunity is there, take it; it might not be there forever.

Another example is Arnie Schwarzenegger. His life reads like a self-help book on how to believe in yourself. When he'd finished with bodybuilding, having been crowned Mr Olympia seven times, and Mr Universe at the age of 20, he set his sights firmly on Hollywood and becoming a leading actor. Despite being constantly overlooked by casting directors because of his extreme body shape and heavily Germanic accent, Arnie would not be deterred. He realised if he wasn't careful he would start believing their suggestions that he should give up and pursue something else.

He was aware that many unknown wannabe actors in Los Angeles became so downtrodden and beaten by all the rejections that they carried them along to the audition like a cloak of shame. After a range of bit parts, he resolved to change this for himself by putting all his endeavours not into acting but starting a building company that would cater to the needs of the well-heeled, sparkly film folk of Bel-Air. He made enough money laying bricks in what he and his business partner jazzed up as 'the European style' that he was able to start buying low-grade, cheap properties as investments. And with a high level of inflation at the time, he was able to make huge profits and upgrade to more and more expensive houses. It wasn't long before he became a millionaire. Around this time he was called to an audition for a film called *Conan the Barbarian*. His plan had been to create a financial platform that would give him the confidence he needed to walk into a big Hollywood meeting as an equal rather than an underling to the casting folk, the director and producer, and he succeeded in this. *Conan the Barbarian* was his first leading role and the major breakthrough for his acting career.

The sooner that we take responsibility for our actions and our lives, the sooner we begin to take some level of control back, rather than getting lost like a wet fart in a swimming pool. Old cliches are there for a reason and that's because they still make sense; we can't control life and what happens to us, but we can control how we deal with it, how we react to it and what we put into it. It's not how many times we get knocked down that counts, it's how many times we get back up again. People think mental health is black and white – you're either happy or sad, you're either fixed or you're not (we'll cover mental health in detail in a later chapter), but life is more complicated than that, with an infinite palette of greys. There's that famous Sisyphean tragedy in which each of us every day of our lives pushes a boulder to the top of a hill only to see the fucker roll back down to the bottom. However, we can choose whether we decide to be one of those who are broken by the action of rolling it back up again, or we can be the positive ones who keep going and say, 'You know what, I'm getting better at this rolling thing, my technique is improving … it might roll down again but I'm getting quicker.'

HOW YOU TREAT OTHERS

Personally I believe it's harder to be a wanker than it is to be a good person. We all judge books by their cover. We're very good at looking through people we feel uncomfortable interacting with, pretending that they're not there, whether it's homeless or disabled people. You are in control of how you treat people, it's that simple. You are a walking business card for yourself. Some people may only get to interact with you once. How do you want them to remember you? How do you want people to think of you?

Humans are predictable: we're born, we grow up, get a job, have kids, build a family and then die. Now, if we're lucky, and the stars and our level of effort and skill align, we might just get to make a mark on humanity. To give life meaning we have art, literature, architecture, music, the beauty of the world. But ultimately, it's all random. If I was struck down by a degenerative illness tomorrow, I could honestly say that I've done all I could to pack as much into my life as possible. Like Mary Schmich says in her essay commonly known as 'Wear Sunscreen', 'The real troubles in your life are apt to be things that never crossed your worried mind; the kind that blindside you at 4 p.m. on some idle Tuesday.' Curveballs creep up on us when we least expect them, bad things happen to good people and there's no evidence of karma at work or the careful design of an intelligent guiding hand. So it is up to us to marshal ourselves, follow values we believe in and live a good life; one that takes others into consideration and doesn't judge or condemn them for being different.

During the Olympics I become obsessed with every sport from canoeing to fencing to everything in between. I love it and I think Olympians are amazing. I watch their sacrifice and see their skill and talent, and I think, 'What I have done with my life? I would love to have done that.' I wish I had performed in the Olympic sevens or been good at other things other than rugby. To be fair, I get like this over any big sporting event or when watching anyone I admire at work. I recently got to watch Fisher, the superstar Australian DJ, perform live at Hi Ibiza and I was like 'Fuuuuuuuck! I want to do that!' He is so good, and I'd love to perform like that and have his life. Now I should have probably spent some time reflecting on my own achievements, saying to myself, 'Well, you haven't done too badly yourself, James,' but I am not great at that. It's something I have worked on in retirement, as you need to enjoy the moment and be proud of yourself. It can't always be about the next thing.

I will say these moments don't dishearten me, far from it; they make me go, 'Right, what do I have to do in my own world to reach those heights?' I don't try and become an Olympian, but I translate those feeling into my own sphere and re-double my energy to be even better and to hopefully one day look at what I have done with the same level of self-esteem. You can't look at others for inspiration for too long, but every now and then it's great fuel. It certainly is for me. I always ask myself, 'Am I doing all I could be doing to get to their level?' If the answer is no, then 'What the fuck are you waiting for? Get on with it!'

Your perception of where you want to be and where you are currently are two different places. You have the control to ask yourself on a regular basis how you can eat, train, sleep, love and be better, but not to the point you lose sight of the fact that you were put on this earth to live a full life and be happy. It's a difficult balancing act that I have certainly not got right at times.

The other day I was MMA training and afterwards my knee joints were absolutely killing me, and I started moaning about it and complaining rather than being thankful for what I've got and recognising that the only reason they are like that is because of the kind of rugby I played and that was my choice.

DON'T FEEL SORRY FOR YOURSELF, LIFE CERTAINLY DOESN'T

I have moments when I feel genuinely sorry for myself. For example, when I'm hobbling along with my limp thinking, 'I used to be able to do this and that.' I was commentating on the British Lions tour when I started writing this book and all I could think about as I was watching these young players was, 'I want to be out there doing it.' I miss being something that I was. I miss my old identity. I had a reputation for being something and then that was taken away. What you believed yourself to be when you look in the mirror is no longer the case, so it's about updating yourself, trying something different, stretching yourself. I have talked a little about this in previous chapters, so you can go back and look at it in more detail. Acceptance of how you are now is important. You can't spend life focusing on how you used to be. It's about where you actually are and where you would like to get to.

Life is not about grandiose gestures or transcendental transformation, or joining a cult in order to feel a part of something; it's about making conscious improvements every day so you can say to yourself, I'm putting the effort in: today I ate slightly better than I did yesterday, I smiled at more miserable people than I usually do, I started reading a book I've been meaning to for ages; I trained a little harder today, hydrated well, ate healthily, told my wife I love her; I was more patient with rude knobheads in white vans who cut me up and *still* gave me the finger; I wrote something creative, booked a music lesson, researched that diving trip to Costa Rica, took the dog for a walk, apologised to a friend I haven't spoken to for three months, checked in on someone who is ill … Whatever it may be, we can all make incremental differences to our day, just by doing something that we wouldn't usually do.

EXERCISE IS FOOD FOR THE SOUL

Find something that switches your focus if you're having a bad day. During the pandemic, people who had never had the time or thought of exercising were given an hour a day to go outside and do just that. Suddenly that 60 minutes became a precious gift to be used carefully. People found themselves saying, 'Bloody hell, I went straight from the couch to doing 1k and now I'm on 5k … and I thought I was too old for that!' or 'I didn't think I was sporty but I'm actually not a bad runner. I feel as if my life has got meaning now, I'm seeing the birds and the bees!'

Two of the things that therapists recommend for anxiety are exercise and cooking. Apparently, kitchen therapy is good for the soul when people get themselves in the flow of baking, beating eggs, kneading dough etc, as it improves concentration and boosts confidence. What most people don't get to do in life is to put themselves through real physical hardship – be it an Ironman Triathlon, mountain climbing, boxing; something extreme that requires huge amounts of energy. That feeling of, 'I can't go on any further, I'm going to drown, I can't breathe' is followed by the elation of endorphins, one of the feelgood hormone chemicals released in the brain that rewards the body after it has been pushed through hell.

Unless they're in a really good team who are defined through trust, shared risk and equal endeavour, the average person in an office has never had to work for anything greater than themselves. When you're part of a sporting team, your actions have an immediately clear and direct impact on everybody else. If the rest of your team is giving 110 per cent and you're not pulling your weight, you stand out and are made to feel bad.

One of the reasons that people love CrossFit gyms is because they are part of a collective, a team, doing something that they feel is bigger than themselves. That's why class-based gyms like F45 have gone through the roof, because they take an average group of like-minded people, give them a goal and then put them through hardship. The average person thinks they train hard, but I have been to enough public gyms and trained enough people to know this is not true. It's hard to really challenge yourself but in these classes the way things are set up means you have to work hard or quit. You have the added element at F45s, for example, to be often put in pairs. Suddenly you are working with a teammate that you can't let down. People find themselves motivated not by themselves but by their responsibility to the team and experience an epiphany. 'God, this is the greatest thing ever!' You don't really know yourself until you have gone through a bit of hardship. A team is never a team until you have been tested and discovered where your weak points are. That's why I always find companies who talk about having a strong team slightly amusing. I am sure a lot of them think they have one, but wait until they really get tested. Will so-and-so have your back or run for the hills and become self-serving? Unless you have had to work for something greater than yourself and done your job to the letter in a selfless way to guarantee the success of your team, through a level of hardship that makes you want to quit, then don't talk about being a tightly knit team. Sports teams in comparison to, say, Special Forces teams are just pretenders to the thrones. We are never in danger of losing our lives and if I fuck up an assignment it won't lead to one of my teammates or all of my team dying. That's a big difference.

Being in a team is something I did my whole sporting life, and looking back, I probably took it for granted. Surrounded by people that you train, eat, play or go to war with brings a feeling of wellbeing, as if you are strengthened and supported by a ring of humanity (or orcs in my case). Orcs or not, they became my friends, and the safety net I needed once I pushed myself out of my comfort zone and played in Japan, France and New Zealand. There is nothing like being on your own in a strange place to find out what you are made of, but it was the team that got me there.

THERE'S MORE TO LIFE THAN RUGBY

I truly believe that one of the things that can help us cope with life is having something outside of what you do on a day-to-day basis. Let's say you have a family and a nine-to-five job – as opposed to a career, which is when you're getting paid to do something you love – and you hate this job and your wife makes you miserable; even if you are the most positive person in the world you will be in hell and your life will feel like shit. But if you've got something outside of these two that doesn't have anything to do with your job or family, something that you can call your own that takes you out of yourself, a passion that challenges and interests you and makes you part of a team whether it's five-a-side footie or sevens rugby, a cycling club with your mates or even fucking croquet – then you will have something you own that is yours, something to fall back on. So if one out of three is going badly, you have the other two to fall back on. If everything in your life is at the whim of others, it's very hard to find balance.

As a player, I was often criticised by old grumpy curmudgeons who said I shouldn't have anything outside of my rugby to distract me. I see these players now who have nothing other than rugby, that's all they do and the problem is when their rugby is going bad they have nothing else to fall back on. I would recommend to any young player to get balance in your life; rugby should not be your everything at all times. You need razor-sharp focus but not all the time. I would find something away from the sport that gives you joy as it's not controlled by others. I do see a lot of sportspeople change after they have had a family. They realise that rugby or the sport they play is not the be-all they thought it was and that there is more to life.

I remember when I was at school, I used to try anything, partly because it was bloody expensive for my parents to send me to boarding school so I had better make the most of it, and partly because I've always wanted to try as many things as possible in order to find something that makes me feel good. Of course, there is a danger of having too many plates spinning at the same time. Which is the thing often levelled against me. I am often talked about as a 'Jack of all trades, master of none'. But if you look at the full unvarnished version of this age-old cliché, it actually reads as 'Jack of all trades is a master of none, but oftentimes better than a master of one.' I actually love all the things I do and until one is detrimental to the others' success I will keep doing them. Nobody said you can only have one thing in your life that you are good at. Life is there to be lived and grabbed by its pendulous pink testicles ...

12

SEEKING FEEDBACK

If a good coach doesn't challenge your perception, they're not a good coach. You don't want to be in a situation where everybody around you is a cheerleader for mediocrity. A major part of self-improvement, as I've touched on in other parts of this book, is found through seeking feedback from the right people. A coach once said to me, 'You're shit, Haskell.' He thought I'd reply with two fingers, but it had the opposite effect. I was de-motivated. What I needed was for him to say, 'Listen, you're doing that well but you're not so good on this, and here's *how* to fix it.' So, then I could go away and work relentlessly on that specific area because I'd been given the tools to remedy it.

SELF-AWARENESS

Self-awareness is paramount to success; self-delusion is not. When you watch something like *The X Factor* or *Britain's Got Talent*, you see people being told by Simon Cowell that they're absolutely awful. The look on their face is priceless as they turn to their parents in the audience as if to say, 'What!? Did you hear what he said, Mum? He said, "I'm awful!" Can you believe that?' You have to ask yourself why they have no idea how bad they are. It's because they've been in this placatory feedback loop where their family has consistently told them they are brilliant.

It's like my mum saying to me, 'You're really handsome, son.' I ask you, how many mothers would actually say, 'Son, you're actually really ugly.' All mums think their sons are Adonises. Asking your mum an objective opinion of anything regarding yourself is probably not the place to go. The other extreme, in my case, was my dad. He was hypercritical after rugby matches: he used to say things like, 'You didn't play well today, you missed lots of tackles and looked off the pace.' So I stopped asking for his opinion. He did get a bit better, but not until Chloe took him to one side and told him how much I looked up to him, and how his feedback was not having the effect that he wanted. It was not helping me get better but actually setting me back.

The X Factor contestants are often asked, 'How did you know you were such a good singer?' and they say, 'Well, I were upstairs in the shower singing and me mam shouted up, "Turn the radio down!" and I say, "That's not the radio, mum, that's me singing." Then she says, "You should join *The X Factor.*"'

If only they had practised a little self-awareness, they could have saved themselves a whole world of pain. The producers of these reality talent contests must be pinching themselves when they see these deluded lunatics walk through the door. Be under no illusion they have already been auditioned before they get in front of the actual TV judges. Tens of thousands turn up to try out for things like *The X Factor* and there is no way Simon Cowell sits through them all. So what happens is you perform in front of members of the crew. They then pass on the best ones and worst ones for the TV judges to look at and for them to be filmed. It's like a driving instructor watching you drive into a wall and then going yep, you are ready for your exam and then letting you loose in front of an examiner. The only person in the melee who doesn't know they are shit and the butt of the joke is the performer. I think it's fair to say we all have suits of armour that deflect harsh realities and protect us from what all the evidence is saying. However, sometimes bits fall off and reality hits us hard. Just in most cases it's not on prime-time TV where you tried to sing and sounded like a cat being microwaved.

To do anything really successfully takes a level of sacrifice and pain. I think to find real happiness in your work you should do something you are passionate about and work at it, accepting that it is not going to be easy, but trusting that the money will take care of itself if the effort is put in. If you don't have a passion for something – whether it's climbing the world's tallest mountain, trying to get through selection for the Special Forces or building your own business up amid a sea of competition – you won't get there as your heart will not be in it. Or you will flog yourself half to death in the doing of it because it's not the right fit for you. If your motivation is for money but you don't love what you do, then I believe you more often than not will never get there. I know so many men in particular who have seen others be successful and have thought, 'Do you know what? I'll have a go at that.' They have poured money into opportunities and got nowhere, because they just don't really care. They aren't prepared to be on site every day, to do the nitty gritty, to have the inner fire to make whatever the project is work. You can't make yourself really care if you don't have the passion for it. They know what result they want, which is always the money, but they don't care for the process. You need to live and breathe your passion to make it work. You need to fail with it and then be able to go again. I do lots of things, but I enjoy all of them. They don't feel like work. Every time I am asked to do something I don't really care about, I always hate it. I turn down work all the time if I just don't care enough about it. I have tried to cut out anything that I don't like from my life and I am lucky to be able to do that. For some they have no choice, but you can start to build something you do care about whatever that is. I have talked about having passions and interests outside of your normal life to give you balance. Make something you love doing one of them, and then one day you may discover there is a career in it for you.

Why spend your life doing something which you absolutely hate? Obviously, it's easier for some to follow their dream than others; I'm not a single mother with three kids to support so I won't be so glib as to suggest a person in that position can just drop a job they hate in order to pursue something they love. However, even amid the struggle of bringing up children and trying to pay the bills, there is no reason why that single mother can't find a little bit of time that she makes her own to pursue her hobby. It might be she can read a book or watch films on Netflix. Anything that you like doing can easily grow, if watered, into something bigger that can change your life and make you a happier, more authentic version of yourself.

When J. K. Rowling was writing the *Harry Potter* books she was a single mum living on benefits and look where that particular interest in writing would eventually take her. She was reportedly worth $1 billion before giving much of it to charity, and has sold over 500 million copies of the *Harry Potter* series. The more focus you place on something the better you get at it.

I heard a great analogy that works in this case and demonstrates the importance of locking in and doing what you love. Say you are running a fish and chip shop and that's your passion, you love it and you want it to be the best fish and chip shop going, but next door they open a Chinese takeaway and you can see queues outside the door and running down the street. Do you suddenly start selling Chinese food or do you look at your passion and make tweaks for it to be the best? If money is all you want, and there is no passion, then you either need to partner with someone who does care or forget it.

There's a great quote from legendary filmmaker Werner Herzog on keeping your focus on what you are doing rather than thinking about how much money it will generate. In this case he is talking about raising funding in order to make a film: 'If your project has real substance the money will follow you like a common cat in the street with its tail between its legs. There is an old German proverb that says, "The Devil always shits on the biggest heap." So get heaping and have faith.'

Like the stoics we read about earlier who prepped for as many things that could go wrong in order that they had less to worry about, Herzog writes of the need to expect trouble. 'Prepare yourself: there is never a day without a sucker punch.' In other words, forewarned is forearmed.

I'm lucky because even though I have a million plates spinning at the same time, they all to some extent involve a level of performance, and satisfy that need I have to get up and express myself. But most importantly, there's nothing I'm currently doing that I don't want to do anymore. I've phased everything out that made me unhappy. I no longer write books on fitness as that doesn't get me excited. Chloe is in that business and she's obviously passionate about it as she takes great pleasure in upskilling herself, listening to podcasts, reading medical papers, whereas I couldn't imagine anything worse. Where I find my attention lies is listening to music, watching live DJ sets and dismantling people's sets to see how they do things. I love making music and being creative in that arena.

When I started DJing in 2012, I mentioned earlier that I tried to learn off-the-cuff and got to shadow and observe some great well-known DJs because of my contacts through rugby. However, that didn't work so I found another DJ teacher and did a course of one-on-one training. I started tracking my hours every day to see how far I was away from the 10,000-hour mark. If you haven't heard of this before, it's the idea put forward in Malcolm Gladwell's 2008 book, *Outliers*, that if you practise at anything for 10 years or 10,000 hours, you will become an expert. According to Gladwell, 'It is the magic number of greatness.'

I applied the same level of dedication and thoroughness in my research with becoming a DJ as I had shown as a rugby player. If I really wanted to get better I needed to seek honest and constructive advice. Just as I had written to Richie McCaw, one of the greatest All Blacks ever to play in the back row, and asked his advice about how I might play the game in a similar way to him, I now sought out the best DJs in the business to ask their advice on how to get to grips with this new artform that I was – and still am – completely obsessed with. I sent off my mixes for their feedback. I used the life lessons I'd learnt from fuck-ups down so many paths to help me on my journey now.

I'm always asking for feedback: how can I get better at this? What am I doing? It's the same when I do an after-dinner speaking gig; I always record it so I can study it, and I'll ask someone I trust and respect what they think I can improve upon. Same goes for my podcasts: if I interview someone, the next day I'll ask the producer what she thinks. Was I going to quickly? Did I give the subject space to answer? Or I might call my co-presenter of *The Good, The Bad & The Rugby*, Alex Payne, who is a brilliant and seasoned presenter. I've asked Chloe's dad, Richard Madeley, his advice on occasions as he has so much experience of interviewing. I'm always interested in what I can improve and hearing it from someone who knows what they are talking about. Those little tweaks that someone might suggest in their feedback may make the difference between you transitioning from good to excellent.

RELATIONSHIP CAPITAL

Remember when you were younger and your mum said, 'Don't hang out with those people, they're bad for you and will get you into trouble.' So, what did you do? You hung around with them and most likely you got into trouble. In more severe cases, kids get swept up into gang culture, suddenly they're selling drugs and end up in prison doing time; all because they lived in the wrong block of flats and were hoovered into a gang with the wrong values.

Equally dangerous to you are those people who have achieved all they're going to achieve or want to achieve. They are always negative, always moaning, and it's always someone else's fault not theirs. Fourteen years in the military, four years in the Parachute Regiment, ten years in the SAS, twice scaled Mount Everest, hero Jay Morton tellingly said in his own podcast, 'You're either a radiator or a drain.'

If you're with people who drain you, you will only rise to their level. The team who we surround ourselves with and the ethos of that team are hugely important to whether we make a success of ourselves or whether we plateau or slide. When Jay appeared on the *What a Flanker* podcast with me, he also said, 'I like to be surrounded by fucking awesome individuals that inspire me to do things that feel good and that I get satisfaction from and to live a good life.'

Your selection of friends should not all be clones but different from each other. We all have our own particular strengths; for instance some people are good with emotions and empathy and are good to turn to when we have a sensitive problem, while other people are great for inspiring you. You need balance and to build up an army of good people around you if you're really going to thrive in life.

Eddie Jones once said, 'When you win everybody wants to talk to you, but when you lose you only hear from your partner and your mum.' Isn't that true? During the Six Nations when we were winning the phone was red hot with people ringing. The real friends in life are there when you're in trouble or when you're down and make time for you and they reach out; they're the ones who stand up for you despite the consequences to themselves. Like Danny Cipriani: when I left Wasps unceremoniously he made a point of walking out of the room with me just to show how badly he felt I had been treated. When you are on top of the world you find you have friends you didn't even know you had. I remember when things went well for me, I would get messages from people I hadn't seen for 20 years saying 'Hi' and 'Well done'. My phone would blow up with well-wishers. I lose a game and, no joke, I'd get a text from Chloe and maybe my mum and that would be about it. It's madness. So many people want to bask in reflected glory, but no-one wants to reach out to a loser; there's no glory in that. Actually, there is if you are a good person.

You need to surround yourself with broad-minded types who are going to stretch you. I love being around successful people who embody who I want to be like. A good example is Special Forces soldiers because they inspire me so much; I have a bit of a man crush on them if I am honest. They have such discipline and push themselves so hard. They are also super-positive and determined. They could not have done what they did if they didn't have, and hadn't actioned, at least 90 per cent of the behaviours, methodologies and practices I talk about in this book. They also deliver not to make money or to be famous, but because their lives and the lives of others depend on it. When you talk about proper legends, for me these guys are the epitome of that word.

HARNESSING NEGATIVITY

I have used every doubter and critic and all their negative comments to fuel me to try harder. Turning negatives into positives is hard but when you look back over your life you will see that there have been so many occasions when you have refused to believe in what was said. On the occasions coaches, fans, trolls and at times those closest to me like my dad told me I wouldn't do this or wasn't good at that, it would make me go the extra mile to prove them all wrong. It's interesting that Ollie Ollerton, Jason Fox and Ant Middleton (all ex-Special Boat Service) were written off by negative people and succeeded in turning this into fuel for their fire. If you're of the mindset that you can always be better, you will find yourself more open to seek to improve than if you think you're the dog's bollocks and have nothing left to learn. Fear of failure is a propellant that has launched stellar careers from the likes of Barack Obama to just about anyone else who has got to the top of their game.

KNOB-HEADS

Humans too easily slide into self-doubting because of what others have said about them, instead of developing a thicker skin to not care about the opinions of those we wouldn't take a piss on if they were on fire. I like that William Blake quote, 'The eagle never lost so much time as when he submitted to learn of the crow.' Fuck the crows! There's also another one I read the other day by Nietzsche: 'The higher we soar, the smaller we appear to those who cannot fly.' In other words, follow your path, be true to yourself and don't worry about those who just don't get you.

Marcus Aurelius says, 'Begin each day by telling yourself, today I shall be meeting with interference, ingratitude, insolence, disloyalty, ill-will and selfishness; all of them due to the offender's ignorance of what is good or evil.'

My take on knob-heads is quite similar; in life I believe there are always going to be tossers that grate on you and people that don't get you. That's fine and actually a good thing; you don't want to be everyone's friend and for everyone to like you. You want to have something about you. The best thing you can do is be aware of these people, and act politely when you're in their company. If they're going to be overtly negative towards you then ignore it; the best revenge is living well. While you are not their cup of tea and they are so focused on you, you should be out there cashing cheques and snapping necks. Whenever I have reacted to those who hate me and dislike me, it has cost me. Never lower yourself to their level of stupidity, or become concerned with them. They are not the ones who count. You have that circle of trusted advisors and people's opinions you respect. There is a great quote that is attributed to Mark Twain that makes the point nicely: 'Never argue with stupid people, they will drag you down to their level and then beat you with experience.'

GRAVEYARDS

The richest places on earth are not gold mines but graveyards, as they are full to the brim of wasted potential and brilliant ideas. Don't waste your time and talent. You only have one life, contrary to whatever you may have read. Now is the time to strike. Don't die wondering and don't die miserable if you can help it.

IT'S GOOD TO HAVE A MOAN SOMETIMES

I love nothing more than sitting down with a few pals having a *sappuccino*, where we have a fucking good moan about life and seemingly sap morale, when actually we are building it over a good laugh and over a posh coffee. It's a bit like draining the sludge that gathers at the bottom of your car's petrol tank. It's a reset and a chance to air all your grievances with each other and the world at large. You wouldn't neglect to check everything was working right on a Formula One car before a race and it should be no different with yourself; how can you perform to your best if you're not running well internally, both physically and mentally? Laughter and piss-taking in any team are essential. Even in relationships you need to shoot the shit, address some stuff, ideally in a jokey way, and then crack on. I am not advocating sitting around moaning about everything and doing nothing about it, but gallows humour can get you through most situations. In most teams I was in, I was chief morale officer. Nobody would escape getting shit from me and I would in turn get shit from everyone. It helps keep a group honest. There is nothing wrong with sitting round and getting stuck into whatever you want as long as you get back up again and crack on.

We all know those people who sap the life out of you and their environment but offer nothing else. I think it was Clive Woodward, the coach of the 2003 World Cup-winning England rugby union team, who talked about energy sappers. Those people who take so much managing and who are so high maintenance they are detrimental to the wider group. You find these people everywhere and my advice is avoid them and get rid of them from your life. If they demand your emotional time, your physical time and offer nothing back, and they moan non-stop, fuck them off and find people who do the opposite. These people never change and negativity can become infectious. I think General Melchett from *Blackadder* summed it up better than I ever could.

GENERAL MELCHETT: Is this true, Blackadder? Did Captain Darling pooh-pooh you?

CAPTAIN BLACKADDER: Well, perhaps a little.

GENERAL MELCHETT: Well, then, damn it all! What more evidence do you need? The pooh-poohing alone is a court martial offence!

CAPTAIN BLACKADDER: I can assure you, sir, that the pooh-poohing was purely circumstantial.

GENERAL MELCHETT: Well, I hope so, Blackadder. You know, if there's one thing I've learnt from being in the Army, it's never ignore a pooh-pooh. I knew a Major, who got pooh-poohed, made the mistake of ignoring

the pooh-pooh. He pooh-poohed it! Fatal error! 'Cos
it turned out all along that the soldier who pooh-
poohed him had been pooh-poohing a lot of other
officers who pooh-poohed their pooh-poohs. In the
end, we had to disband the regiment. Morale totally
destroyed … by pooh-pooh!

When you meet an impasse, you need to blow off a bit of
steam, then pick up your toys, put them back in the pram and
get back on your path. I have never once said in this book that
you can't be upset, sad, hacked off, depressed, disappointed or
display any of the plethora of humans emotions at your
disposal. Having emotional reactions is good, you need them.
They can help shape your response. You need to feel. Always
allow yourself to express the emotion you feel.

Knowing when you have gone off-task is equally important.
In the British Army, when soldiers get lost in the fog out in the
wilds during a map-reading exercise, they're taught not to
panic but to find their way back to their last known waypoint.
I think this is the same in life: when you find that you've lost
your way, think back to when you were on course and were
happy, then try and return to that place in order to get yourself back on track.

No person is an island; you need to have people around
you who will not only support you but challenge you when
you're wrong. It's not that you're relying on others to complete
your puzzle; that's dangerous as you can be over-reliant and
at worst co-dependent. If your life is completely tied up in
someone else's that's no good, as you are putting so much
emphasis on the other person who you can't control. It's
lovely if you can find the yin to your yang – my life is definitely better with my wife than without her – but it doesn't

mean I'm looking for her to fulfil me all the time. I don't think you should ever look to anyone else to make your life what you want it to be. Only you can do that. Relationships like that are bound for failure. Chloe at times hates my independence and the fact that I don't really rely on anyone but myself in an emotional sense. Don't get me wrong, Chloe is not dependent on me in any way but she emotionally leans on me more than I do her. Whenever this comes up as an issue, I have said to her that while I can give you some short-term reassurance, only *you* can fix you.

PILLAR IV
CHANGE

If big success is built on granular modifications in our behaviour then what needs to change in our approach? What habits do we need to put in place so we can lead a more useful life? Our work on ourselves is never finished, and as motivational speaker and life coach Paul Mort says, 'As we expand, everything else has to change too, and evolve with us.' Nothing should be stagnant. We should look at ourselves as works in progress that need constant attention and remodelling. A Formula One car keeps changing, with racing teams constantly looking for milliseconds of micro-improvement: better grip, acceleration, quicker responsiveness ... There are always things that can be finessed, and collectively these granular actions make a big difference. Here are a few areas we can look to improve in.

MIND

What are my thoughts doing? What am I feeling? What have I done for my mind recently? Am I feeding and stimulating it with positive thinking? What am I reading? What am I writing? Am I sufficiently decluttering my mind of shit so I have the bandwidth to pause, reset and come up with new ideas? Am I organised in my affairs or are they distracting me from what I could be doing? Am I curious and interested in new things, or am I letting my mind slide back into autopilot mode? Pensioners who read, exercise and socialise are less prone to dementia than those who sit and stare into the middle distance. Given that the mind is master over the body and dictates everything we feel, we need to take better care of it.

BODY

We should always keep an eye on how we're faring physically. Ask yourself: am I taking care of my body? Am I eating the right food to give me energy for the day? Am I getting enough sleep? Am I pushing myself too hard? Do I feel stressed? Do I need to exercise more? Do I need a physical challenge?

We now know that there are as many neurons in our gut as there are in a cat's brain. You heard it right – your stomach is as clever as your cat. So what we put into our gut to a great degree dictates how intelligent our gut is able to be. Now, I'm not suggesting that the more bananas you eat the more likely your stomach will be able to solve complex algebra, but what I'm talking about in terms of intelligence is the more aware we are of the quality of food that we are putting into our stomach, the better it is able to work on our behalf. Our gut controls our energy levels, our sense of get up and go. How easily we digest our food, how well the body functions, as well as avoiding things like constipation and bowel cancer, to a large extent depends on what we put into our bodies.

PLASTICITY

In his excellent book *Battle Ready*, ex-Special Forces operative Ollie Ollerton recounts a period of focused isolation he imposed on himself in a cottage in Cornwall to put a plan together for what has now become a successful training company. He crystallised what his major goal was, then worked backwards, noting down the mini-goals he needed to fulfil en route to getting there. Drawing a circle, he dissected it into twelve sections like a clock face; at midnight he wrote his most important goal, and then from 1 to 11 p.m. he listed in order of importance, the steps/obstacles he had to take/beat to reach that goal. Then on each section he wrote what he wanted as if he had already achieved it: 'I have money in the bank; I'm in a loving relationship; I'm drinking less ...' This is pure visualisation, and by the Power of Grayskull, it works!

The mind is incredibly powerful. It can reinforce unhelpful thoughts just as it can forge positive new ones. This is called *plasticity*. And what my therapist Dr Jill Owen got me to do was if I imagined myself missing a tackle, she got me to rewind and replay the tackle successfully. Strangely, your mind fights you because it seems to be congenitally tied to worry, anxiety and negative pathways. But if we visualise something enough times the brain – for fear of going absolutely insane – will try to bridge the disconnect between where we are and where we're telling it to be.

I therefore got into the habit of stopping myself every time I self-sabotaged and began to think that I couldn't do something; I learnt to immediately rethink the situation, but this time I imagined myself doing it properly and successfully. I didn't just do this visually; I also tried to imagine how I would feel in the moment as well, almost so I could taste the event in my mind. You are what you think.

MUSIC

Music is a great emotive tool for flipping your mood and distracting you from negative thoughts you might be experiencing. Hearing a song you haven't heard for a while can immediately make you feel better because it reminds you of a better time, but then its magic only lasts for so long and then its impact, like a dream, disappears. I'd create playlists in the days before I became a DJ, specifically designed to wake me up and motivate me. Two of my top 20 most listened-to songs were 'If I Could Turn Back Time' by Cher, and Katy Perry's 'Firework'. I don't listen to the lyrics but just the melody. Pre-match music shifted my state, taking my attention away from any negatives.

Let's imagine I was just about to play a game and I'd just had an argument with my partner; how did I stop my mood from damaging my performance? The answer was, notes I referred to that helped change my thinking, and music I listened to in order to direct my internal feelings.

HAVE A RECAP

- **Changing focus to avoid feeling negative** – remember, where focus goes, energy flows, so you need to watch or listen to something that will make you laugh or smile; anything that will distract you from self-sabotaging thoughts.
- **Goal setting** – There are goals within goals, so make sure you're not utterly overwhelmed by the end goal

and break it down into a series of smaller goals. If you're in a really bad place in yourself, the most depressed you've ever been, there's no point you saying to yourself, 'I'm going to be really happy,' because that's just too much of a stretch. So instead, we break down the route to happiness and start to list things that are specific, measurable and achievable: today I'm going to eat well, I'm going to speak to somebody who makes me happy, I'm going to listen to a song I really love. At the end of the day, you are slightly happier than you were at the beginning.

- **Process-driven behaviour** – it seems a much over-used phrase, but the journey is so much more important than the destination. The journey is the process, and I think life is about refining the process so you can get out of it the things that you want.

- **Taking responsibility** – The first thing that we do when we do something wrong is we look to pass the blame to somebody else and make excuses to get us off the hook. Let's imagine it's tackling and you just missed one. You tell yourself the problem was 'The guy on the inside, me and him didn't communicate properly … I was tired, training has been really tough this week …' You have to remember what you did control in that moment – maybe you didn't chase your feet, you ran too quickly, you dipped too early; there will be something you didn't do. Add some structure through analysing what went wrong.

ARISTOTLE'S 12 VIRTUES

One of the ways that we can maintain a sense of control in our lives is by sticking to a set of principles or values that we hold ourselves accountable to. Aristotle believed a list of noble behaviours would help guide his students to live a better life. To keep his students on the right track he indicated what too much or too little of each model behaviour would look like. So for example, on the subject of courage, too little of it results in cowardice but too much results not in bravery but rashness. Finding the middle ground is the key.

EXCESS	BALANCE	DEFICIENCY
Rash	Brave	Cowardly
Ascetic	Temperate	Addictive
Extravagant	Generous	Stingy
Boastful	Truthful	Self-deprecating
Buffoonish	Witty	Boorish
Bootlicking	Friendly	Quarrelsome
Boisterous	Spirited	Melancholy
Deferential	Conscientious	Depraved
Retributive	Indignant	Envious
Self-sacrificing	Benevolent	Mean
Single-minded	Industrious	Lazy
Shy	Modest	Shameless

When somebody is described as 'walking the talk', it means they are practising what they preach and living to their values. The ancient Greek word for 'habit' is *ethos*. We are all malleable and our brains, as we've already seen, are capable of plasticity, which means we can always improve, always learn and always create new neural pathways. If you asked a stoic whether they believed in nature or nurture, they would certainly go for nurture; with practice, moral fibre is something that you can continually work on with great results.

Of his 12 Virtues, Aristotle wrote, 'We acquire the virtues by practice, we cannot take refuge in theory like patients that listen attentively to the doctors but do none of the things they're told to do.' The philosopher believed the only way to establish a positive set of behaviours was through direct action, developing a kind of ethical muscle memory.

THE MYERS–BRIGGS TEST

The Myers–Briggs psychometric test was developed in the 1940s based on the theories of Carl Jung and is still used today as a guide to characterising different personalities. Imagine the four colours blue, red, green and yellow represent types of personalities. We are all made up of all the colours, but there are certain traits that are constant in us on a day-to-day basis, our sort of default behaviour. The beauty of this model is it makes you empathise with others' styles. If you can work out what they need and how they operate, there's more chance you can relate to them.

THINKER

BLUE: Analytical	RED: Driver
Likes detail. Organised. Dry wit. Needs proof, data. Can over-think. Doesn't like being in big groups. Can slow you down. **Famous blue: Obama**	Likes being in control. Can offend others with their abruptness and candour. Task-focused. Determined. Good in a crisis. **Famous red: Churchill**

INTROVERSION   **EXTROVERSION**

GREEN: Amiable	YELLOW: Expressive
Concerned more about harmony of the group than results. Patient. Kind. Avoids conflict, easy to get on with. Can be over-emotional, holds grudges. Loves chat. **Famous green: Tindall**	Storyteller. Entertainer. Likes being centre of attention. Sometimes doesn't know when to be quiet. Can resort to sarcasm if not having fun. **Famous yellow: Haskell!**

FEELER

MIND MAPS

When we create order and clarity, we create an environment in which effective change can happen. A great way to start thinking of where you are now and where you want to go is to create a mind map, whereby you jot down on a piece of paper the things you need to take care of to get there. (Sorry, a Triumph Bonneville motorbike, a bumper pack of Viagra and a one-way ticket to Bangkok are not on the list.) A friend of mine is single for the first time in years. He currently has his head in the sand and is a bit of a rabbit in the headlights. He became so used to his wife organising all the bills and direct debits that he now doesn't have a clue how to go about setting up his utilities in his new flat. He needs to get himself sorted and organised but just doesn't know where to start. A good way to ease the feeling of being overwhelmed is to create a 'mind map' where you streamline what needs to be done in bubbles under headings, and in each heading write down the next steps. Create separate bubbles or silos for each thing that needs addressing and within that bubble break it down.

My friend's first bubble heading might be 'Money', beneath which he can write how much money he's got coming in, or how much he is going to have to pay his wife every month, how much money he needs for his own rent and how much his living costs will be: council tax, electricity, gas etc. That's one major subject covered. He can now start to think about other areas that need dealing with, such as work, mental health, family, fun things … and create new bubbles accordingly.

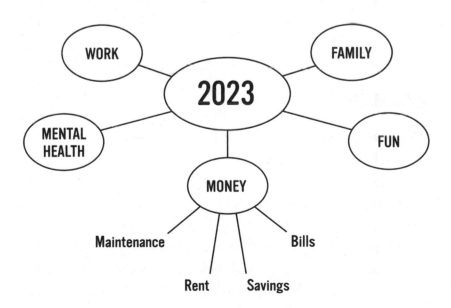

It's only when you start to organise yourself that you can then free up the time to really make the most of life.

There are so many things in life that we can't control – we can't stop ourselves getting ill, being cheated on, becoming heartbroken or being knocked down by a runaway bus – but we can on a daily basis try to be the very best person possible, accept where we are in life and make plans to change what we want to. All we can do is try. People are hard on themselves and diminish their achievements, instead of creating a positive dialogue with themselves. You cannot live your life trying to be protected from negative things happening to you. If you worry about being cheated on, you will never give yourself to someone completely and be vulnerable. If you don't leave your house, you may not get hit by a bus or other disasters may not befall you, but what kind of life is that? You need to throw yourself into living wholeheartedly. If you have your heart broken, it's sad and awful and hurts like hell but you have to move on. The lessons you learn from that experience can shape you and help you find someone who won't do that to you again and can be a positive, but like everything in this book it will take work. It's the rich tapestry of life and it's full of ups and downs that you cannot avoid. You have very little control over anything other than what I have described in these pages, so dive in head first and make every moment count. Fail, win, love, hate, and everything in between; you can always get up and go again.

THE PROCESS TRAIN

A process is a system that you create and then follow to achieve your goal; it's the 10,000 hours you put in to become an expert. Competition is healthy as it pushes you forward into new ground and forces you to consider what else you can try that you haven't done already. The journey is much more important than the goal, it's never the future you should live in but the present, trusting in the process that will get you to the finish. The idea of this book is to make that journey from A to B easier, to help you re-address areas in which you are holding yourself back and to manage some of the natural human emotions that you have.

It is the journey from failure to success through negativity and adversity that counts. Imagine your passion or purpose as being like a train carrying gold bullion. In order to get out of the station you need tracks to follow, a clear route map of where you're headed. Before you lay your routines down you need to look at the lie of the land: has anyone else been through there before, how did they fare and at which point did they fail? The chances of no-one ever having had your goal before are really slim, so do your homework and find out who got the closest and ask if they can help you. Also consider if there's an easier route than tunnelling through the mountain. For fuel you'll need plenty of self-belief and self-discipline to power you.

Life being what it is, along the route you will have things that delay you, leaves on the track or people from Extinction Rebellion tying themselves to the line. You'll have to stop and assess these situations and deal with them before you resume your journey. You will also pass through stations of delight, progress waypoints that are to be savoured like the small sips of water a fighter has in his corner between rounds, with the knowledge that that moment will be sweet and worth every bead of sweat and punishment.

If you are going to cut through difficulties effectively and execute what you need to do, your process needs to be constantly refined. It's an ever revolving door of revisiting your relationship capital, seeking out people to help you improve with their feedback, using negativity as a tool that spurs you on and allowing yourself to be a bit down in order that you can then pick yourself up and start off being positive again. And don't forget to enjoy those waypoints.

You can apply a process to any skill execution, whatever that might be. You can find out the best way of doing something and the best way of doing it for you. You can then tailor that process and break it down into steps so that when you come to review what you have done you can see where errors have come in and whether you missed out a step somewhere. Most mistakes you will make I bet are because there is something missing from your process. The process may not just be the action, it is everything that leads up to it. Did you prepare, did you get feedback, did you cover all bases ready for that skill execution? If one piece is missing, it falls apart. If you physically nail everything then you need to look at your mental process. Where were there weaknesses in that area? I guarantee if you underperform there is something not right in your process. If you have never bothered to analyse how you do things, take some time; it will save you when the pressure comes on. You always have your process to fall back on whatever happens.

KEY TAKEAWAYS FROM PILLAR IV: CHANGE

- Visualise a successful outcome.
- Learn from your mistakes.
- You can be a hero too.
- Embrace the unknown and keep moving through fear.

- Mind map your life.
- Endeavour is your best friend.
- Exercise is food for the soul.
- Develop your process.
- Constantly seek feedback from others.
- Give yourself a life audit – are you surrounded by the right people?

13

FINDING YOUR *WHY*

REDISCOVER YOUR MOJO

The Roman stoic philosopher Seneca the Younger once said, 'If a man knows not to which port he sails, no wind is favourable.' In other words, without purpose we are destined to drift around in circles if we have no direction. As Tyson Fury, the current two-time and linear world heavyweight boxing champion says, 'In life you either have a target or you don't. Ninety-nine per cent of the time if you spend enough effort and determination, you will reach that target. But a person without a target won't hit anything because there's nothing to aim for.'

If you find yourself shuffling from one drama to the next, it's because you're putting your attention on negatives and are passive to your self-sabotaging thoughts; after all nobody sets out to be apathetic or miserable on purpose. And that last word is massively important. *Purpose.* At the root of individual existential discontent (aka feeling shit) is a lack of a sense of purpose. When a sportsman attains a long-hoped-for goal, when he's put everything into it and succeeded, he needs to have another fresh goal to attempt soon after to give him purpose, otherwise he's going to very quickly have a fall. We'll explore Tyson Fury's dramatic crash in a minute.

It's the same with a writer who basks in the glory of his first novel but then knows he needs to get back to writing the next one. We all fear wasting our life and being useless; it's as if we need goals to be happy, to take pride in ourselves. And the goal, though crucial to the formula of contentedness, is less important than the purpose; it's the positive feeling we get from being in flow with ourselves when we are serving our purpose. You know the phrase he/she/it 'has served its purpose'. In other words, he/she/it is now redundant. We are happiest when we are challenged in a way that utilises our skills and knowledge.

When you've lost your mojo, it's often because your expectations of yourself are not being met. But once you have found something worth doing that you really enjoy, be it a new hobby or career change, you set yourself a goal. 'This time next year I want my golf handicap to be x,' 'I'm writing short stories but my goal is to write my first book by y.' Being excited by our purpose makes us glow inside. It's what all really successful people have in common: they have a vision, a clear set of coordinates to follow, and they are prepared to put the required work in to make it happen. The inspiration they receive while realising their vision lubricates the wheels of endeavour so it no longer feels like work. If you're really lucky, your hobby may become a passion. That's great, but passions take a lot out of you and can eventually die; like fireworks they are beautiful but short-lived and must eventually burn themselves out. In *Blade Runner*, when the blond replicant (android) Roy Batty tracks down his designer, Eldon Tyrell, and demands more life, his maker's reply is, 'The light that burns twice as bright burns half as long.' To go back to writers, I read that Lee Child, author of the hugely popular *Jack Reacher* novels, handed the character over to his brother to continue writing, as he had lost his passion for him and he had become just a meal ticket. He was honest enough with himself to know that if he carried on, it would be downhill in terms of the quality of the plots and writing. Hopefully, he'll find his purpose with a new character.

We all need something meaningful to move towards, a reason to be, and when we gather momentum and find ourselves it feels like a piece of our missing puzzle has been found. But if you've got nowhere in particular to aim for, you'll just end up focusing on the things that are wrong with your life and the sense of unfulfillment will only get worse. I think when our minds are bored and unemployed we attract problems. Where attention goes, energy flows.

Imagine the following hypothetical conversation:

'Why do you want to study law for four years, another year at the bar, and end up with a huge debt for your studies?'

'Because I want to earn enough money to have a good life and I'm interested in law.'

'And *why* are you interested in law?'

'Because I think it's a job that I can make a difference in.'

'*Why* do you want to make a difference?'

'Because I hate injustice.'

'And *why* do you hate injustice?'

'Because as a kid I saw decent honest people being ripped off and I suppose I want to do my best to help them.'

'So, you're saying you want to use being a lawyer to help others?'

'Yes.'

Having a purpose is tantamount to having a point, a reason for doing something. It's your *why*. Sometimes it takes a little longer to find the why behind the what, but if you ask yourself enough questions, you will.

MEANINGFULNESS AFTER A FALL

What drove Tyson Fury to beat Wladimir Klitschko and win the world heavyweight boxing title in 2015? As a young boxer he grew up in the heavyweight division that was utterly dominated by two seemingly unbeatable Ukrainian giants cut from rock, the Klitschko brothers. The whole purpose of his training, all the hours he suffered doing sit-ups and stomach crunches, long runs in all weathers, skipping, sparring and finessing his technique, was geared towards the sole purpose of beating Wladimir Klitschko, who by the time they fought had reigned and successfully defended the heavyweight crown for 11 years.

All the hard work Fury had put in paid off, but having fulfilled the challenge, the ultimate goal he set himself, there was no Plan B. Having climbed that considerable mountain and beaten the champ with such ease and style there was no-one left for Fury to fight. And it was at that point his bipolar condition got the better of him and he began his slide. Life lost its meaning as he didn't have anything else to aim for, and no upcoming fight to channel his considerable skills towards. What followed was the sorry tale of a talented man who lost his way to drink and drugs, and almost killed himself behind the wheel of his speeding car.

What saved Tyson was his determination to show the world that no matter how far you may drop it is still possible to drag yourself up again. The fighter had ballooned to 28 stone, but in the space of less than two years he returned from retirement and addiction, got back to his fighting weight of 18.5 stone and made a bid for the world title against Deontay Wilder, which ended in a draw. A rematch followed and in 2018 Fury became the linear and WBC heavyweight champion of the world, a title he successfully defended against Wilder in the autumn of 2021. His new purpose was not only to become a world champion for the second time, but to be a voluble champion for those like himself suffering with mental health. 'If I can drag myself back from the abyss, so can you.'

Success does not come to us, we have to grab it by the throat and make it happen. We can't just be reactive in our life, we need to be brave enough to sit down, face reality and ask ourselves what we want out of it. And once you've decided to do that, you are going to need purpose to fight the obstacles blocking your path to achieving your goals. Without purpose you're just tumbleweed rolling blindly from one place to the next. Humans are at their best when they are driven by a vision to change things, build empires and pioneer ideas. We love creating, we love having a why.

We need to stop being passive observers of our lives, get on the pitch and drive our own game. In rugby the ball doesn't come to you, you have to fight for it. Nietzsche said, 'He who has a why in life can tolerate almost any how.' Your *why* is your North Star and true purpose in life, and once you're aligned to it you can tolerate any hardship, no matter how painful, on your journey to fulfil that purpose.

A 2010 study published in the *Journal of Applied Psychology* suggested that individuals with a high level of wellbeing – defined as having a sense of purpose and feeling that the job you do is worthwhile – tend to live longer, experiencing fewer strokes, heart attacks and dementia.

Meaningfulness or purpose involves putting something or someone before yourself. Helping others, whether it's doing a shop for an elderly person, helping a stranger on the side of the road whose car has broken down, donating money to charity, all these acts of kindness give a sense of meaning to your life and help you develop your why.

Finding your purpose can take a lifetime of searching, but one way to help you focus on finding it sooner rather than later is to actively consider what excites you in life. What subjects do you talk about with the most enthusiasm? When left to your own devices what do you look at on the web? Milfs and Big Naturals aside, what sites do you visit the most? Maybe it's cycling, shooting, running, sculpture, classic cars or motorcycles; whatever it might be, try to home in on the thing that gives you the most pleasure in life, and then begin to ask yourself questions about what it would look like if you were able to make money out of this hobby. How would you feel if you could leave your nine-to-five job and focus purely on exploring a passion, and how can this passion help other people?

People in life who know their purpose tend to be more comfortable with themselves as they know who they are, why they're here and what needs to be done. It's as if the pieces in their life have meshed neatly together. When you find and flow with your *why* you are constantly evolving.

THE HERO'S JOURNEY

Your inner self knows what your true purpose is and will often make itself known to you in the most inconvenient and unexpected moments. It's usually when your exterior world and your exterior self are completely out of sync with your inner self. Author Joseph Campbell says, 'The privilege of a lifetime is being who you are,' and that, 'if you do pursue your passion, you follow your bliss and put yourself on a kind of track that's been there all the while, waiting for you, and the life that you want to be living is the one you are living.'

Some people are lucky enough to find their purpose and passion early on in life. Jack Canfield, author of *Chicken Soup for the Soul*, says we are born with a set of talents that we then practise so they become skills. Aside from being a natural pain in the arse, which I'd like to think I worked at and honed to a fine art, I found my other talent was playing rugby, which became my *what*. Canfield was fascinated by human behaviour, how we set goals and interact with each other, and while at college human psychology became his passion. Over the following years he realised his true purpose in life was to inspire others and help them become their best selves. Canfield says, 'When seeking your true passion there will always be problems or obstacles that come up and hold you back. Pressure from outside influences is often the root cause that leads people down life paths they don't enjoy. Another is that people often prioritize things such as money and prestige above doing what they love.'

If we can identify things that might have held us back from finding our true purpose in life, we can then silence them and get back on track. Our inner compass, the needle that flickers between happiness and discontent, tells us when we're on the right path when what we're doing makes us happy, because we seem to lose ourselves in it completely and time passes quickly. Is that because it burns twice as bright? This is called being in flow with ourselves.

According to Hungarian psychologist Mihaly Csikszentmihalyi, *flow* occurs when skills and the challenge at hand are equal. If they are not, i.e. the challenge is too difficult for the skills, the person will become overawed, if too easy they will become bored. Having experienced pain and suffering growing up in wartime Europe during the Second World War, Csikszentmihalyi began investigating happiness. He concluded that happiness was an internal state that could be consciously manifested with effort, and he interviewed athletes, musicians and artists to establish when they were at their most productive and happiest. The common response was that they entered a place in themselves where their work sort of flowed out of them and they simply forgot about everything else; they were 'in the zone'.

Canfield suggests a 10-point plan to find our purpose:

1. Explore the things you love to do.
2. What two qualities do you most enjoy expressing in the world? E.g. love and joy.
3. Create a life purpose statement (your perfect world).
4. Decide where you want to go.
5. Be clear about your life's purpose.
6. Conduct a passion test. Fill in the blank for the following statement: '*My life is ideal when I am –*' For example: 'My life is ideal when I am helping others.' Do this 15 times, creating a new statement each time. The words you choose must contain a verb.
7. Conduct a joy review. Think of all the times in your life when you were at your happiest. Write down what you were doing, and then look for a pattern.
8. Take time for yourself.
9. Align your goals with your life purpose.
10. Lean in to your life purpose.

In the absence of my own venerable quote, I'll finish with the words of another, Picasso. 'The meaning of life is to find your gift. The purpose of life is to give it away.'

14

THE PROBLEM WITH MEN: THINGS WE DARE NOT TELL

'We see but pride in a selfish breast, while a heart is breaking there; Oh, the world would be such a kindly world if all men's hearts lay bare! We live and share the living lie, we are doing very well; While they eat our hearts as the years go by, do the things we dare not tell.'

Henry Lawson, the Australian poet, highlights the fact that men are crap at letting their guard down, admitting weakness to one another and letting people in when they really need help. The principles of taking control over your life apply to both men and women. But because men are traditionally supposed to be strong and silent when it comes to their own fears, we hide them like an abscess that we're afraid to treat, and only face these issues when it's often too late and they have grown into monsters that are too big to deal with. Being a man has its trials. In this chapter we'll consider some of the subjects guys hate to talk about but are often desperately in need of sharing: feeling suicidal, admitting having anxiety attacks or suffering depression, coming out, being bisexual, hair loss, erectile dysfunction, the inability to cry, suffering midlife crises and abandonment issues ... to name but a few.

THOUGHT FOR THE DAY: MALE PRIDE

I remember talking to Ian Wright about this in the jungle during *I'm a Celebrity* … Why do men say shit to someone, most likely their partner, and realise that they've caused hurt and pain, but fail to reach out and fix it even though they know it's the right thing to do? Is it because of male pride, the fear of being emotional and vulnerable? Is it in our genetic makeup?

In 'Boys Keep Swinging' David Bowie sings: 'Heaven loves ya, the clouds part for you, nothing stands in your way, when you're a boy. Clothes always fit ya, life is a pop of the cherry, when you're a boy …' Bowie, that brilliant chameleon of visages, alter egos and musical genres, was being ironic when he wrote this, as he was openly bisexual, sometimes wore a dress and played with gender roles throughout his amazing career.

Have you ever noticed the way females can find something in common on a surface level with other female strangers and bond extremely quickly, and yet men in a gym, for instance, are more inclined to remain aloof, marking neutral territory with silence and grunts? It's interesting that women don't feel the need to do this. Psychological research has now revealed that the emotional differences between men and women stem more from socialisation than biology. That said, women produce less testosterone than men, an excess of which gives rise to violence. It's also the case that in our pre-cognitive networks men are more oriented towards violence and aggression than women are; however, once provoked, women can be just as ugly as men, though it tends to be in response or retribution to something a man has done.

Think about it for a second: for every Boadicea or Amazonian warrior in history, there are a hundred Genghis Khans and Attila the Huns. By and large men are war-makers and women are peace makers. That's historical fact. In a study focusing on data from the FBI over a 10-year period from 1976 to 1986, only 14 per cent of homicides were committed by women. Again, for every Rose West or Myra Hindley, there are scores more Ian Bradys and Yorkshire Rippers.

The first academic paper published on female serial killers was by Eric Hickey in 1985. Warning: this might make you look at your missus in a different light, but the criminologist discovered in his research – which spanned all the way back to the 1800s – that we shouldn't assume that women are not capable of the depravity required to commit such horrific crimes. He also discovered that there had always been female serial killers but the fact was their existence had been largely covered up or just not acknowledged as such; like a case he was working on with a woman who had murdered eight people over two years by poisoning them. Hickey concluded that women are as perfectly capable of atrocious crimes as men, but they tend to be more subtle in their modus operandi.

Aggression displayed by a woman is less likely to be physical and more passive–aggressive, whereby they harm another through gossiping, spreading false rumours and excluding others socially – which is exactly what is happening on social networks! Are we growing more sly and less physical in our aggression as men? Nah, we're just finding new ways to be nasty. Remember when you were back at school, how many girls did you see in a fight, pulling hair and scratching each other like wildcats? In your dreams maybe. Can't remember one? Now, how many boys' fights did you witness or get into? I think I've probably got into more scraps than I actually observed, and my personal experience was that having got it out of our system – whatever the beef was that started it – me and my male opponent tended to shake hands and, a little bit like a deer that shakes off the stress of just being chased by a lion, or a grizzly that has just lost to another skulks off until he tries to oust the reigning alpha bear on another occasion, once we were done with the violence, it was all over and we just moved on.

I understand from girlfriends that back at school it was much more likely that a beef with another girl would not be over so quickly and with such clear, forgiving parameters; instead, it would be snide and sly, toxic and longer lasting. I know which one I'd prefer: a quick, honest scrap and then transparency. Joe Marler and I are now friends. Enough said.

Is it the way men have been socialised or are we genetically more suited to do what we do? The woman with her maternal instinct and ability to feed her young does a better job of caring for a baby's needs, while the male, though larger and stronger, falls behind in so many emotional areas.

Women find it much easier to open up and cry compared with men. For hundreds of thousands of years, being a boy has involved following an unspoken code of holding your emotions in check and not showing weakness. The men go hunting and take all the risks, while the women cook, clean the cave and take care of issues requiring emotions. And while women have been encouraged to express themselves and embrace their emotions, men have been conditioned to do the opposite: a guy who cries is a pussy, while the one who buries his feelings, grits his teeth and never complains is considered an exemplary man. And in the process of manning up, fear and anxiety bottled up beneath the surface create a fractured psyche. Don't get me wrong, I'm not advocating we take ourselves off to evening support groups to get bear-hugged by a guy with bitch tits like Meat Loaf in *Fight Club*, but when the upshot of internalising our feelings is that suicide among young men is now the number one killer in the UK, we're doing something very wrong.

SUICIDE AMONG MEN

According to the World Health Organisation, over 800,000 people die each year from suicide worldwide, most of them men. In the UK, a study conducted by the Samaritans in 2017 reported 6,213 suicides in the UK and Republic of Ireland; and while suicide is the number one killer of men under the age of 45, it's men aged 45 to 49 – that dangerous period of middle-age – that are most under threat. The causes of suicide were listed as:

- Mental health problems.
- Bullying or discrimination.
- Abuse, including domestic, sexual or physical.
- Bereavement, including losing a loved one to suicide.
- End of a relationship.
- Long-term physical pain or illness.
- Adjusting to a big change, such as retirement or redundancy.
- Money problems.
- Housing problems, including homelessness, isolation or loneliness.
- Being in prison.
- Feeling inadequate or a failure.
- Addiction or substance abuse.
- Doubts about sexual gender identity.

- Cultural pressure, such as forced marriage.
- Eating disorders.

DEPRESSION

There are different kinds of depression, some more severe than others. **Chronic depression,** now known as **major depression,** is when you feel depressed most of the time, and often for no good reason. **Manic depression,** now known as **bipolar disorder,** is when you have extreme mood fluctuations, from feeling intensely happy with extreme highs followed by extreme lows.

People suffering from chronic or major depression have often lost interest in life and the things they used to enjoy. They have very little sleep, and extreme weight loss or weight gain is common. There's also a feeling of worthlessness and excessive thoughts of suicide.

With manic depression or bipolar disorder, the mood swings can be problematic. Some of the behaviour of people when in elevated moods might appear selfish, and in a hypomanic state somebody with bipolar disorder can behave without a filter in social situations, being sexually disinhibited or have grandiose self-delusions. Because it's such a rollercoaster of emotions, the comedown from the high is terrible. The creativity associated with the high phase can be overrated, as a person with bipolar can find it impossible to concentrate long enough to be able to get their ideas down on paper. Charles Dickens and Beethoven were both believed to have had bipolar disorder, and celebrities Kanye West and Stephen Fry are both sufferers.

Symptoms of depression to look out for are:

- Finding it hard to get out of bed.
- Losing interest and the ability to take pleasure in favourite activities.
- Loss or weight gain.
- Broken sleep or insomnia.
- Drop in energy, mentally and physically.
- Feelings of worthlessness.
- Suicidal thoughts.
- Loss of interest in personal hygiene.
- Disorganisation.
- Sudden mood changes.
- Withdrawal from friends and family.
- The feeling that life has no purpose.
- Sudden rage.

If you're suffering from any of these symptoms, the best thing you can do is talk to somebody. Depression is so common these days that you should feel no shame if you're in a low state; but it won't go away on its own and by suppressing it you are only making it worse. Thanks to major celebrities from Leonardo DiCaprio to Brad Pitt and sporting stars such as Tyson Fury admitting that they have had problems with their mental health, it has made it easier for men to open up about it without feeling like failures.

ANXIETY

Without sharing with another person what is troubling us, the risk of developing a number of anxiety disorders increases. Today's news is often bleak and admittedly there's a lot to be anxious about. But so much of what is perfectly normal is now being labelled as anxiety. It's one of the most overused words in common use right now. You tell yourself, 'I'm anxious before a game' but you're not, you're just a bit nervous and that's normal. When I'm going onstage to do a speaking gig my stomach has butterflies. Again this is just healthy nerves, it's not anxiety. If I felt nothing then that would probably mean I'm not switched on and energised enough. The brain learns more when it is in an unpredictable situation. According to a Yale study on cognition, 'We may crave stability but the brain benefits from volatility,' so these flutters of nervousness are a good sign so long as they don't overpower and take us over.

We're supposed to go through this stuff and come out the other end. Yes, there's an awful lot of anxiety going around, but let's not mistake something that is perfectly normal like butterflies for anxiety. It's like that other generalisation often used to describe someone who is not a great communicator or seems slightly different, 'Must be on the spectrum,' we now say. Everybody is suddenly an amateur shrink these days. We're all on the spectrum apparently!

Roughly one in three people will experience an anxiety disorder over the course of their lifetime, and very often if you're susceptible to one disorder you'll develop another if you don't get a handle on it. Fortunately, our understanding of the brain is pretty extensive these days and treatment to cure anxiety is usually possible. The term 'anxiety' is a huge umbrella under which reside various types of disruptive mental disorders. According to the *Diagnostic and Statistical Manual of Mental Disorders*, these include the following.

Phobias

The word 'phobia' comes from the ancient Greek *phobos*, meaning fear or aversion. A phobia is a type of panic disorder and an irrational fear of something that is unlikely to happen. We haven't got enough space in this book to list all of them – there are over a hundred – but among the top ten according to a YouGov poll are: fear of failure (atychiphobia), fear of death (thanatophobia), fear of spiders (arachnophobia), fear of enclosed spaces (claustrophobia) and fear of flying (aerophobia). An estimated 30 per cent of Americans suffer from some kind of phobia at any one time (I wonder if *donaldphobia*, a fear of bullshitting, has joined the ranks?). One of the treatments for dealing with phobias is 'exposure therapy'. (No, we're not talking getting your old chap out on *Naked Attraction*. There really should be a phobia just dedicated to *Naked Attraction*. What kind of person would stand behind a screen and have their cock discussed in front of millions of viewers by a prospective date as if she was wondering whether to buy a Cumberland or Old Spot sausage?) Exposure therapy involves a gradual interaction with the sufferer and the thing they are terrified of.

Social anxiety

This is yet another form of panic disorder. According to the NHS, it's a 'long-term overwhelming fear of social situations, a common problem that usually starts during the teenage years'. For some it gets better over time, but for others it doesn't go away without treatment. If you have a fear of meeting strangers, starting conversations or going to parties and are constantly worrying that you might say something stupid, you're probably suffering from social anxiety. You'll probably be experiencing panic attacks and experience symptoms like sweating, shaking or a rapidly pounding heartbeat. Your GP very often can't be bothered to do anything more than write you a prescription for Prozac, but don't let them get off the hook so easily. You can self-apply to the NHS psychological therapy service without a reference from your GP. Aside from antidepressants you can try cognitive behavioral therapy (CBT), which helps you identify negative thought patterns and change them. Once you've got the hang of it, you can practise this anywhere.

General anxiety disorder

This is to do with worrying for the sake of worrying. With a heightened state of anxiety about many things, the sufferer feels near-constant unease. If you're suffering from GAD your symptoms will include difficulty concentrating, finding it hard to sleep, dizziness and restlessness. Research suggests that general anxiety disorder is caused by an imbalance of the brain chemicals known as serotonin and noradrenaline, which control our mood.

Panic attacks

Feeling anxious and suffering a panic/anxiety attack are continents apart and shouldn't be confused. With normal anxiety you might have sweaty palms, your voice might tremble and your heart might be going quicker than usual, but with a panic attack you're completely out of control, you experience a vertigo kind of a feeling and shortness of breath, and your heart feels in pain as if you are having a heart attack. You think you are going to die. Your first panic attack is usually the most frightening because it's unprecedented – you've never experienced one before.

Panic attacks are caused by a buildup of stress and last anything between ten minutes to one hour, the average being about half an hour. Panic attacks can be random, but they are often caused by an underlying mental health disorder like obsessive-compulsive disorder (OCD), depression and post-traumatic stress disorder (PTSD).

In order to be diagnosed as a panic attack any four of the following criteria need to be present:

- Palpitations.
- Pounding heart or accelerated heart rate.
- Sweating.
- Trembling or shaking.
- Feeling of choking.
- Chest pain.
- Abdominal distress.
- Feeling sick, dizzy, unsteady.
- Experiencing a feeling of going mad.
- Tingling or numbness.

COMING OUT

There's probably never been a better time to come out as a gay. It's just been announced that the new Superman, Clark Kent's son, is gay, and earlier this year the new incarnation of *Batman & Robin* saw Batman's sidekick as gay. Recognition and acceptance of gay mainstream superheroes is a major shift. *Strictly Come Dancing* in 2022 featured the first same-sex pairing and it's a given that many adverts now feature same-sex couples. Things couldn't be more different than just over 50 years ago when it was a criminal offence in England for one man to sleep with another. Up until 2000, gay and bisexual men and women were banned from serving in the Army. Sadly, despite all this, recent figures compiled by

Gallup show that homophobic attacks increased 147 per cent in the three months after the Brexit vote. Hate crime is not confined to Islamophobia and racism.

Despite my fallout with Stonewall, the LGBTQ+ charity, I fully support people who wish to express their sexuality however they want. I think it's a shame that people even feel the need to have to come out. It should be a normal part of our lives. When people realise that sexuality is not black and white but a myriad of greys, the world will be a better place. We need to stop trying to define everything to give those who are uncomfortable or those who are naïve something to grasp onto. My younger brother Edward is gay and based on his experiences I know how difficult it is to admit that you're different to your family, friends and work colleagues. Edward came out to me, and I could tell he was super-nervous. Would his meathead, alpha male, rugby-playing brother go mental and beat him up? To be honest, I couldn't have cared less about it. I told him I loved him and I wanted him to be happy and I was here for him. His sexuality was never a problem for me and never will be. What I am more interested in is how hard he works and whether he makes the most of his potential.

Being honest about your sexual orientation makes a huge difference to you being able to lead a happy, fulfilling life, rather than suffering in isolation. There's a very high risk of suicide in young LGBTQ+ people aged between 16 and 25; recent research by the Department of Health revealed that 25 per cent of people didn't ask for help when they were feeling suicidal because they didn't want to reveal that their sexual orientation was the cause of their own unhappiness. Twice as many young people are now coming out than those over 25. For those who find it hard to understand all this, I think of it in this way. Imagine going to work every day and being around your friends every day, but you couldn't be yourself. You had to play this role the whole time. You were never able to express yourself and be true to yourself, to love who you wanted and dress like you wanted. How hard would that be, what a toll it must take on you. As you have read in the pages of this book, it's hard enough for you to get being *you* right, let alone trying to be someone else.

There's no simple way of coming out. It's not as if you can CC everyone on an email because you will always be meeting new people you'll want to tell. As to how you tell your family is another consideration. In the world of men's professional rugby, you can count on one hand players who've been brave enough to admit that they are gay. Actually, never mind one hand, two fingers are all you need – Gareth Thomas and Dan Palmer. The same goes for men's boxing and MMA. But the male sport that is clearly the most homophobic is football; of the 60,000 professional players worldwide, only a couple have come out as gay while playing, Jake Daniels and Josh Cavallo. More have come out since retiring, but there's still clearly a long, long way to go.

HAIR LOSS

For those of you lucky enough to still have hair like Clint Eastwood in *Dirty Harry*, a bonce so thick you could rest a new-born baby on it in a wind-lashed storm, you're unlikely to empathise with the anguish experienced by us blokes with receding lids. When your hair starts thinning under a bright overhead lamp and you see your scalp peeking through like a furless new-born mouse, it's a crushing moment, a shiver of your own mortality. If the deadfall of hair begins in your mid-twenties or early thirties, it feels like your prime is prematurely on its way out. It's odd because men don't talk about hair loss, but it's one of the biggest insecurities men have (aside from the size of their penis). Women have the menopause that we hear plenty about. But going bald is awful for so many. It destroys your confidence and your identity. You see all sorts of elaborate ways of trying to make a dire situation better. The fact that the more testosterone you have in your body, the more you are likely to lose your hair, doesn't really give you much succour; nor that women find bald men no less attractive than those with Samson locks. As far as you're concerned you're going fucking bald and that's the end of it. And unless you have no vanity whatsoever – which is very unusual – not a day goes by that you don't obsessively observe your hair getting thinner and migrating to the plughole in the shower, or find yourself getting envious over Italian waiters with their crow-black sheen of pomaded hair. Jesus H, you even envy ginger people with a thick head of fiery curls!

Your options are many: first up you can embrace the baldness as it begins its autumnal decline on your scalp, you decrease the graded numbers of your clipper blades in parallel with your hair loss, from grade three to grade two, to grade one, to grade nought. After that it's a case of shaving it off like Marlon Brando in *Apocalypse Now*. Sadly, some of you, depending on the shape of your head and nose, will end up looking more like Nosferatu then Jason Statham.

Your second option is to pack yourself off to Istanbul where you can get a very credible hair transplant at affordable rates that won't make you look like Russ Abbot back in the last millennium, when his forehead was as perforated as a pin cushion. These days there are two kinds of treatments you can have: FUT and FUE. With an FUT (follicular unit incision) transplant the surgeon removes a strip of donor skin from a concentrated area at the back of your head in order to remove individual follicular units that are then placed in the recipient areas where there is hair loss. FUE (follicular unit extraction) treatment, on the other hand, involves the removal of tiny follicular units extracted directly from all over the scalp, and what this means is you won't see the obvious Nike-shaped scar that FUT leaves behind if you have your hair cut really short. The FUE approach is the newer technique, and as a result is a little bit more expensive. This technique can also be performed by a robot. Even then it does price people out, and depending how it's done it can still look dodgy. Some teammates of mine have had amazing bits done, while others look like they left their lids out by the bins and the council did them.

The days of wigs and hairpieces are long gone – some of our favourite actors had to put up with these, including the likes of Sean Connery, Burt Reynolds, Richard Harris and John Travolta. Even Richard Burton had his makeup artist paint his scalp with black paste to hide the pink of his bald spot. A number of people who've had hair transplants come to mind, including Mel Gibson, Billy Bob Thornton, Jimmy Carr, Frank Skinner, James Nesbitt, Matthew McConaughey, Gordon Ramsay and Jamie Foxx, plus a great many more who have had the treatment before anybody realised they were losing their hair. I haven't made my mind up yet on what to do as regards my own hair, which is slowly going. The odd thing is it affects so many men, yet they are the first to absolutely destroy anyone with a hint of a receder. I look back on teammates that I grilled about their hair and think what a prick I was, now I am heading albeit slowly the same way. Men are very odd at times. I get messages telling me, 'I think it's time you shaved your head,' or 'Come on mate, get a transplant,' from people I have never met. I think they consider it as 'banter', a word that is now basically used as an excuse for being a massive cunt to anyone. It's a get-out-of-jail-free card wielded by the moronic and lazy. I can't stand it.

MIDLIFE CRISIS

The definition of a midlife crisis according to the Collins dictionary is 'a period of doubt and anxiety that some people experience in middle age when they think about whether their life is the kind of life that they want'. It's a phenomenon that occurs in males and females more commonly between the ages of 45 and 55, a yearning for one's youth and a grieving for the loss of the golden years when we were in shape, hopeful, idealistic and at our most attractive. Clearly, they're rose-coloured glasses we're looking through, but when a midlife crisis hits it can be extremely destructive. A man who's worked hard for the last 20 years to create a family, a decent position at work and establish loving trust with his wife can suddenly find himself feeling detached, empty and driven by a strange voice that trades on the fear that the best of his life is over, which then pushes him into a rollercoaster ride of risk. Common symptoms are:

- Apathy.
- Feeling unfulfilled.
- Intense nostalgia, chronic reminiscence about the past.
- Feelings of emptiness and meaninglessness.
- Impulsive, often rash actions.
- Dramatic changes in behaviour and appearance.
- Marital infidelity or constant thoughts about infidelity.

- Constantly comparing oneself with others, who seem happier or more fulfilled.
- Intense feelings of regret.

Add to this erectile dysfunction, loss of testosterone (which is a huge one) and sex drive. Women can also suffer from a midlife crisis. And if they're really unlucky, they can go through perimenopausal depression – caused by fluctuations of oestrogen, as their eggs dry up in preparation for their periods to stop – at the same time as a bloke has his midlife crisis. This starts at around 50 and can last for years, with horrible symptoms like hot flushes, intense irritability and severe mood swings. Life can get pretty testing for both man and woman if they're simultaneously going through changes, with the woman lashing out and the man getting progressively lonely and down. According to the Centers for Disease Control and Prevention, white men between the ages of 45 and 49 have the highest rates of suicide. Not surprisingly, divorce rates among men aged 45 to 49 are the highest too.

What is less talked about is that men go through a version of the menopause; although it should be pointed out that this is not the case for every man and even then it's not at the same rate as women. However, men's testosterone can diminish from the age of 30. This affects all manner of things: mood, sex drive, sleep, recovery, bone mass, fat distribution, muscle mass and strength, and the production of red blood cells and sperm. All pretty key things for men. In Hollywood, most of the actors you see that are older but still look great are, among other things, probably on TRT (testosterone replacement therapy) and HGH (human growth hormone) treatment. But treat with caution. Once you mess around with your body's homeostasis you throw things out of kilter and sometimes they don't go back. Of course, if you feel tired all the time, your mood is awful, you have no drive, then you should look into getting your levels tested, and if they are low you can go on TRT under medical guidance – but whatever you do, don't take advice from the local meat head at the gym.

Against this backdrop of doom is a sense that time is running out. It catalyses an act of desperation as we attempt to recapture the excitement of youth and in the process we can make some very damaging self-sabotaging decisions. Decisions that at the time seemed worth the risk: like having an affair, online gambling, going to see a prostitute or making impulse purchases. Ex-Special Forces soldier Ollie Ollerton says, 'Nothing screams louder than that which is about to die,' and I think this applies to the male midlife crisis, because it's as if the last vestiges of our youth are calling for our attention, for one last fandango; maybe we're just big kids that don't want to grow up. Hopefully, you can avoid it before it unravels the life you've carefully put together over the last 20 years.

ERECTILE DYSFUNCTION

Erections develop when mental or physical stimulation prompts your central nervous system to release nitrous oxide, which encourages the arteries that supply your penis with blood to widen, allowing blood to infuse the soft tissue that lines your penis. Not getting or being able to sustain an erection is the bête noire for guys, straight or gay. We've all experienced it at some stage, be it through too much drink, from depression, because we got stage fright, or suffered extreme fatigue, or maybe because of illness-related medicines. Whatever the reason, it's extremely common. In

Germany, an estimated 6 million men suffer from ED but the figure is likely to be much higher, given that many men feel too ashamed to talk about it. Studies conducted in China, Europe, the USA and Brazil show that it affects up to 40 per cent of the adult male population, with approximately 150 million new cases reported every year.

Diet, exercise, training your pelvic floor muscles, keeping trim and avoiding obesity are some of the ways it can be prevented, as well as not drinking too much alcohol and avoiding nicotine. If – or rather when – it happens, ED can be deeply troubling. Performance anxiety is sometimes the culprit for ED; this happens when you put pressure on yourself to perform and start overthinking things. Even a slight bit of worry over performance can bloom into a full-blown neurosis on a one-night stand or in a steady relationship. The good news is these days Viagra is available over the counter in chemists, so if you're going through needless worry, buy yourself some and keep it handy as insurance, and in the safe knowledge you've got a back-up plan you'll soon forget your worries. In other cases, it may be something to do with your heart and the regulation of blood flow, which is more serious. According to livehealthily.com other causes of ED might be:

- **Atherosclerosis,** which causes your arteries to narrow and harden, limiting the amount of blood that can reach your penis.
- **Diabetes,** which affects both the blood supply and the nerve endings in your penis.
- **High blood pressure,** which can damage the arteries that feed the penis.
- **Multiple sclerosis,** which affects your central nervous system.

- **Parkinson's disease**, which can affect your brain's ability to release important hormones.
- Nerve or spinal injuries.
- Hormonal conditions like **hyperthyroidism** or **Cushing's syndrome**.
- **Peyronie's disease**, which affects the tissues in the penis.

Certain medications are known to cause temporary erectile dysfunction in men, including some anti-hypertensives, diuretics, antidepressants, antihistamines and medications that contain steroids, among others. Science has progressed to the point where there are plenty of ways to treat ED. It may be a case of trying CBT (cognitive behavioral therapy) to master your thinking patterns, so you're not worried about getting an erection before having sex. But don't suffer in silence; life is too short, so go see your doctor who can refer you to a sex therapy counsellor.

EATING DISORDERS

You may think that eating disorders are the sole preserve of women, but the truth is men are equally susceptible to bulimia and anorexia, and account for 15 per cent of all those suffering. The problem with men is that they think it's a woman problem, which makes them even more ashamed to go and seek help. Anorexia, bulimia and binge-eating disorder are all mental health conditions. Many people will develop them as coping mechanisms – ways to take control of our life when everything else seems beyond our grasp. There can also be aesthetic factors at play; for example many men develop these disorders as a result of obsessing about muscle definition.

These days everybody seems to want a six-pack and to achieve the perfect body. For the most part, having a six-pack all year round is pretty hard to maintain, unless you're genetically gifted. Don't ever get confused with being lean and being healthy – these are two *very* different physical goals. Add to that, depending on your body type, achieving a physique goal may well be harder for you than other men. There are three somatotypes, but between each one is a vast spectrum of body type, and most of us will be a combination of one and two, or two and three.

Ectomorphs tend to be long, lean and wiry. On the one hand, they are to be envied as they can eat a hell of a lot of calories and struggle to gain weight. But on the other hand, they can lift weights until the cows come home, and still struggle to build any significant muscle mass. In the bodybuilding world, these men are called 'hard gainers', and unfortunately, they are unlikely to have much success in the sport without the assistance of anabolic steroids.

Mesomorphs are considered to be the genetically gifted. However, while they may find muscle building somewhat easy, mesomorphs can also carry significantly more body fat than ectomorphs, so need to remain aware of energy balance (calories in vs calories out) if they want to show off the muscle definition they are so capable of amassing.

Endomorphs can gain body fat very easily. Their physiques tend to be less angular and more rounded. However, endomorphs tend to be stronger than mesomorphs and ectomorphs – after all, mass moves mass; think sumo wrestlers.

A good example of the somatotypes in the professional sports world would be Tyson Fury and Deontay Wilder. Fury is a classic endomorph, and no matter how much hell he puts himself through, he will always lack definition unless he wants to compromise his performance as a boxer. Wilder is a meso-morph and looks as if he's been carved out of mahogany.

The reason that I mention these different body types is because I want to highlight that everybody is different and each somatotype has its own advantages and disadvantages. An ecto can eat what they want. A meso can gain muscle mass. And only an endo will win the title of World's Strongest Man. On the flipside, an endo can't gain muscle mass easily if at all. A meso likely has to calorie count all year round to stay in shape, and an ecto will struggle to ever see the muscle mass all those deadlifts are building.

It's important to remember that there is life beyond how you look, and not to make yourself miserable trying to tick one box, when there are so many others out there that will bring joy to your life.

Eating healthily, working out and looking good are things we all aspire to; the problem is today's society only really cele-brates an ideal physique and doesn't take into account the fact that we're all built differently. The seed this sows among many men is that they are not good enough. Some will express this anxiety through excessive exercise, through steroids, starving themselves or making themselves sick. Thanks to brave celebrities like Freddie Flintoff, who confounded us all with his frank and heartbreaking documentary on bulimia, men are beginning to realise that an eating disorder is nothing to be ashamed of, but it will not disappear on its own. You need help to combat it.

PILLAR V
PROGRESS

Learning to grow older with grace and ease takes practice and a shift in mindset, shedding an old skin so a new one can come through. Recalibrating is about finding new things to make you tick. The Japanese word *ikigai* roughly translates as a 'reason for being' and finding an inner sense of purpose. It makes sense that if we find something we love doing we will get better at it the more we do it. And if you can get paid for it and it benefits others then that's real success. Life is about doing things that make us happy, and as I mentioned earlier, we are at our happiest when we are challenged and stretching ourselves and *in the flow* – that brilliant state where time seems to disappear and you experience a sense of calm and fulfilment …

The more we align what we believe in to the job that we do, the happier and more successful we'll be in doing it. In his now legendary 2005 Stanford Commencement Address, Steve Jobs was a great advocate of finding your *why*. We should not settle for a job we care little about he tells us. 'Your work is going to fill a large part of your life, and the only way to be truly satisfied is to do what you believe is great work. And the only way to do great work is to love what you do. If you haven't found it yet keep looking, don't settle. As with all matters of the heart, you'll know when you find it. And, like any great relationship, it just gets better and better as the years roll on. So, keep looking until you find it. Don't settle.'

Nietzsche also said that we cannot find our purpose unless we find ourselves first. We can ask ourselves a few tough questions in order to unwrap what our why is:

- Have you made the best of the gifts that life has given you?
- What must you do for you to be proud of yourself?
- What would make you feel more powerful?
- What do you have to accomplish?
- What would the most amazing goal for your life be?

Joseph Campbell believes we all have the choice to become our optimum selves; it is up to us whether we commit to following a calling that takes us into the unknown, or whether we choose to hold ourselves back, resist the adventure and stick to the known, predictable and safe. He calls the first option 'the hero's journey'. 'A hero,' he says, 'is someone who's given his or her life to something bigger.' The evolution to becoming one is composed of certain key steps. As you read through the list below, think about some of your favourite movies – in my case, the likes of *Star Wars*, *Lord of the Rings*, *Karate Kid* … all of them use Campbell's blueprint, the stages of the hero's journey, which has now become a standard in Hollywood scriptwriting:

- The call to adventure.
- The quest.
- The person is afraid and refuses the opportunity.

- A mentor appears and allays their fears, convincing them to embrace the adventure.
- On their journey they meet enemies but also allies.
- A battle, ordeal or challenge must be faced.
- Despite their worst fears they survive and are transformed by the experience.

We need to find a way to make it okay to talk frankly about mental health, just as we need to progress and engender a more permissive environment in which young men can express themselves emotionally so they don't end up in that dark space in the first place. *Restrictive emotionality* describes someone who inhibits their expression of intimate feelings. It's a term generally used to describe men. I'm glad to say that thanks to men in the public spotlight, from A-listers to sporting giants (literally) opening up about their own mental health issues, things are gradually improving. Sadly, for some it's not quick enough.

In the Appendix at the end of this book, I have compiled a list to help you find someone who will listen to you and give you much-needed compassion and advice. I have always said that if you want it, there is help out there. You are never alone and there is a way out of even the bleakest situations, so that you can press on and progress with your life. Good luck.

KEY TAKEAWAYS FROM PILLAR V: PROGRESS

- If you haven't found your life ambition, don't worry, keep looking until you find it.
- Pay attention to your inner compass.
- Don't be afraid to seek help from the professionals. Only when you know your weakness can you work on it.
- Look for the truth in yourself, to find what gives you a sense of meaning.
- Reframe problems as opportunities.
- Be willing to do it in a different way in order to progress.

EPILOGUE

We are all on our own individual journeys trying to get from A to B, and we need to learn to become more tolerant of people who are not the same as us, who might have different beliefs, different sexual orientations or differently coloured skin. In the current cancel culture when a group of people feel oppressed, they fight back by cancelling individuals, but in doing so are displaying the same kind of malicious behaviour that they purport to despise. Trying to shut people down aggressively just because they have a different belief than us is wrong.

J. K. Rowling got herself in very hot water with the LGBTQ+ community on Devex, a media platform, when she tweeted in protest at the use of the word *people* rather than *women*, as if *women* was now deemed to be a non-inclusive, dirty word. She wrote, 'People who menstruate. I'm sure there used to be a word for those people. Someone help me out. Wumben? Wimpund? Woomud?' The LGBTQ+ community branded her tweet 'transphobic'. An organisation that helps distribute menstrual hygiene supplies to girls replied, 'Not all women menstruate and not all who menstruate are women. There are many girls, non-binary folk, trans boys, and trans men who also get a period.'

Rowling tried to defuse the backlash by further tweeting, 'I respect every trans person's right to live any way that feels authentic and comfortable to them. I'd march with you if you were discriminated against on the basis of being trans. At the same time, my life has been shaped by being female. I do not believe it's hateful to say so.' Fortunately, it's not that easy to cancel the most popular writer on the planet but the after-shocks continue.

Other notables who have suffered at the hands of toxic LGBTQ+ fanatics include Sir Philip Pullman, author of *His Dark Materials*, and *Father Ted* creator and writer, Graham Linehan. The latter dared to question the validity of the third sex, trans, and very quickly everything he'd ever worked for was stripped away; he lost his marriage when his wife who had become a victim of LGBTQ+ trolls – by pure association – just couldn't bear the abuse any longer and divorced him; then TV execs began stonewalling him, and his forthcoming West End play adaptation was cancelled.

As I *finally* finish this book (it feels as if I've been writing it since the Jurassic period!), Johnny Depp vs Amber Heard has just ended in Virginia, nearly two years after Depp lost his libel case in the UK against the *Sun* for calling him a 'wife beater'. This time Depp was suing Ms Heard for an article she wrote for the *Washington Post* in which she claimed to be a victim of domestic abuse. Live footage of the courtroom drama went viral. The sad thing is Miss Heard is clearly not well, and the cracks appearing in her allegations and the mistruths were as clear as day. Having been tested for PTSD, she was unfortunately diagnosed as having borderline personality disorder, the symptoms of which are a fear of abandonment and violent tendencies caused by intense and highly changeable moods. The diagnosis was put forward by an expert for Depp, but was challenged by Heard. While her illness is regrettable, her actions have directly resulted in Depp being cancelled. He may never get his life fully back. It's clear to see that they were both pretty awful to each other, and Depp has blame in the matter ending up where it did, but should it have led to him being cancelled or to him losing his lucrative acting role in the *Pirates of the Caribbean* franchise and in J. K. Rowling's *Fantastic Beasts*? Or the damage it has caused to his ex-wife and children? The answer in any sane mind is or course, no. The court of public opinion should not have been able to cause so much havoc until the legal system had done its job. I truly believe than no-one should ever have their name printed in the papers and released to the public until they are found guilty.

At the San Sebastian Film Festival in 2021, where Depp received the Donostia Lifetime Achievement Award, he used the platform to speak out about the cancel culture movement and 'this instant rush to judgement based on what essentially amounts to polluted air'. He added, 'It takes one sentence and there's no more ground, the carpet has been pulled. It's not just me that this has happened to, it's happened to a lot of people, women and men. Sadly, at a certain point they begin to think that it's normal. Or that it's them. When it's not.'

Black comedian Dave Chappelle appalled the Jewish community with his joke about *Space Jews*, a fictional movie idea about the oppressed becoming the oppressors after leaving earth and returning there to claim it; a thinly veiled swipe at the Zionist movement in Palestine taking over and claiming the land of the Palestinians while effectively imprisoning them in the Gaza Strip, the world's largest open-air jail. Chappelle was basically shining a light on the hypocrisy of the fact that Jews were persecuted in the Holocaust and then have become the persecutors themselves.

It was a very brave move, after which Chappelle said, 'I'm not gonna do any more comedy.' Chappelle was using comedy as a device to open debate on verboten subjects like Palestine, or the often militant and vitriolic LGBTQ+ community. When you start censoring comedy, that's the end of democracy; it's the one medium that should be free of rules. And trying to destroy somebody just because they hold a different view to you is plain backward and arrogant. Now you may not like what Dave says – and the man that most recently stormed Chappelle's new stage show *Netflix Is a Joke* with a knife strapped to a fake gun to kill him certainly didn't – but it's okay to disagree. It's just that when you do disagree, walk away; there's no need to inflame and attack. Ricky Gervais uses the example of piano lessons advertised as you walk down the street. If you don't want piano lessons just walk past the advertisement. You don't have to call the person up and scream, 'I don't want fucking piano lessons, how dare you?!'

Chappelle was cancelled by the LGBTQ+ community and his new show *The Closer* was turned down by every TV company for fear of recrimination from the gay lobby; everyone, that is, apart from Netflix. Somebody has to break the cycle. This caused a huge stir at Netflix, with angry staff walking out and even storming the top executives' meeting. Some staff were duly suspended amid a huge outcry that Netflix was transphobic. It was quickly pointed out that they were suspended not because of their gender or sexual orientation but because they disrupted a meeting, which is against the company rules. The streaming service outlined its anti-censorship stance in an internal memo that was sent to staff. 'If you'd find it hard to support our content breadth, Netflix may not be the best place for you.'

Ted Sarandos, co-chief executive at Netflix, was quoted as saying, 'We're programming for a lot of diverse people who have different opinions and different tastes and different styles, and yet we're not making everything for everybody. We want something for everybody, but everything's not going to be for everybody.'

That right there is the key to this whole issue. *Everything's not going to be for everybody.* There is another quote that makes it even clearer, if you think TV and film are evil: 'Every great library contains something to offend.'

Until companies follow the lead of Netflix, grow some balls and stand up for common sense and what's right instead of always being seen to be doing the right thing, the man in the street will have the power to cancel at will. It's all well and good winning the libel case or getting an apology on page 18, but you were being slandered on the front page. Once the genie is out the bottle, in the court of public opinion there is no way to get it back in.

Look, we are all having different human experiences and we should respect each other's journeys. American rapper DaBaby said something at a gig about gay people and AIDS that even Dave Chappelle thought he had gone too far with. The upshot was DaBaby had to sit down with the gay community and apologise, explaining that he didn't understand what he was saying and he'd made a big mistake. Dave Chappelle said of the DaBaby cancelling, 'In our country you can shoot and kill a nigga but you better not hurt a gay person's feelings', referring to the fact that DaBaby had once shot and killed a man in Walmart and yet this fracas with the gay community had caused him much more bother.

Why do I care? Well, people have tried to cancel me a few times, luckily for nothing bad, but I have faced my fair share of the rough side of public and media opinion. I don't hold extreme views. I don't go out of my way to join up to certain crusades. I am too busy trying to get the most out of my life, but what I do have is an opinion, common sense, a big mouth and a dodgy sense of humour, which is not always a good recipe for life in 2022 and beyond. I see everyone getting so caught up in this chaos. I see people lose their jobs and livelihoods, people who can't get work because they are not what is on trend. I know people who have taken their lives because of social media and this global mess we have got into. We have to change things and it goes beyond using # and virtue signalling. Like everything, we need action not just words.

Somewhere between wokeness and narrow-mindedness there is an equilibrium. It's up to us to find it in ourselves. Let's try not to judge others when so many of us are the unfinished article and have more flaws than the Empire State Building. Worry about yourself first; look in, not out. Don't jump on the bandwagon of hate, don't pile on to people on social media. Don't walk past things you know to be wrong. The world is an amazing place and you have such an opportunity to be better every day, which in turn will give your life meaning, direction, pleasure and so much more. Worry about only what you can control and forgot about what you can't. You can control how you treat your body, your mind, how hard you work and how you treat others. That is it, no more, no less.

Reach out for help and offer help to those around you. Get feedback from those you respect. Have a plan and stick to it, and remember you are never the finished article. Aim to be better than you were yesterday, that's all you can do. Finally, let's try and operate from a place of honesty and kindness; speaking candidly but in a way that doesn't end up being confrontational. Life is too brief to spend it feeling constantly enraged. Let's live and let live.

APPENDIX

HELPLINES AND CRISIS CONTACTS

This book is about getting back control of our lives, but sometimes we might need a helping hand on the journey. Don't hesitate to reach out to these organisations – their specialist care services are there for you.

If you are concerned about your health or the health of a friend or family member, you may find useful information from one of the sources below.

In an emergency, call 999 or go to your local A&E department.

If you're in crisis and need to speak to someone, call NHS 111 (for when you need help but are not in immediate danger).

Contact your GP and ask for an emergency appointment.

Use the 'Shout' crisis text line: text SHOUT to 85258.

Samaritans

Available 24 hours a day to provide confidential emotional support for people who are experiencing feelings of distress, despair or suicidal thoughts.
www.samaritans.org
Helpline: 116 123 (free to call from within the UK and Ireland), 24 hours a day
Email: jo@samaritans.org

Mind

Mind offers advice, support and information to people experiencing a mental health difficulty and their family and friends. Mind also has a network of local associations in England and Wales to which people can turn for help and assistance.
Open Monday to Friday 9 a.m. to 6 p.m. (except bank holidays)
www.mind.org.uk
InfoLine: 0300 123 3393 to call, or text 86463
Email: info@mind.org.uk

Rethink Mental Illness (*formerly* National Schizophrenia Fellowship)

Rethink Mental Illness works to help everyone affected by severe mental illness, such as schizophrenia and bipolar disorder, recover a better quality of life. It provides effective services and support, and campaigns for change through greater awareness and understanding.
www.rethink.org
National Advice Service: 0300 5000 927 (Open Monday to Friday 9.30 a.m. to 4 p.m.)
Email: advice@rethink.org

PAPYRUS UK

PAPYRUS is the national charity dedicated to the prevention
of young suicide. They support young people under 35
who are experiencing thoughts of suicide, as well as
people concerned about someone else.

Open 9 a.m. until midnight every day of the year (including
weekends and bank holidays)

www.papyrus-uk.org

Helpline: 0800 068 4141

Text: 07860 039 967

Email: pat@papyrus-uk.org

Young Minds

Committed to making sure all young people can get the
mental health support they need.

Parents helpline: 0808 802 5544

Open Monday to Friday 9.30 a.m. to 4 p.m. (excluding bank
holidays)

Young Minds Crisis Messenger: text YM to 85258 (available
24/7)

Campaign Against Living Miserably (CALM)

A helpline for people in the UK who are down or have hit a
wall for any reason, who need to talk or find information
and support.

www.thecalmzone.net

Helpline: 0800 58 58 58

Webchat: www.thecalmzone.net/help/webchat/

Open 5 p.m. to midnight, every day of the year

SANE

SANE services provide practical help, emotional support and
specialist information to individuals affected by mental
health problems, their family, friends and carers.
www.sane.org.uk
Helpline: 07984 967 708
Textcare: www.sane.org.uk/what_we_do/support/textcare/

Anxiety UK

Advice and support for people living with anxiety.
www.anxietyuk.org.uk
Helpline: 0344 775 774
Text: 07537 416 905

British Association for Counselling and Psychotherapy (BACP)

Professional body for therapy and counselling. Provides
information and a list of accredited therapists.
www.bacp.co.uk
Helpline: 01455 883 300
Open Monday to Friday 10 a.m. to 4 p.m.

No More Panic

Information, support and advice for those with panic
disorder, anxiety, phobias or OCD, including a forum and
chat room.
www.nomorepanic.co.uk

No Panic

Step-by-step programmes and support for people with
anxiety disorders.
www.nopanic.org.uk
Helpline: 0300 772 9844

Triumph Over Phobia (TOP UK)

Self-help therapy groups and support for those with OCD,
   phobias and related anxiety disorders.
www.topuk.org
Helpline: 01225 571 740

Beat (*formerly* Eating Disorders Association)

Can help you overcome an eating disorder through their self-
   help groups and helplines. There's also a wealth of
   information on their website.
www.beateatingdisorders.org.uk
Helpline: 0808 801 0677

ACKNOWLEDGEMENTS

Wow, book seven and we are still going. Thank you to all those who make it possible for me to fulfil one of my biggest passions, which is to write. Thank you to Oliver Malcolm and the team at HarperCollins for having the faith in me to write a different kind of book. *Approach With(out) Caution* is a real pivot away from my first two offerings, yet you all embraced it in the same way. Working with you for the last three books has been amazing and a real pleasure.

Thank you to Richard Waters for your incredible hard work on this book. Without your writing, knowledge and skill, *Approach With(out) Caution* would not exist. You are one of the most interesting people I have worked with, and I loved our chats. Even if it was just me ranting at you for hours on end. You have the patience of a saint.

Thank you to Clare Hulton, my amazing literary agent. You always do a fabulous job and get me the best possible deals. Thank you for helping me get this very different book into print.

Lastly, to my amazing wife Chloe, thank you for helping me understand the world better and for your incredible support. Thank you for giving me the best present in the world – our wonderful daughter Bodhi, who I hope will get to read this one day.